T0182034

# Putting Systems and Complexity Sciences Into Practice

Joachim P. Sturmberg

Editor

# Putting Systems and Complexity Sciences Into Practice

Sharing the Experience

 Springer

*Editor*
Joachim P. Sturmberg
School of Medicine and Public Health
Faculty of Health and Medicine
University of Newcastle
Newcastle, NSW, Australia

Foundation President, International Society
for Systems and Complexity Sciences
for Health
Newcastle, NSW, Australia

ISBN 978-3-030-08825-5       ISBN 978-3-319-73636-5   (eBook)
https://doi.org/10.1007/978-3-319-73636-5

# Preface

> *Our world is not shaped by those who think similarly,*
> *but by those who dare to think differently.*
>
> Unknown

The theme of the *2nd International Conference on Systems and Complexity Sciences for Health* in Billings, Montana, in November 2016 focused on sharing the experiences of *putting systems and complexity sciences into practice*. Systems and complexity thinking are still widely seen as an esoteric pastime by the large majority who cling to the Newtonian reductionist way of thinking.

This book highlights 16 different ways of applying systems and complexity thinking to problems spanning topics from the philosophy of health, understanding health and disease, the provision of patient care and patient engagement, health professional education and ethics, and health system organization and improvement to the link between arts and science. Readers ready to try out "systems and complexity thinking" in their domain will find lots of helpful tips and tricks to get started in *putting systems and complexity sciences into practice*.

I would like to thank my editors Janet Kim and Christina Tuballes for their assistance in compiling this book as well as their enthusiasm and support in promoting *The Value of Systems and Complexity Sciences for Healthcare* and *Health System Redesign. How to Make Health Care Person-Centered, Equitable, and Sustainable*. My thanks also go to the Springer production team for their work on shaping the layout of *Putting Systems and Complexity Sciences Into Practice: Sharing the Experience*.

Holgate, NSW, Australia                                   Joachim P. Sturmberg
September 2017

# Contents

**1    Putting Health Back into the Healthcare System** ...................... 1
Joachim P. Sturmberg
1.1    Exploring Our Mindsets ........................................... 1
1.2    Why Are Health Systems Focused on Disease? ................... 2
1.3    The Need to Refocus on the Person/Patient ....................... 4
1.4    The Person/Patient at the Centre: Connecting the Subjective
        with the Objective ................................................ 4
1.5    Conclusions ....................................................... 6
References ................................................................ 8

**Part I    Patient Care**

**2    Healthy Smoker: An Oxymoron? Maybe, But It Is More
       Complicated Than That** ............................................. 11
Jeanette M. Bennett, Lydia G. Roos, Joseph S. Marino,
Nicolas Rohleder, and Maren J. Coffman
2.1    Introduction ...................................................... 11
2.2    Methods ........................................................... 14
2.3    Results ............................................................ 17
2.4    Discussion ........................................................ 19
2.5    Conclusions ....................................................... 22
References ................................................................ 24

**3    From Microbes to Models: How Coping with Ear Infections
       Led to a New Paradigm** ............................................. 29
Alonzo H. Jones
3.1    Introduction ...................................................... 29
3.2    The Body's Defenses .............................................. 29
3.3    Strengthening our Defenses: The Prototype Model .............. 33
3.4    Strengthening Nasal Defenses ..................................... 34
3.5    Bacterial Adherence and Infectious Disease: A New Model
        that Honors Complexity and Adaptation ......................... 36

3.6     Conclusion........................................................................  38
References....................................................................................  41

**4    Suspending Hierarchy, Liberating Innovation: Personal
      Reflections on the Triple Chronotherapy Journey** ......................  43
Diane Hurd, Nicholas Coombs, Cara Fairbanks, Heather Landon,
Andrea Macdonald, Kyle Luraas, and Keri Cross
4.1     Introduction.........................................................................  43
4.2     Reflections..........................................................................  44
Reference....................................................................................  49

**5    Supporting Complex Dynamic Health Journeys Using
      Conversation to Avert Hospital Readmissions from the
      Community: An Ecological Perspective Incorporating
      Interoception** ..............................................................................  51
Carmel Martin, Joachim Sturmberg, Keith Stockman, Donald
Campbell, Lucy Hederman, Carl Vogel, and Kevin Smith
5.1     Background.........................................................................  51
5.2     Health Journeys, Resilience, Interoception, and Anticipatory
        Systems .............................................................................  54
5.3     Conversations Provide Insights ....................................  55
5.4     Implementing the Patient Journey Record System (PaJR) in
        Ireland and Australia .............................................................  56
5.5     Falling Between the Silos of "Evidence-based" Care ..............  60
5.6     PaJR: The Principles ................................................  60
5.7     Complex Adaptive Care and Feedback Loops: Preliminary
        Analysis from Pilot Studies....................................  62
5.8     Discussion ..........................................................................  66
5.9     Conclusions.........................................................................  68
References....................................................................................  70

**6    Transforming Monitoring and Improving Care with
      Variability-Derived Clinical Decision Support** ..........................  73
Christophe L. Herry, Nathan B. Scales, Kimberley D. Newman,
and Andrew J. E. Seely
6.1     Introduction.........................................................................  73
6.2     Our Approach .....................................................................  74
6.3     Example of a Clinical Application: Weaning and Variability
        Evaluation (WAVE) ...............................................  77
6.4     Conclusions.........................................................................  79
References....................................................................................  80

**7    Linking Gulf War Illness to Genome Instability, Somatic
      Evolution, and Complex Adaptive Systems** ............................  83
Henry H. Heng, Guo Liu, Sarah Regan, and Christine J. Ye
7.1     Introduction.........................................................................  83
7.2     The Unexpected Journey of Studying GWI ........................  84

7.3 The Complex Features of Chromosomal Aberrations
in GWI Patients...................................................... 86
7.4 GWI: A Case Study of Somatic Evolution and Complex
Adaptive Systems ................................................... 87
7.5 Search for the General Model for Common and Complex
Diseases/Illnesses .................................................. 89
7.6 Conclusions........................................................ 91
References................................................................ 93

8 The Key to Implementing an Accessible Information Standard
Across Complex Adaptive Health and Social Care Organisations .... 97
Beverley Ellis, John Howard, and Howard Leicester
8.1 Introduction........................................................ 97
8.2 Study Context ..................................................... 103
8.3 Methods........................................................... 104
8.4 Ethics ............................................................. 104
8.5 Results from the Workshop Sessions.............................. 105
8.6 Recommendations.................................................. 110
8.7 Achievements so Far .............................................. 110
8.8 Conclusion........................................................ 112
References................................................................ 114

Part II   Education and Healthcare Organisation

9 Transforming Health Education to Catalyze a Global
Paradigm Shift: Systems Thinking, Complexity, and Design
Thinking ................................................................ 119
Chad Swanson and Matt Widmer
9.1 Introduction........................................................ 119
9.2 A Systems Approach............................................... 121
9.3 Barriers to Change: We Are All Invested ......................... 125
9.4 Conclusion........................................................ 130
References................................................................ 131

10 New Ways of Knowing and Researching: Integrating
Complexity into a Translational Health Sciences Program ............ 133
Paige L. McDonald and Gaetano R. Lotrecchiano
10.1 Introduction........................................................ 133
10.2 A Complex Task at Hand .......................................... 134
10.3 Addressing the Needs of Diverse Stakeholders ................... 134
10.4 The Emerging Learning Model ..................................... 136
10.5 The "Hidden" Creative Tensions in the Model .................... 138
10.6 Conclusion........................................................ 142
References................................................................ 144

**11   Complexity of Knowledge in Primary Care: Understanding
      the Discipline's Requisite Knowledge—A Bibliometric Study** ........  147
Frauke Dunkel and Martin Konitzer
11.1   Starting the Quest to Understand the Requisite Knowledge
       for Family Medicine ...............................................  147
11.2   What Was Known? ..................................................  149
11.3   The New Approach: Professional Levels, Equivalents
       of Knowledge, and Bibliometric Method ...........................  150
11.4   Outcomes .........................................................  153
11.5   Comparing Corpora ................................................  157
11.6   Discussion .......................................................  159
11.7   Conclusions ......................................................  161
References .................................................................  163

**12   Journey to Refine Acute Care Hospital Process Improvement
      Projects for Ethically Complex Patients: Applying Complexity
      Tools to the Problem of Identifying Which Patients Need a
      Little More Attention than Most** ....................................  165
Evan G. DeRenzo
12.1   Introduction .....................................................  165
12.2   The Association Between Risk-Related Variables and
       the Cost of Legal Claims: A Proof-of-Concept Study at
       MedStar Washington Hospital Center (2012) .........................  167
12.3   Ethically Complicated Cases (ECC) Feasibility Study:
       Ethics, Electronic Medical Records, and Quality Markers .........  171
References .................................................................  175

**13   Relationship Between Health Outcomes and Health Factors:
      Analysis of 2016 Data in the Pacific Northwest Robert Wood
      Johnson Foundation** *County Health Rankings and Roadmaps* ........  177
Russell S. Gonnering and William J. Riley
13.1   Introduction .....................................................  177
13.2   County Health Rankings and Roadmaps ..............................  178
13.3   Conclusions ......................................................  185
13.4   Recommendations ..................................................  185
References .................................................................  186

**14   Positive Deviance in Health Care: Beware of Pseudo-Equifinality** ....  189
David C. Aron, Brigid Wilson, Chin-Lin Tseng, Orysya Soroka,
and Leonard M. Pogach
14.1   Introduction .....................................................  189
14.2   Methods ..........................................................  192
14.3   Analyses .........................................................  193
14.4   Discussion .......................................................  194
References .................................................................  196

**15  Understanding the Emergency Department Ecosystem Using
     Agent-Based Modelling: A Study of the Seven Oaks General
     Hospital Emergency Department** ........................................ 199
     Oluwayemisi Olugboji, Sergio G. Camorlinga,
     Ricardo Lobato de Faria, and Arjun Kaushal
     15.1  Introduction ........................................................ 199
     15.2  Agent-Based Models ................................................ 200
     15.3  Modeling and Simulation of the SOGH-ED ......................... 206
     15.4  Conclusions ........................................................ 210
     References .................................................................. 214

**Part III   The Art-Science Project**

**16  Leo's Lions: An Art-Science Project** .................................... 217
     Bruno Kissling and Esther Quarroz
     16.1  Introduction ........................................................ 217
     16.2  Leo's Story ......................................................... 218
     16.3  Inner Pictures and Illness Narratives .............................. 219
     16.4  The Art-Science Dialogue Project: Billings–Bern ................. 220
     16.5  Conclusions ........................................................ 226
     References .................................................................. 229

**The Programme** ................................................................. 231

**Index** ........................................................................... 241

# Contributors

**David C. Aron** Department of Veterans Affairs, Louis Stokes Cleveland VA Medical Center, Cleveland, OH, USA

Case Western Reserve University School of Medicine, Cleveland, OH, USA

**Jeanette M. Bennett** Department of Psychological Science and Health Psychology PhD Program, The University of North Carolina at Charlotte, Charlotte, NC, USA

**Sergio G. Camorlinga** Department of Applied Computer Science, University of Winnipeg, Winnipeg, MB, Canada

**Donald Campbell** Monash Medical Centre, General Medicine Offices, Clayton, VIC, Australia

**Maren J. Coffman** School of Nursing and Health Psychology PhD Program, The University of North Carolina at Charlotte, Charlotte, NC, USA

**Nicholas Coombs** Billings Clinic, Psychiatric Center, Billings, MT, USA

**Keri Cross** Billings Clinic, Psychiatric Center, Billings, MT, USA

**Ricardo Lobato de Faria** Seven Oaks General Hospital, University of Manitoba, Winnipeg, MB, Canada

**Evan G. DeRenzo** John J. Lynch, MD Center for Ethics, MedStar Washington Hospital Center, Washington, DC, USA

**Frauke Dunkel** Praxis Drs Sieker, Thale, Germany

**Beverley Ellis** Health Informatics Team, School of Health Sciences, UCLan, Preston, UK

**Cara Fairbanks** Billings Clinic, Psychiatric Center, Billings, MT, USA

**Russell S. Gonnering** Arizona State University, Elm Grove, WI, USA

**Lucy Hederman** Centre for Health Informatics (CHI), Trinity College Dublin, The University of Dublin, College Green, Dublin 2, Ireland

**Henry H. Heng** Center for Molecular Medicine and Genetics, and Department of Pathology, Wayne State University School of Medicine, Detroit, MI, USA

**Christophe L. Herry** The Ottawa Hospital Research Institute, Clinical Epidemiology Program, Ottawa, ON, Canada

**John Howard** Health Informatics Team, School of Health Sciences, UCLan, Preston, UK

**Diane Hurd** Billings Clinic, Psychiatric Center, Billings, MT, USA

**Alonzo H. Jones** Common Sense Medicine, Plainview, TX, USA

**Arjun Kaushal** George & Fay Yee Centre for Healthcare Innovation, Winnipeg, MB, Canada

**Bruno Kissling** Elfenau Praxis Bern, Switzerland

**Martin Konitzer** Academic Teaching Practice, Medizinische Hochschule Hannover, Schwarmstedt, Germany

**Heather Landon** Billings Clinic, Psychiatric Center, Billings, MT, USA

**Howard Leicester** Health Informatics Team, School of Health Sciences, UCLan, Preston, UK

**Guo Liu** Center for Molecular Medicine and Genetics, Wayne State University School of Medicine, Detroit, MI, USA

**Gaetano R. Lotrecchiano** Department of Clinical Research and Leadership, George Washington University School of Medicine and Health Sciences, Washington, DC, USA

**Kyle Luraas** Billings Clinic, Psychiatric Center, Billings, MT, USA

**Andrea Macdonald** Billings Clinic, Psychiatric Center, Billings, MT, USA

**Joseph S. Marino** Department of Kinesiology, The University of North Carolina at Charlotte, Charlotte, NC, USA

**Carmel Martin** Monash Medical Centre, General Medicine Offices, Clayton, VIC, Australia

**Paige L. McDonald** Department of Clinical Research and Leadership, George Washington University School of Medicine and Health Sciences, Washington, DC, USA

**Kimberley D. Newman** The Ottawa Hospital Research Institute, Clinical Epidemiology Program, Ottawa, ON, Canada

**Oluwayemisi Olugboji** Department of Applied Computer Science, University of Winnipeg, Winnipeg, MB, Canada

**Leonard M. Pogach** Department of Veterans Affairs, New Jersey Healthcare System, East Orange, NJ, USA

Department of Biostatistics, School of Public Health, Rutgers University, Piscataway, NJ, USA

**Esther Quarroz** Perspectiven Entwickeln, Bern, Switzerland

**Sarah Regan** Center for Molecular Medicine and Genetics, Wayne State University School of Medicine, Detroit, MI, USA

**William J. Riley** Arizona State University, Tempe, AZ, USA

**Nicolas Rohleder** Department of Psychology and Sports Science, Friedrich-Alexander-University of Erlangen-Nürnberg Erlangen, Erlangen, Germany

Department of Psychology, Brandeis University, Waltham, MA, USA

**Lydia G. Roos** Health Psychology PhD Program, The University of North Carolina at Charlotte, Charlotte, NC, USA

**Nathan B. Scales** The Ottawa Hospital Research Institute, Clinical Epidemiology Program, Ottawa, ON, Canada

**Andrew J. E. Seely** The Ottawa Hospital Research Institute, Clinical Epidemiology Program, Ottawa, ON, Canada

**Kevin Smith** Research Computing Centre Level 5, The University of Queensland, St Lucia, QLD, Australia

**Orysya Soroka** Department of Veterans Affairs, New Jersey Healthcare System, East Orange, NJ, USA

**Keith Stockman** Monash Medical Centre, General Medicine Offices, Clayton, VIC, Australia

**Joachim P. Sturmberg** School of Medicine and Public Health, University of Newcastle, Newcastle, NSW, Australia

Foundation President, International Society for Systems and Complexity Sciences for Health, Newcastle, NSW, Australia

**Chad Swanson** Arizona State University School for the Science of Healthcare Delivery, Utah Valley Hospital, Provo, UT, USA

**Chin-Lin Tseng** Department of Veterans Affairs, New Jersey Healthcare System, East Orange, NJ, USA

Department of Biostatistics, School of Public Health, Rutgers University, Piscataway, NJ, USA

**Carl Vogel** Trinity Centre for Computing and Language Studies, Trinity College Dublin, The University of Dublin, College Green, Dublin 2, Ireland

**Matt Widmer**  Romney Institute of Public Management, Brigham Young University, Provo, UT, USA

**Brigid Wilson**  Department of Veterans Affairs, Louis Stokes Cleveland VA Medical Center, Cleveland, OH, USA

**Christine J. Ye**  The Division of Hematology/Oncology, Department of Internal Medicine, Comprehensive Cancer Center, University of Michigan, Ann Arbor, MI, USA

# Chapter 1
# Putting Health Back into the Healthcare System

Joachim P. Sturmberg

> *The good physician treats the disease;*
> *the great physician treats the patient who has the disease.*
>
> William Osler

What should be the focus of the healthcare system? This question arose when Susanne (not her real name), a 24-year-old dying from cancer, ask me the week prior to her death: *Doc, I know I am dying, but can you tell me why I am feeling so healthy?*

One might think that this is a rather paradoxical question; however, it is a question that challenges the fundamental assumptions we hold about the nature and purpose of what we call "the healthcare system".

## 1.1 Exploring Our Mindsets

Mindsets define a particular way of thinking; they allude to our attitudes and opinions about things. Three common worldviews that determine one's approach towards Susanne's question—*can one be healthy at the time of dying from cancer*—can be categorised as:

- The *objectivist's worldview*—clearly, this is a paradoxical statement
- The *person-centred worldview*—health is an experiential state, one's experiences occur in various contexts, and the context of dying can be experienced in Susanne's way

J. P. Sturmberg (✉)
School of Medicine and Public Health, University of Newcastle, PO Box 3010, Newcastle, NSW 2260, Australia

Foundation President, International Society for Systems and Complexity Sciences for Health, Newcastle, NSW, Australia
e-mail: jp.sturmberg@gmail.com

© Springer International Publishing AG, part of Springer Nature 2018
J. P. Sturmberg (ed.), *Putting Systems and Complexity Sciences Into Practice*,
https://doi.org/10.1007/978-3-319-73636-5_1

1

- The *professional worldview*—if Susanne feels healthy in the final stages of her life, then we must have provided exceptional care

## 1.2 Why Are Health Systems Focused on Disease?

Why are the objectivist and professional worldviews so prevalent, and why is it so hard for essentially all "health system professionals" to adopt a person-centred perspective?

This question is even more perplexing when one considers the philosophy and history of health care[1] which has largely been about *caring for the person/patient*. It is only for the past 175 years that a shift in focus on the *object of disease* became possible. There are a number of reasons for this including:

- The classification of the "patient's condition" as diseases (*taxonomy*)
- The discovery of the "causative organisms" responsible for most of the diseases of the time (*aetiology*)
- The correlation of the clinical picture of the suffering patient with the "seat of disease" in the post-mortem study [1] (*pathology*)

### 1.2.1 Progress at a Price

Undoubtedly these developments have made medicine suddenly much more effective and have saved many lives, but at a price. The price became obvious to many eminent clinicians very early on during the phase of unprecedented scientific and technological advancement (Fig. 1.1).

For example, Rudolph Virchow, while deeply interested in studying disease mechanisms, was far more interested in the causes of ill health in the community. While accepting the infectious mechanisms of disease and discovering immunological ones, he recognised that the living and working conditions of the people are much more important in causing disease. As he famously pointed out health professionals have much larger responsibilities in keeping people healthy:

> Medicine is a social science, and politics is nothing else but medicine on a large scale. Medicine, as a social science, as the science of human beings, has the obligation to point out problems and to attempt their theoretical solution: the politician, the practical anthropologist, must find the means for their actual solution ... Science for its own sake usually means nothing more than science for the sake of the people who happen to be pursuing it. Knowledge which is unable to support action is not genuine - and how unsure is activity without understanding ... If medicine is to fulfill her great task, then she must enter the political and social life ... The physicians are the natural attorneys of the poor, and the social problems should largely be solved by them.
>
> (1848), in Virchow's weekly medical newspaper Die Medizinische Reform

---

[1] *Health care* refers to the act of caring; *healthcare* to the institution.

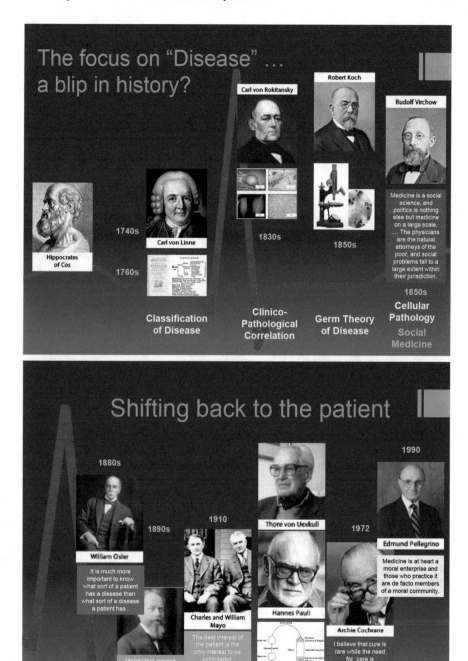

**Fig. 1.1** The temporal nature of "disease" in the history of healthcare

## 1.3 The Need to Refocus on the Person/Patient

Since the 1850s the need for medicine to refocus on the *care of the patient* rather than his diseases has been emphasised by a long list of eminent physicians and philosophers alike:

- William Osler—*It is much more important to know what sort of a patient has a disease than what sort of a disease a patient has.*
- Edmund Husserl [2]—*Merely fact-minded sciences make merely fact-minded people.*
- The Mayo brothers [3]—*The best interest of the patient is the only interest to be considered.*
- Thure von Uexküll and Hannes Pauli [4]—*For the science of medicine, however, the aspect of the subjective universe is especially important because all studies show that people do not necessarily respond to the objectively determinable occurrences of the environment but to what the occurrences mean to them subjectively.*
- Archie Cochrane [5]—*I believe that cure is rare, while the need for care is widespread and that the pursuit for cure at all cost may restrict the supply of care.*
- Edmund Pellegrino and David Thomasma [6]—*Medicine is at heart a moral enterprise, and those who practice it are* de facto *members of a moral community.*

Despite these passionate pleas for a humanistic and holistic approach to health care, the focus of healthcare systems remains on managing diseases. Thus, a more apt way of describing what we have would be "disease management systems". And unsurprisingly, being concerned with the object of disease detracts—or even makes it undesirable and unnecessary—to appreciate the consequences of the object, disease, on the subject affected, the person or patient.

## 1.4 The Person/Patient at the Centre: Connecting the Subjective with the Objective

Connecting the subjective with the objective is the basis of health care or as Uexküll and Pauli put it: *The experience of sharing a common reality with the physician is of great importance to the patient. It is part of each therapy* [4].

Making this a common reality, the "system of healthcare" needs to shift its focus back on the person/patient; in other words: we need to *redesign health systems* [7–10].

### 1.4.1 Complex Adaptive Health Systems

Health systems are a form of organisational systems. Complex adaptive organisational systems function based on three key principles:

- *The definition of its purpose and goals*
- *The definition of its value and "simple (operating) rules"*
- *The alignment of its subsystems with the system's overarching purpose, goals and values framework*

Of note, a complex adaptive health system is an umbrella system that contains the many diverse subsystems, subsubsytems and so forth of a "health system". The health system maintaining the focus on these three key principles allows the emergence of a seamlessly integrated health system, both within and across its multiple organisational levels.

Importantly, the "healthcare system" is only ONE of the many subsystems of a complex adaptive "health system". It is that part of the health system that delivers a wide range of health professional—colloquially known as *medical*—care.

Primary care, secondary care and tertiary care in turn are organisational and functional subsystems of the "healthcare system". Each of these subsystems has a particular focus and role in the "care of a person/patient" and, when properly integrated, provides a seamless "health care experience".

### 1.4.2 Complex Adaptive "Person-Centred" Health Systems

Putting health—defined as the "experience of health" by the person—back into the health system can be conceptualised through the health vortex model [11–13] (Fig. 1.2). The health vortex has at its focal point "the needs of the person/patient". As the vortex builds upwards, the organisational layers of healthcare, community health and prevention and finally the health policy domain emerge. As a "person-centred" system, all organisational layers maintain their focus on "the needs of the person/patient"—such a health system is vertically and horizontally seamlessly integrated.

### 1.4.3 Connecting the Subjective with the Objective

Health, like illness and disease, are themselves highly complex adaptive states and must be distinguished from the less complex state of disease [14]. It is the loss of complexity that creates the "patterns of diagnosable diseases". Health care facilitates the re-emergence of a new highly complex adaptive state resulting in "healing the person/patient".

## The Patient's Health Experience Driving the Health Care Vortex

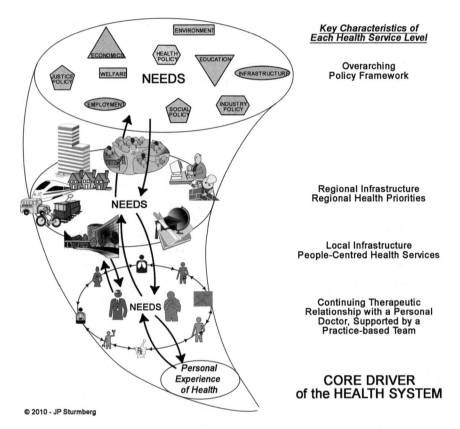

Fig. 1.2 Health at the centre of the health (and healthcare) systems

## 1.5 Conclusions

It would appear that the prevailing pre-eminent focus on the *object of disease* may well be no more than a *blip on the timeline of the history of medicine*. As in every complex adaptive system, perturbations leave their mark—being able to understand the causes and temporal consequences of some diseases has had dramatic effects; however, the central concern of medical care remains the person affected by the disease. The recent findings of the psychoneuroimmunological pathways [15, 16], and in particular the influence of the "social determinants of health" [17] on these pathways, as the drivers of disease processes, and the understanding of modulating these pathways through social, emotional and cognitive based interventions, have opened the door to much more effective care for the many people experiencing illness without disease.

These insights have also opened doors to the redesign of health systems around the person and his health experiences; the health vortex model offers a tangible framework to guide the redesign of health systems that make *health* the driver in the pursuit of achieving highly integrated, constantly adapting health systems that *meet the needs of the person/patient*.

## The Journey

My journey into systems and complexity sciences entails two childhood experiences and a crisis in the early years as a medical practitioner. I learnt from my father, a mechanical engineer, the notion of unintended consequences; his designs of new machinery to make it possible to build very high precision products, like the spindles for the canal lift at Henrichenburg, close to where I grew up, or the magnets for the first hadron collider at CERN, meant that highly qualified tradesmen would lose their jobs, and with it manufacturing would lose a unique set of valuable but underappreciated skills solely residing in these men, something that weighed heavily on his social conscience.

The exposure to Donella Maedows' *Limits to Growth* provided a different way of seeing and thinking, that of interconnected and interdependent systems and their nonlinear system dynamics behaviour.

Unfortunately medical school pushed all of this to the side, only to hound me in my early career in general practice. At the time of crisis, Ian McWhinney and Ed Pellegrino came to my rescue.

Ian McWhinney helped me to understand my role in healthcare. He emphasised the importance of understanding the contextual dimensions and the underlying feedback relationships that characterise the patient's illness experience. Ed Pellegrino opened my eyes to the epistemology of medicine as a discipline whose essential focus is on both health and disease.

The journey into health-related systems and complexity sciences from the start was a collaborative effort with my close friend and colleague Carmel Martin— we co-edit the *Forum on Systems and Complexity in Health* within the *Journal of Evaluation in Clinical Practice* and co-edited the *Handbook of Systems and Complexity in Health*. The network grew slowly over time, and its interactions have shaped my understandings and insights of health and illness and what this means in terms of shaping a person-centred health system. Important collaborators along the way include amongst others Di O'Halloran, Jeanette Bennett, Andrew Miles, Ruben McDaniel, Henry Heng, Bruno Kissling, Andrew Seely, Bruce West, Geoff McDonnell, Curt Lindberg, Stefan Topolski and Stephen Lewis.

The "rediscovery" of the interconnected nature of the world, and in particular that of the patient, has opened my eyes to the great deficiencies of and the need for the redesign of our approaches to healthcare and the healthcare system, resulting in the recently published book *Health System Redesign: How to Make Health Care Person-Centered, Equitable, and Sustainable* [10].

Take-Home Message

- A "health-focused" health system requires a *person-centred* mindset
- The developments and discoveries of taxonomy, aetiology and pathology gave rise to the *focus on the object of disease*
- A health system that puts the focus on *health as a person's experiential state* does not undermine the role of "disease-focused" care where needed
- Putting health back into the healthcare system requires a *collaborative redesign effort*

# References

1. Sedivy R. Rokitansky und die Wiener Medizinische Schule. Von der Naturphilosophie zur Naturwissenschaft. Wien Med Wochenschr. 2004;154(19–20):443–53.
2. Husserl E. The basic problems of phenomenology: from the lectures, winter semester, 1910–1911. Dordrecht: Springer; 2006.
3. Mayo Clinic Health Policy Centre. Building a New Vision for Health Care in America. Your Voice. New Vision. www.mayoclinic.org/healthpolicycenter.
4. Uexküll Tv, Pauli HG. The mind-body problem in medicine. Adv J Inst Adv Health. 1986;3(4):158–74.
5. Cochrane A. Effectiveness and efficiency. Random reflections on health services. London: The Nuffield Provincial Hospitals Trust; 1972.
6. Pellegrino E, Thomasma D. A philosophical basis of medical practice. Towards a philosophy and ethic of the healing professions. New York: Oxford University Press; 1981.
7. Institute of Medicine. Crossing the quality chasm: a new health system for the 21st century, 2001. Available at: www.iom.edu/file.asp?id=27184.
8. Jones P. Design for care: innovating healthcare experience. New York: Rosenfeld Media; 2013.
9. Kolko J. Design thinking comes of age. Harv Bus Rev. 2015;93(9):66–9.
10. Sturmberg J. Health system redesign: how to make health care person-centered, equitable, and sustainable. New York: Springer; 2017.
11. Sturmberg JP, O'Halloran DM, Martin CM. People at the centre of complex adaptive health systems reform. Med J Aust. 2010;193(8):474–8.
12. Sturmberg JP, O'Halloran DM, Martin CM. Understanding health system reform - a complex adaptive systems perspective. J Eval Clin Pract. 2012;18(1):202–8.
13. Sturmberg JP, O'Halloran DM, Martin CM. Health care reform - the need for a complex adaptive systems approach. In: Sturmberg JP, Martin CM, editors. Handbook of systems and complexity in health. New York: Springer; 2013. p. 827–53.
14. Katerndahl DA. Is your practice really that predictable? Nonlinearity principles in family medicine. J Fam Pract. 2005;54(11):970–7.
15. Kemeny M. Psychoneuroimmunology. In: Friedman H, editor. Oxford handbook of health psychology. New York: Oxford University Press; 2011. p. 138–61.
16. Sturmberg JP, Bennett JM, Martin CM, Picard M. 'Multimorbidity' as the manifestation of network disturbances. J Eval Clin Pract. 2017;23(1):199–208.
17. Slavich GM, Cole SW. The emerging field of human social genomics. Clin Psychol Sci. 2013;1(3):331–48.

# Part I
# Patient Care

In the seven contributions in this first part of *Putting Systems and Complexity Sciences into Practice*, the authors share their experiences about a better understanding of their patients' needs.

- Can smokers be healthy, or are they as unhealthy as lonely people?
- Is there an effective way of preventing middle ear infections in babies and young children reducing the need for repeated courses of antibiotics?
- How to respond to a desperate patient who wants to try a so far unproven treatment for his depression that has failed all known treatment protocols?
- Can continuing monitoring of self-rated health prevent unnecessary hospitalizations?
- How can heart and respiratory rate variability analysis enhance clinical decision-making of the critically ill patient?
- What happens to the genome of as yet unexplained complex diseases like Gulf War illness?
- Providing access to health information for people with any form of disability, developing and implementing an "accessible information standard."

These examples highlight that healthcare does not have to fail the patient as Michael Porter[1] suggested: *Ultimately, health care fails the most basic test. It's not organized around the needs of the patient.*

---

[1]Rose C. Charlie Rose Talks to Harvard's Michael Porter. Bloomberg News. 1-Mar-2013. https://www.bloomberg.com/news/articles/2013-02-28/charlie-rose-talks-to-harvards-michael-porter.

# Chapter 2
# Healthy Smoker: An Oxymoron? Maybe, But It Is More Complicated Than That

Jeanette M. Bennett, Lydia G. Roos, Joseph S. Marino, Nicolas Rohleder, and Maren J. Coffman

## 2.1 Introduction

Today, diseases that contribute to morbidity and mortality have significantly changed from infectious agents as the main culprit to chronic conditions, in which pathogenesis occurs over years [1]. Using a biopsychosocial approach to disease, the level of one's psychological stress can exacerbate or slow the dysregulation of the body as it ages, either hastening or delaying the development of chronic conditions

J. M. Bennett (✉)
Department of Psychological Science and Health Psychology PhD Program, The University of North Carolina at Charlotte, 4049 Colvard, 9201 University City Blvd, Charlotte, NC 28223, USA
e-mail: jbenne70@uncc.edu

L. G. Roos
Health Psychology PhD Program, The University of North Carolina at Charlotte, 4018 Colvard, 9201 University City Blvd, Charlotte, NC 28223, USA
e-mail: ljames38@uncc.edu

J. S. Marino
Department of Kinesiology, The University of North Carolina at Charlotte, 254 Cameron, 9201 University City Blvd, Charlotte, NC 28223, USA
e-mail: jmarin10@uncc.edu

N. Rohleder
Department of Psychology and Sports Science, Friedrich-Alexander-University of Erlangen-Nürnberg Erlangen, Nägelsbachstr. 49a, Raum 3.114, 91052 Erlangen, Germany

Department of Psychology, Brandeis University, Waltham, MA, USA
e-mail: nicolas.rohleder@fau.de

M. J. Coffman
School of Nursing and Health Psychology PhD Program, The University of North Carolina at Charlotte, 423A CHHS Building, 9201 University City Blvd, Charlotte, NC 28223, USA
e-mail: mjcoffma@uncc.edu

© Springer International Publishing AG, part of Springer Nature 2018
J. P. Sturmberg (ed.), *Putting Systems and Complexity Sciences Into Practice*,
https://doi.org/10.1007/978-3-319-73636-5_2

such as cardiovascular disease, obesity, type 2 diabetes, and major depression [2, 3]. This stress activates physiological systems evolved to support survival [4].

Stress is ubiquitous in life; however, rarely does an individual find themselves in a life-or-death situation, needing to survive. Yet, once stress is perceived, a cascade of biobehavioral adjustments occur which assist the individual's ability to engage with or retreat from the situation [5, 6]. Regardless of whether one engages or retreats, our bodily systems have the same response for managing the stressor: (1) activation of the sympathetic nervous system (SNS), (2) withdrawal of the parasympathetic nervous system (PNS), and (3) stimulation of the hypothalamic-pituitary-adrenal (HPA) axis [7, 8]. These neuroendocrine changes modulate a variety of hormone levels that affect the functionality of the entire body at inter- and intracellular levels.

Acute stress reactions are often advantageous as they assist the individual's ability to handle the situation successfully. Physiological systemic variability (e.g., cardiovascular and neuroendocrine reactivity) is necessary to navigate acute stressful experiences allowing individuals to identify, respond to, and recover from stress. However, chronic stimulation results in excessive demand on multiple bodily systems, leading to reduced variability in these physiological systems and, consequently, loss of adaptive function and more psychological stress [5, 9, 10], creating a vicious negative cycle that continually dysregulates the system as the "resting" state moves toward the activated state (see Fig. 2.1). *This physiological shift wreaks* havoc *on human health.*

The link between physiological dysregulation and stress has been observed in many populations, including individuals with major depression and anxiety disorders [11–14]. Even psychosocial factors such as loneliness and socioeconomic status are related to the negative physiological adaptations [15–17]. However, examining this stress evolution on physiological systems (Fig. 2.1; large red arrow) in humans can be difficult because life stressors are unpredictable, and psychological stress depends on the individual's perception. In addition, factors like depression, anxiety, loneliness, and chronic health conditions that are reliably associated with physiological dysregulation do not have precise start and end points for researchers to investigate changes linked to cyclic depressive episodes or disease flare-ups [11–14]. Thus, a human model of how acute stress transitions to chronic stress is critical to advance our fundamental understanding of how stress and psychosocial factors modulate physiological functioning (red arrow in Fig. 2.1).

Cigarette smoking has identifiable start and end dates; smokers can typically recall when they started and possibly stopped using cigarettes [18]. In addition, it is reliably linked to the "wear-and-tear" or dysregulation of multiple bodily systems (e.g., cardiovascular, immune, endocrine, etc.) [19] that mirrors the effects of stress on the body. Data from our lab suggest that before observable dysregulation (e.g., no current mental or physical health diagnosis or pharmacological treatment), *immune cells from smokers are less affected by stress hormones such as cortisol when compared to nonsmokers' immune cells* when controlling for known confounds like current depressive symptoms, childhood trauma, and recent stressful life events [20]. Immune cells resistant or insensitive to cortisol's effects also known as glucocorticoid resistance (GR) are a factor related to chronic disease [12]. GR

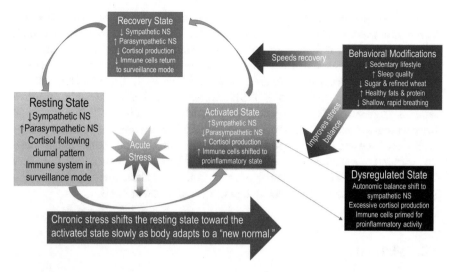

**Fig. 2.1** Stress system activation and regulation. For non-stressed individuals, the body exists at rest for the majority of time. A stressful encounter drives the body into the activated state; the sympathetic nervous system and HPA axis activate to manage the stressor. The body moves into recovery and eventually returns to rest. This ability to move through activation and recovery fairly quickly demonstrates variability and less dysregulation (indicated by thicker blue arrows). However, in chronically stressed individual, their body spends less time at rest, slowly shifting their new baseline toward the activated state. If this process continues (along the red arrow), the individual's body adapts to a point where it becomes rigid and inflexible (indicated by the thin straight lines), maintaining a physiological state that is dysregulated until failure or disease development. However, via behavioral modification, an individual's system can reverse the dysregulation and approach the healthy, non-stressed stress system activation. Notably, the ability of an individual to make behavioral modifications is driven by the self, but the psychosocial environment (e.g., employment, leisure time) and sociocultural influences (e.g., public policy, government law) dramatically affect permanent lifestyle improvement. *NS* nervous system; *HPA* hypothalamic-pituitary-adrenal

reduces one of the body's most potent anti-inflammatory regulators, thereby driving physiological dysregulation.

Furthermore, we have explored the role psychosocial factors, such as loneliness, might play in this relationship. In our preliminary investigation [21], the interaction of *loneliness* and smoking status predicted changes in the immune cells' sensitivity to cortisol. Specifically, nonsmokers who reported greater loneliness had immune dysfunction mirroring that of smokers, suggesting that *loneliness in nonsmokers changed physiological functioning similarly to smoking cigarettes*. Since factors like smoking and loneliness have similar modulating effects on the immune system, we also investigated whether an individual's self-rated health might be a better predictor of immune dysregulation than simply smoking behavior.

Self-rated health (SRH) reliably predicts morbidity and mortality risk, especially among stress-related chronic conditions [22–24]. Outlined in a review, individuals who report higher SRH are more likely to participate in better health behaviors, report less psychological distress, and have greater socioeconomic status. Although these unique factors are associated with SRH, none of them explain all the variability observed within SRH [25]. Moreover, neither physician's rating of patient's disease nor clinical physical assessments reflect a patient's SRH or actual disease progression. This discrepancy highlights the disconnect between the current clinical practice and how the body is functioning. With this and the biopsychosocial lens in mind, we examined whether SRH was a better predictor of physiological functioning than a single health behavior: smoking. We also mirrored our smoking by loneliness interaction analysis by replacing smoking with SRH.

## 2.2 Methods

### 2.2.1 Participant Screening

We screened potential participants for medication use, current diagnosis or treatment for chronic diseases that influences neuroendocrine function or inflammatory outcomes, and lifetime tobacco smoking behavior. Twenty-four eligible smokers were brought into the lab immediately, while eligible never smokers were placed in a sample pool until they matched a smoker on sex, age, and body mass index (BMI). All sample characteristics are summarized in Table 2.1. Following a smoking participant session, we immediately contacted a matching never smoker to complete the lab session.

### 2.2.2 Laboratory Protocol

After a 12-h fast, participants arrived in the lab between 7 and 9 AM and provided their informed consent. Final eligibility requirements were reviewed with participants, including body temperature assessment, expired carbon monoxide levels to confirm smoking status (elevated in current smokers), and for females, screening for the presence of human chorionic gonadotropin (hCG) in their urine. Following eligibility confirmation, a blood sample was collected via venipuncture for immunoassay into lavender-topped blood collection tubes. Participants were provided with a variety of options for a pre-packaged breakfast and beverage. Sociodemographic and psychosocial questionnaires were completed after their meal and received compensation of $35 for their time.

**Table 2.1** Average sample characteristics and change in inflammatory gene expression [mean ± SEM or number (%)] by smoking status and the overall sample

| | Smokers ($n = 24$) | Never smokers ($n = 24$) | Overall ($n = 48$) |
|---|---|---|---|
| Age (years) | 30.62 ± 1.64 | 30.50 ± 1.65 | 30.56 ± 1.15 |
| BMI (kg/m$^2$) | 26.41 ± 1.07 | 26.67 ± 1.05 | 26.54 ± 0.74 |
| Sex (female) | 10 (41.7%) | 10 (41.7%) | 20 (41.7%) |
| Race (white) | 17 (70.8%) | 13 (54.2%) | 30 (62.5%) |
| Education complete | | | |
|   Some college or less | 9 (37.5%) | 8 (33.3%) | 17 (35.4%) |
|   Bachelor's degree | 13 (54.2%) | 11 (45.8%) | 24 (50.0%) |
|   Graduate degree | 2 (8.3%) | 5 (20.8%) | 7 (14.6%) |
| Pack-years | 9.42 ± 1.88 | | |
| Nicotine addiction | 3.34 ± 0.40 | | |
| Systolic BP (mmHg) | 118.93 ± 1.84 | 116.22 ± 1.81 | 117.57 ± 1.29 |
| Diastolic BP (mmHg) | 71.46 ± 1.31 | 71.22 ± 1.91 | 71.34 ± 1.14 |
| Heart rate (bpm)** | 80.13 ± 1.73 | 71.29 ± 2.25 | 75.72 ± 1.55 |
| Recent stressful life events* | 2.79 ± 0.28 | 1.67 ± 0.33 | 2.23 ± 0.23 |
| Childhood trauma* | 44.25 ± 3.18 | 34.70 ± 1.79 | 39.57 ± 1.96 |
| Depression** | 12.79 ± 1.78 | 5.46 ± 0.81 | 9.13 ± 1.11 |
| Perceived stress | 20.00 ± 0.62 | 19.96 ± 0.36 | 19.98 ± 0.36 |
| Anxiety** | 30.21 ± 1.34 | 24.71 ± 0.72 | 27.46 ± 0.86 |
| Sleep quality* | 6.25 ± 0.60 | 4.37 ± 0.55 | 5.31 ± 0.43 |
| Loneliness* | 42.25 ± 2.38 | 35.33 ± 1.85 | 38.79 ± 1.57 |
| Self-rated health* | 58.33 ± 3.25 | 69.79 ± 3.98 | 64.06 ± 2.67 |
| Cytokine mRNA expression | | | |
| $\Delta$TNF-$\alpha$* | 8.09 ± 1.81 | 18.90 ± 4.07 | 13.50 ± 2.34 |
| $\Delta$IFN-$\gamma$* | 3.31 ± 0.86 | 6.84 ± 1.42 | 5.04 ± 0.85 |
| $\Delta$IL-6 | 243.94 ± 157.49 | 273.14 ± 88.63 | 258.54 ± 89.42 |

*Note.* Group difference indicated: *$p < 0.05$; **$p < 0.01$
*BMI* body mass index; $kg/m^2$ kilograms per meter squared; *BP* blood pressure; *mmHg* millimeters of mercury; *bpm* beats per minute; $\Delta$ change from LPS gene expression to LPS+DEX gene expression; *TNF-$\alpha$* tumor necrosis factor-alpha; *IFN-$\gamma$* interferon-gamma; *IL-6* interleukin-6

## 2.2.3 Questionnaires

Participants self-reported their highest education level to estimate socioeconomic status, as education is considered less vulnerable to acute current economic conditions compared to income and job status [17]. In addition, they confirmed their sex and age as well as their smoking history for calculation of pack years as an estimate of lifetime tobacco exposure (i.e., number of packs smoked per day * number of years smoking). The Fagerström Test for Nicotine Dependence was used to assess smokers' dependence on nicotine [26]. Values were indicated as low (1–2), low to moderate (3–4), moderate (5–7), and high (8+) levels of dependence; higher values indicate greater dependence.

Primary predictors were assessed via the following measurements. The UCLA Loneliness Scale was used to measure subjective feelings of loneliness and social isolation [27]. The scale is highly reliable and demonstrates good construct and convergent validity [27]. Higher scores indicate more subjective loneliness. Self-rated health was captured via a single item "In general, you would say your health is": with a 5-point Likert scale (poor, fair, good, very good, excellent) from the Medical Outcomes Study short-form 36 (SF-36) [28]. Higher values indicate better self-rated health.

Secondary factors were measured via the following questionnaires. Depressive symptoms experienced within the past week were captured using the 20-item Center for Epidemiologic Studies Depression Scale (CES-D; [29]). It is a highly reliable and well-validated scale across many populations with a score of 16 established as a clinical cutoff indicating at risk for depression [30]. Values range from 0 to 60 with higher values indicating more depressive symptoms. Recent stressful life events encountered over the past 12 months were captured using a modified version of the Life Events Scale [31, 32]. Given the young adult to adult population, 14 life events focusing on interpersonal relationships and job-related issues were assessed. Participants had an option to provide up to three additional life events beyond the scope of events listed. Endorsed life events were summed, resulting in a range from 0 to 17. The Childhood Trauma Questionnaire (CTQ; [33]) was used to determine history and severity of five types of maltreatment during childhood: emotional abuse, physical abuse, sexual abuse, and emotional and physical neglect. It is a reliable scale with 4-month test–retest reliability and correlated well with structured interview-based rating of childhood abuse [33, 34]. The self-report measure uses a 5-point Likert scale with higher scores indicating greater exposure to childhood trauma. Sleep quality was assessed via the Pittsburgh Sleep Quality Index (PSQI), a well-validated and reliable measure of sleep with a cutoff suggesting clinical sleep disturbances [35]. Higher values indicate poorer quality sleep.

### 2.2.4 Glucocorticoid Receptor Sensitivity Assay

A modified version of the immunoassay previously reported to detect glucocorticoid receptor sensitivity was used [36]. Whole blood was diluted with phosphate-buffered saline (PBS) and exposed to one of the following treatments: no treatment (PBS), 100 nM dexamethasone (DEX), 1 ng/mL lipopolysaccharide (LPS), and DEX+LPS for 2 h at 37 °C with 5% $CO_2$. Following incubation, white blood cells were isolated, washed, and lysed to harvest cytokine mRNA via the PerfectPure RNA blood kit (5 PRIME, Gaithersburg, MD). Cytokine (IL-6, TNF-$\alpha$, and IFN-$\gamma$) mRNA was quantified with real-time PCR, and each participant's data were normalized to their control treated value. For more specific details, please see our description in a previous publication [20].

### 2.2.5  Data Analysis

To examine glucocorticoid receptor sensitivity, we calculated the change in mRNA expression from LPS-treated immune cells to LPS+DEX-treated immune cells, resulting in positive change scores as all participants' immune cells were at least minimally sensitive to DEX. Separate hierarchical linear regressions were used to examine smoking status or self-rated health interactive effects with loneliness on the DEX suppression change score.

## 2.3  Results

Participants ($n = 48$) were $30.6 \pm 1.2$ years old, overweight (BMI $= 26.5 \pm 0.7 \, \text{kg/m}^2$), and primarily identified as White (62.5%) and had completed a college degree (64.6%). In addition, 20 participants were female (41.7%). Smokers averaged $6.6 \pm 1.4$ years since starting smoking, and tobacco history ranged from 1–40 pack years with an average of $9.4 \pm 1.9$. Smokers were low to moderately dependent on nicotine (Fagerström score $= 3.3 \pm 0.4$). Compared to never smokers, smokers reported more depressive symptoms, higher number of childhood traumatic experiences and recent stressful life events, and poorer sleep and had an elevated heart rate ($t \, s(46) > -2.58, p \, s < 0.05$). In addition, all expected zero-order relationships among psychosocial variables existed (see Table 2.2). Critical to the primary predictors, better self-rated health was associated with never smoking ($r = -0.31, p < 0.05$).

Using hierarchical linear regression controlling for recent negative life events and childhood traumatic experiences, loneliness interacted with SRH to predict a significant change in TNF-$\alpha$ gene expression ($p = 0.002$), mirroring our previous finding with the interaction between loneliness and smoking [21]. Specifically, among those with higher SRH, as loneliness increased, the change in inflammatory gene expression in between LPS and DEX + LPS was smaller. However, there was no relationship between loneliness and immune function among those with poorer SRH (see Table 2.3 and Fig. 2.2). Importantly, the overall model including self-rated health explained more of the variance in the change in inflammatory gene expression in between LPS and DEX + LPS compared to smoking status, $R^2 = 0.26$ and $R^2 = 0.21$, respectively. For the change in IFN-$\gamma$ and IL-6 gene expression, the patterns with smoking and SRH interacting with loneliness were similar but did not reach statistical significance.

**Table 2.2** Summary of all zero-order correlations among study variables

| Variable | 1 | 2 | 3 | 4 | 5 | 6 | 7 | 8 | 9 | 10 | 11 | 12 | 13 | 14 | 15 | 16 | 17 |
|---|---|---|---|---|---|---|---|---|---|---|---|---|---|---|---|---|---|
| 1. Age (years) | – | 0.16 | 0.24 | 0.08 | 0.63** | 0.26 | -0.21 | -0.06 | -0.28 | -0.15 | -0.06 | 0.01 | -0.15 | 0.03 | 0.09 | -0.16 | -0.02 |
| 2. BMI (kg/m$^2$) |  | – | -0.15 | -0.06 | 0.20 | 0.00 | 0.00 | 0.19 | -0.26 | -0.21 | -0.24 | -0.03 | -0.21 | 0.18 | -0.01 | -0.15 | 0.01 |
| 3. Gender (female) |  |  | – | 0.04 | 0.04 | 0.07 | -0.35 | -0.26 | 0.08 | 0.02 | 0.09 | 0.00 | 0.18 | -0.04 | 0.06 | 0.08 | 0.07 |
| 4. Race (white) |  |  |  | – | -0.05 | -0.05 | 0.06 | -0.16 | -0.03 | 0.01 | -0.02 | 0.17 | -0.04 | -0.05 | 0.17 | 0.16 | 0.19 |
| 5. Pack-years[a] |  |  |  |  | – | 0.15 | 0.19 | 0.27 | -0.21 | 0.07 | 0.28 | N/A | -0.30 | 0.10 | 0.28 | -0.16 | -0.07 |
| 6. Nicotine addiction[a] |  |  |  |  |  | – | -0.10 | 0.01 | -0.39 | -0.30 | -0.38 | N/A | -0.35 | 0.19 | 0.09 | -0.12 | -0.20 |
| 7. Stressful life events |  |  |  |  |  |  | – | 0.18 | 0.28 | 0.31* | 0.14 | 0.36* | 0.12 | -0.11 | -0.11 | 0.05 | 0.20 |
| 8. Childhood trauma |  |  |  |  |  |  |  | – | 0.46** | 0.40** | 0.48** | 0.36* | 0.35 | -0.37 | -0.14 | -0.15 | -0.17 |
| 9. Depression |  |  |  |  |  |  |  |  | – | 0.82** | 0.65** | 0.48** | 0.75 | -0.46 | -0.12 | -0.11 | 0.21 |
| 10. Anxiety |  |  |  |  |  |  |  |  |  | – | 0.64** | 0.47** | 0.62** | -0.41** | 0.03 | 0.01 | 0.20 |
| 11. Sleep quality |  |  |  |  |  |  |  |  |  |  | – | 0.32** | 0.42** | -0.41** | 0.03 | 0.01 | 0.20 |
| 12. Smoker (yes) |  |  |  |  |  |  |  |  |  |  |  | – | 0.32** | -0.31** | -0.34** | -0.31** | -0.02 |
| 13. Loneliness |  |  |  |  |  |  |  |  |  |  |  |  | – | 0.50** | -0.22 | -0.11 | 0.03 |
| 14. Self-rated health |  |  |  |  |  |  |  |  |  |  |  |  |  | – | 0.14 | 0.04 | -0.03 |
| 15. ΔTNF-α |  |  |  |  |  |  |  |  |  |  |  |  |  |  | – | 0.67** | 0.43** |
| 16. ΔIFN-γ |  |  |  |  |  |  |  |  |  |  |  |  |  |  |  | – | 0.37* |
| 17. ΔIL-6 |  |  |  |  |  |  |  |  |  |  |  |  |  |  |  |  | – |

*Note.* $N = 48$

*BMI* body mass index; $kg/m^2$ kilograms per meter squared; *mRNA* messenger ribonucleic acid; Δ change from LPS mRNA to LPS+DEX mRNA; *TNF-α* tumor necrosis factor-alpha; *IFN-γ* interferon-gamma; *IL-6* interleukin-6

* $p < 0.05$; ** $p < 0.01$

[a]Indicates correlations with only smokers $n = 24$

**Table 2.3** Summary of hierarchical linear regressions examining the interaction between smoking status and loneliness (left) and self-rated health and loneliness (right) on the change in TNF$\alpha$ gene expression from LPS to LPS + DEX

| Predictor | $b$ | SE | $R^2$ | $\Delta R^2$ | Predictor | $b$ | SE | $R^2$ | $\Delta R^2$ |
|---|---|---|---|---|---|---|---|---|---|
| Stage 1 | | | 0.03 | | Stage 1 | | | 0.03 | |
| (Intercept) | 21.017** | 7.701 | | | (Intercept) | 21.017** | 7.701 | | |
| SLEs | −0.860 | 1.496 | | | SLEs | −0.860 | 1.496 | | |
| CT | −0.154 | 0.180 | | | CT | −0.154 | 0.180 | | |
| Stage 2 | | | 0.12 | 0.09 | Stage 2 | | | 0.08 | 0.05 |
| (Intercept) | 26.219* | 9.916 | | | (Intercept) | 19.508 | 18.922 | | |
| SLEs | 0.032 | 1.533 | | | SLEs | −0.679 | 1.492 | | |
| CT | 0.009 | 0.192 | | | CT | −0.033 | 0.196 | | |
| Loneliness | −0.243 | 0.233 | | | Loneliness | −0.266 | 0.253 | | |
| Smoking | −8.364 | 5.341 | | | SRH | 0.101 | 0.157 | | |
| Stage 3 | | | 0.21$^\dagger$ | 0.09* | Stage 3 | | | 0.26* | 0.18** |
| (Intercept) | 8.340 | 8.370 | | | (Intercept) | 11.337 | 7.715 | | |
| SLEs | 0.337 | 1.481 | | | SLEs | −0.619 | 1.352 | | |
| CT | 0.053 | 0.1852 | | | CT | −0.003 | 0.178 | | |
| Loneliness | −0.385 | 0.234 | | | Loneliness | −0.453$^\dagger$ | 0.237 | | |
| Smoking | −7.920 | 5.138 | | | SRH | 0.119 | 0.143 | | |
| Loneliness X Smoking | 0.967* | 0.458 | | | Loneliness X SRH | −0.034** | 0.011 | | |

*Note.* $N = 48$. The model with SRH interacting with loneliness predicts $\sim$26% of the changes in TNF-$\alpha$ gene expression, while the model with smoking status interacting with loneliness predicts $\sim$21% of the changes in TNF-$\alpha$ gene expression

*DEX* dexamethasone; *SLEs* recent stressful life events; *CT* childhood trauma; *SRH* self-rated health; *b* unstandardized regression weight; $\Delta R^2$ change in $R^2$ from prior stage

$^\dagger p < 0.10$; $^* p < 0.05$; $^{**} p < 0.01$

## 2.4  Discussion

Self-rated health (SRH) is a better predictor of psychological health and neuroendocrine to immune communication than smoking. Our data corroborate previously published data [24, 25, 37, 38] as SRH was more strongly related to depressive symptoms and loneliness compared with smoking status. SRH did interact with loneliness to predict the anti-inflammatory effect of glucocorticoids on immune cells, mirroring smoking status, and explained more of the variance between individuals' immune cell function. However, when examining the zero-order correlation, SRH did not predict physiological functioning, such as heart rate or immune function, like smoking status. This inconsistency appears to reinforce that SRH is a proxy for something greater than just individual health behaviors. Could SRH be estimating the "power" of thinking one is healthy or unhealthy?

Smoking tobacco cigarettes enables the absorption of nicotine, a potent physiological modulator. Nicotine is a sympathomimetic [39]; its effects on the body mimic that of the sympathetic nervous system. For example, smokers often have an

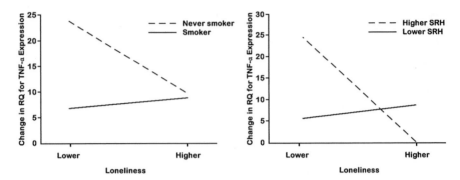

**Fig. 2.2** The moderating effects of smoking (left) or self-rated health (SRH) (right) on the relationship between loneliness and change in TNF-$\alpha$ gene expression from LPS to LPS + DEX. On the left, the moderating effect of smoking on the relationship between loneliness and change in tumor necrosis factor-alpha ($\Delta$TNF-$\alpha$) gene expression. The line representing the never smoker group suggests that as loneliness increases, the change in TNF-$\alpha$ gene expression diminishes ($b = -0.878, t(41) = -2.34, p = 0.02$). On the right, the interactive effect of self-rated health (SRH) and loneliness on $\Delta$TNF-$\alpha$ gene expression. The line representing higher SRH levels suggests that as loneliness increases, the change in TNF-$\alpha$ gene expression diminishes ($b = -1.06, t(47) = -2.89, p < 0.01$). Both analyses controlled for recent stressful life events and childhood trauma exposure. The solid lines representing smoking group (left) or lower SRH levels (right) do not significantly differ from zero, indicating there is no relationship between loneliness and the change in TNF-$\alpha$ gene expression. IFN-$\gamma$ and IL-6 results followed the same pattern for both analyses; however, the interaction did not reach statistical significance

elevated resting heart rate [40, 41], suggesting that repetitive nicotine use shifts the autonomic nervous system into a state of imbalance like sympathetic dominance, creating dysregulation within the cardiovascular system. Cigarette smoking has also been linked to alterations in HPA activity compared to nonsmokers [42–46]. Finally, nicotine can directly communicate with immune cells via the alpha7 nicotinic acetylcholine receptor ($\alpha$7 nAChR) [47, 48]. When stimulated by nicotine, these receptors diminish the inflammatory response [49]. Thus, a pharmacological factor like smoking tobacco can still be more related to health biomarkers than a global health measure, SRH. These results add to the difficulty of understanding the complex construct of health.

### 2.4.1 Why Loneliness?

Humans are social beings, and this desire for connection can be a motivator of behavior [50]. Throughout evolution, likelihood of survival increased when humans were part of a network that was invested in their welfare and cared about their well-being [51]. Over time, this ultimately led to a fundamental need to form close and caring bonds with other people [52]. Failure to fulfill this need may be detrimental to homeostasis and challenge our stress systems, resulting in chronic physiological activation.

Loneliness has a substantial link to stress and physiological dysregulation on par with the adverse effects of obesity and inactivity [53]. Moreover, loneliness has been associated with premature death especially when comorbid with depression [54], mirroring accelerated death observed in tobacco smokers [55]. However, little research investigates the mechanism of physiological dysregulation prior to confounding factors like aging or major stressful life events (e.g., natural disaster or chronic disease diagnosis) [15, 56–60]. Thus, our data showing that, similar to smoking, having lower SRH and elevated loneliness alters the communication between the neuroendocrine and immune systems and should give pause to clinicians and the general population. Moreover, future health studies should continue this line of research and collect data on psychosocial factors as well as the traditional health behaviors and SRH question.

## 2.4.2   Importance of an Acute to Chronic Stress Model in Humans

Chronic stress and physiological dysregulation are linked to disease pathogenesis and mortality [1]. Evidence points to faulty neuroendocrine regulation of the immune system [12, 61]. Yet our understanding about how or when acute stress activation transitions to chronic stress dysregulation is poor. Psychological stress is difficult to investigate because perception, including coping skills and life experiences, plays such a dominant role in the physiological response. Our previous reports [20, 21] combined with this data suggests that tobacco smoking may provide an avenue to observe early dysregulation as it develops. Further, glucocorticoid sensitivity appears to be similarly affected by pharmacological and psychosocial stressors. Overall, these findings may support the theory that stress activation, regardless of source, ultimately ends up challenging our physiology via the same pathways.

If we discover how physiological systems begin to lose variability or become dysregulated, then we can focus on ways to halt or slow this change. A system's ability to vary in its functionality is related to its ability to adapt and successfully manage the situation. This general rule applies to most living organisms as well as physical systems in nature [9]. Hence, discovering a human model to investigate the loss of physiological variability could yield novel ways to inhibit, slow, or repair the physiological dysregulation.

The current literature examining stress and physiological dysfunction lacks a good human model. Chronic stress is pervasive and unpredictable, making it difficult to methodically examine the development of physiological dysregulation. Animal models can provide great insight into human physiology, but they have limitations including direct application of face valid acute or chronic stressors. Specifically, psychological and psychosocial stress is difficult to create when working with rodents, and efforts to do so often incorporate some form of a physical stressor.

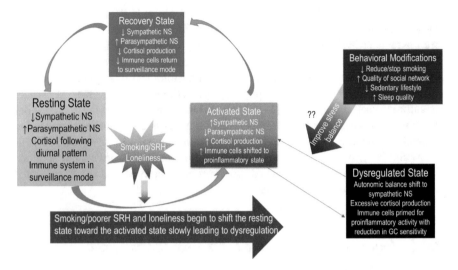

**Fig. 2.3** Current study data and stress system activation and regulation. Displaying our findings in the context of the model described in Fig. 2.1, chronic stress as indexed by tobacco smoking, self-rated health (SRH), or loneliness begins to shift the individual's physiology toward the dysregulated state, which was measured by immune cells' sensitivity to lipopolysaccharide (LPS) and change in tumor necrosis factor-alpha (TNF-$\alpha$ gene expression from LPS to LPS+DEX exposure. It is hypothesized (indicated by ??) that reduction in smoking or a successful quit attempt would reverse the observed immune dysregulation. In addition, lowering loneliness via enhancing social connectedness and increasing SRH would also result in reversal of the insensitive immune cells. *NS* nervous system; *DEX* dexamethasone

Cigarette smoking behavior represents a naturally occurring phenomenon to examine initial physiological changes. Physiological dysfunction observed in smokers does not start on day one of smoking initiation; reduction in system flexibility, or dysregulation, occurs over years of smoking behavior, allowing the observation of the transition from acute stress to chronic stress. This slow progression makes smokers an ideal group with which to investigate how these changes occur and what factors outside of smoking might hasten or delay dysregulation. In addition, physiological recovery from chronic stress might be exhibited following smoking cessation in former smokers, as highlighted in Fig. 2.3.

## 2.5  Conclusions

Health is "complicated." As clinicians and researchers, we must focus on the physical and mental health with a complexity lens that appreciates all aspects of each individual [62]. Based on our data, "healthy smoker" is an oxymoron since compared to never smokers, smokers had reduced glucocorticoid sensitivity prior to clinical disease diagnosis. When does the dysregulation start? It is uncertain as the variability among our smokers' tobacco history was limited and we could not examine relationships between the immune outcomes and tobacco exposure characteristics; thus, more research is necessary. However, healthiness is not as simple as one behavior or one label, like "smoker." Our data also supports the potent role of perceived factors like SRH and loneliness, a psychosocial stressor, among never smokers on the balance between neuroendocrine and immune communication. Taken together, stress influences neuroendocrine system's anti-inflammatory effect on the immune system, which may be the beginning of chronic disease development.

**Acknowledgements** All work was supported by internal funds awarded via competitive opportunities within the University of North Carolina at Charlotte including the Faculty Research Grants, ARCHES, and the Department of Psychological Science. We thank the dedicated assistance of past and present StressWAVES BRL research assistants who supported the data collection for this project.

# The Journey

Dr. Bennett's Journey: "Complexity from Theory to Practice"

I was "systems" focused long before I could fathom what that meant. Being raised in a traditional patriarchal household and one of five kids with only one brother, I started to see systems—biases, symbiosis, imbalances, etc.—at a young age. I rarely took my parents' responses at face value and pushed to understand more. During my undergraduate training, I decided that a single major wasn't going to prepare me to address current health problems. So, I added psychology to my premedical biology training—I began to learn about young new fields, like health psychology and psychoneuroimmunology, that examine the complex interactions of multiple systems involving inter- and intra-level phenomena, also labeled as "cell to society" or "neuron to neighborhood." After a series of complex psychosocial events in my life (i.e., getting married and the birth of my son), I attended graduate school at Penn State and earned my PhD in Biobehavioral Health. There, my training included the reading of Don Ford's *Humans as Self-constructing Living Systems* [63], giving words and conceptualization of how the human and its behavior are the product of multiple physiological systems interacting with the environment, which has multiple levels and systems that influence the human's behavioral choices—a never ending cycle.

Narrowing my focus, I developed a greater appreciation for connections between the neuroendocrine and immune systems as well as how psychological and social factors lead to changes in the stress response. Stress allows the outside world into our body whether it is psychological, social, physical, or pharmacological, leading to an evolutionarily engrained and relatively predictable response that supports survival. Today, the stress systems are activated too often and for too long, resulting in negative adaptations that are linked and may drive development of chronic illness—physical and mental illnesses. Here I am now trying to develop a way to compare psychological or subjective stress to an objective stress like nicotine exposure via tobacco use—thinking it will give us a glimpse into how acute stress transitions into chronic stress. If I'm on to something, the complexity surrounding stress and health will unfold as my career continues.

Take-Home Message

- Stress drives development and progression of today's most prevalent diseases.
- Little is known about the transition from the healthy acute stress response to the dysregulated chronic stress response.
- Loneliness, a psychosocial stressor, appears to be just as detrimental on immune function as tobacco smoking, a pharmacological stressor.
- Self-rated health, a sum greater than its parts, is a better predictor than smoking status, a single negative health behavior.
- Health must be viewed as the culmination of the body interacting with its environment—external (e.g., social relationships, socioeconomic status, etc.) and internal (e.g., communication between the nervous and immune systems) factors.

# References

1. Guyer B, Freedman MA, Strobino DM, Sondik EJ. Annual summary of vital statistics: trends in the health of Americans during the 20th century. Pediatrics. 2000;106(6):1307–17.
2. Kiecolt-Glaser JK, Wilson SJ. Psychiatric disorders, morbidity, and mortality: tracing mechanistic pathways to accelerated aging. Psychosom Med. 2016;78(7):772–5.
3. Glaser R, Kiecolt-Glaser JK. Stress-induced immune dysfunction: implications for health. Nat Rev Immunol. 2005;5:243–51.
4. Dickerson SS, Kemeny ME. Acute stressors and cortisol responses: a theoretical integration and synthesis of laboratory research. Psychol Bull. 2004;130(3):355–91.
5. McEwen BS, Gianaros PJ. Central role of the brain in stress and adaptation: links to socioeconomic status, health, and disease. In: Adler NE, Stewart J, editors. Biology of disadvantage: socioeconomic status and health, vol. 1186. Malden: Wiley; 2010. p. 190–222.
6. Sapolsky RM. Stress and the brain: individual variability and the inverted-U. Nat Neurosci. 2015;18(10):1344–6.
7. McEwen BS. Physiology and neurobiology of stress and adaptation: central role of the brain. Physiol Rev. 2007;87(3):873–904.
8. Thayer JF, Lane RD. A model of neurovisceral integration in emotion regulation and dysregulation. J Affect Disord. 2000;61(3):201–16.
9. Sturmberg JP, Bennett JM, Picard M, Seely AJ. The trajectory of life. Decreasing physiological network complexity through changing fractal patterns. Front Physiol. 2015;6:169.
10. Heng HHQ, Liu G, Stevens JB, Bremer SW, Ye KJ, Abdallah BY, Horne SD, Ye CJ. Decoding the genome beyond sequencing: the new phase of genomic research. Genomics. 2011;98(4):242–52.

11. Miller G, Cohen S, Ritchey A. Chronic psychological stress and the regulation of pro-inflammatory cytokines: a glucocorticoid-resistance model. Health Psychol. 2002;21(6):531–41.
12. Cohen S, Janicki-Deverts D, Doyle WJ, et al. Chronic stress, glucocorticoid receptor resistance, inflammation, and disease risk. Proc Natl Acad Sci. 2012;109(16):5995–9.
13. Maltese P, Palma L, Sfara C, et al. Glucocorticoid resistance in Crohn's disease and ulcerative colitis: an association study investigating GR and FKBP5 gene polymorphisms. Pharmacogenomics J. 2012;12(5):432–8.
14. Yang N, Ray DW, Matthews LC. Current concepts in glucocorticoid resistance. Steroids. 2012;77(11):1041–9.
15. Jaremka LM, Fagundes CP, Glaser R, Bennett JM, Malarkey WB, Kiecolt-Glaser JK. Loneliness predicts pain, depression, and fatigue: understanding the role of immune dysregulation. Psychoneuroendocrinology. 2013;38(8):1310–7.
16. Jaremka LM, Fagundes CP, Peng J, et al. Loneliness promotes inflammation during acute stress. Psychol Sci. 2013;24(7):1089–97.
17. Fagundes CP, Bennett JM, Alfano CM, et al. Social support and socioeconomic status interact to predict epstein-barr virus latency in women awaiting diagnosis or newly diagnosed with breast cancer. Health Psychol. 2012;31(1):11–9.
18. Bernaards CM, Twisk JWR, Snel J, Van Mechelen W, Kemper HCG. Is calculating pack-years retrospectively a valid method to estimate life-time tobacco smoking? A comparison between prospectively calculated pack-years and retrospectively calculated pack-years. Addiction. 2001;96(11):1653–61.
19. Adamopoulos D, Van De Borne P, Argacha JF. New insights into the sympathetic, endothelial and coronary effects of nicotine. Clin Exp Pharmacol Physiol. 2008;35(4):458–63.
20. Bennett JM, Marino JS, Peck B, Roos LG, Joseph KM, Carter LB, et al. Smokers display reduced glucocorticoid sensitivity prior to symptomatic chronic disease development. Ann Behav Med. 2018; Advanced publication online. https://doi.org/10.1093/abm/kax058.
21. Bennett JM, Marino JS, Canevello AB, Roos LG, Coffman MJ, Rohleder N. Loneliness analogous to smoking? Lonely never smokers and smokers exhibit similar immune dysregulation. 2018; (under review).
22. Stenholm S, Kivimäki M, Jylhä M, Kawachi I, Westerlund H, Pentti J, Goldberg M, Zins M, Vahtera J. Trajectories of self-rated health in the last 15 years of life by cause of death. Eur J Epidemiol. 2016;31(2):177–85.
23. Mavaddat N, Parker RA, Sanderson S, Mant J, Kinmonth AL. Relationship of self-rated health with fatal and non-fatal outcomes in cardiovascular disease: a systematic review and meta-analysis. PLoS One. 2014;9(7):e103509.
24. Wu S, Wang R, Zhao Y, Ma X, Wu M, Yan X, He J. The relationship between self-rated health and objective health status: a population-based study. BMC Public Health. 2013;13(1):320.
25. Picard M, Juster R, Sabiston C. Is the whole greater than the sum of the parts? Self-rated health and transdisciplinarity. Health Aff. 2013;5(12A):24–30.
26. Heatherton TF, Kozlowski LT, Frecker RC, Fagerstrom K-O. The Fagerstrom test for nicotine dependence: a revision of the Fagerstrom tolerance questionnaire. Br J Addict. 1991;86(9):1119–27.
27. Russell DW. UCLA loneliness scale (version 3): reliability, validity, and factor structure. J Pers Assess. 1996;66(1):20–40.
28. Ware JE, Sherbourne CD. The MOS 36-Item-Short-Form Health Survey (SF-36): I. Conceptual framework and item selection. Med Care. 1992;30(6):473–83.
29. Radloff LS. The CES-D scale: a self-report depression scale for research in the general population. Appl Psychol Meas. 1977;1(3):385–401.
30. Basco MR, Krebaum SR, Rush AJ. Outcome measures of depression. In: Strupp HH, Horowitz LM, Lambert MJ, editors. Measuring patient changes in mood, anxiety, and personality disorders. Washington, DC: American Psychological Association; 1997. p. 207–45.
31. Dohrenwend BP. Inventorying stressful life events as risk factors dor psychopathology: toward resolution of the problem of intracategory variability. Psychol Bull. 2006;132(3):477–95.

32. Dohrenwend BS, Krasnoff L, Askenasy AR, Dohrenwend BP. Exemplification of a method for scaling life events: the PERI life events scale. J Health Soc Behav. 1978;19(2):205–29.
33. Bernstein DP, Fink L, Handelsman L, Foote J, Lovejoy M, Wenzel K, Sapareto E, Ruggiero J. Initial reliability and validity of a new retrospective measure of child abuse and neglect. Am J Psychiatr. 1994;151(8):1132–6.
34. Bernstein DP, Fink L. Childhood trauma questionnaire: a retrospective self-report. San Antonio, TX: The Psychological Corporation; 1998.
35. Buysse DJ, Reynolds CF, 3rd, Monk TH, Hoch CC, Yeager AL, Kupfer DJ. Quantification of subjective sleep quality in healthy elderly men and women using the Pittsburgh Sleep Quality Index (PSQI). Sleep. 1991;14(4):331–8.
36. Burnsides C, Corry J, Alexander J, Balint C, Cosmar D, Phillips G, Marketon JI. Ex vivo stimulation of whole blood as a means to determine glucocorticoid sensitivity. J Inflamm Res. 2012;5:89–97.
37. Jarczok MN, Kleber ME, Koenig J, Loerbroks A, Herr RM, Hoffmann K, Fischer JE, Benyamini Y, Thayer JF. Investigating the associations of self-rated health: heart rate variability is more strongly associated than inflammatory and other frequently used biomarkers in a cross sectional occupational sample. PLoS One. 2015;10(2):e0117196.
38. Jylhä M. What is self-rated health and why does it predict mortality? Towards a unified conceptual model. Soc Sci Med. 2009;69(3):307–16.
39. Rollema H, Russ C, Lee TC, Hurst RS, Bertrand D. Functional interactions of varenicline and nicotine with nAChR subtypes implicated in cardiovascular control. Nicotine Tob Res. 2014;16(6):733–42.
40. Harte CB, Meston CM. Effects of smoking cessation on heart rate variability among long-term male smokers. Int J Behav Med. 2014;21(2):302–9.
41. Dinas PC, Koutedakis Y, Flouris AD. Effects of active and passive tobacco cigarette smoking on heart rate variability. Int J Cardiol. 2013;163(2):109–15.
42. Childs E, de Wit H. Hormonal, cardiovascular, and subjective responses to acute stress in smokers. Psychopharmacology. 2009;203(1):1–12.
43. al'Absi M, Wittmers LE, Erickson J, Hatsukami D, Crouse B. Attenuated adrenocortical and blood pressure responses to psychological stress in ad libitum and abstinent smokers. Pharmacol Biochem Behav. 2003;74(2):401–10.
44. Kirschbaum C, Strasburger CJ, Langkrar J. Attenuated cortisol response to psychological stress but not to CRH or ergometry in young habitual smokers. Pharmacol Biochem Behav. 1993;44(3):527–31.
45. Kirschbaum C, Scherer G, Strasburger CJ. Pituitary and adrenal hormone responses to pharmacological, physical, and psychological stimulation in habitual smokers and nonsmokers. Clin Investig. 1994;72(10):804–10.
46. Childs E, de Wit H. Effects of acute psychosocial stress on cigarette craving and smoking. Nicotine Tob Res. 2010;12(4):449–53.
47. Wang H, Yu M, Ochani M, Amella CA, Tanovic M, Susarla S, Li JH, Wang H, Yang H, Ulloa L, Al-Abed Y, Czura CJ, Tracey KJ. Nicotinic acetylcholine receptor α7 subunit is an essential regulator of inflammation. Nature. 2003;421(6921):384–8.
48. Tracey KJ. Physiology and immunology of the cholinergic antiinflammatory pathway. J Clin Investig. 2007;117(2):289–96.
49. Dao DQ, Salas R, De Biasi M. Nicotinic acetylcholine receptors along the Habenulo-interpeduncular pathway: roles in nicotine withdrawal and other aversive aspects. In: Lester R, editor. Nicotinic receptors. New York, NY; Humana Press; 2014. p. 363–82.
50. Leary MR, Cox CB. Belongingness motivation: a mainspring of social action. Handbook of motivation science. New York: Guilford Press; 2008. p. 27–40.
51. Tooby J, Cosmides L. Friendship and the banker's paradox: other pathways to the evolution of adaptations for altruism. Paper presented at: Proceedings British Academy; 1996.
52. Baumeister RF, Leary MR. The need to belong: desire for interpersonal attachments as a fundamental human motivation. Psychol Bull. 1995;117(3):497.

53. Holt-Lunstad J, Smith TB, Layton JB. Social relationships and mortality risk: a meta-analytic review. PLoS Med. 2010;7(7):e1000316.
54. Holwerda TJ, van Tilburg TG, Deeg DJH, Schutter N, Van R, Dekker J, Stek ML, Beekman AT, Schoevers RA. Impact of loneliness and depression on mortality: results from the Longitudinal Ageing Study Amsterdam. Br J Psychiatry. 2016;209(2):127–34.
55. Doll R, Peto R, Boreham J, Sutherland I. Mortality in relation to smoking: 50 years' observations on male British doctors. Br Med J. 2004;328(7455):1519.
56. Sugisawa H, Liang J, Liu X. Social networks, social support, and mortality among older people in Japan. J Gerontol. 1994;49(1):S3–13.
57. Thurston RC, Kubzansky LD. Women, loneliness, and incident coronary heart disease. Psychosom Med. 2009;71(8):836–42.
58. Dixon D, Cruess S, Kilbourn K, Klimas N, Fletcher M, Ironson G, Baum A, Schneiderman N, Antoni MH. Social support mediates loneliness and human herpesvirus type 6 (HHV 6) antibody titers. J Appl Soc Psychol. 2001;31(6):1111–32.
59. Hawkley LC, Masi CM, Berry JD, Cacioppo JT. Loneliness is a unique predictor of age-related differences in systolic blood pressure. Psychol Aging. 2006;21(1):152.
60. Hawkley LC, Thisted RA, Masi CM, Cacioppo JT. Loneliness predicts increased blood pressure: 5-year cross-lagged analyses in middle-aged and older adults. Psychol Aging. 2010;25(1):132.
61. Shields GS, Moons WG, Slavich GM. Inflammation, self-regulation, and health: an immunologic model of self-regulatory failure. Perspect Psychol Sci. 2017;12(4):588–612.
62. Sturmberg JP, Bennett JM, Martin CM, Picard M. 'Multimorbidity' as the manifestation of network disturbances. J Eval Clin Pract. 2017;23(1):199–208.
63. Ford DH. Humans as self-constructing living systems. 2nd ed. State College, PA: Ideals; 1994.

# Chapter 3
# From Microbes to Models: How Coping with Ear Infections Led to a New Paradigm

**Alonzo H. Jones**

## 3.1 Introduction

Ear infections and other upper respiratory problems have been increasing in the USA and worldwide for several decades. The long-term study of asthma discharges from the University Hospital in Charleston, South Carolina, shows the trend best (Fig. 3.1), beginning in the mid-1960s [1]. A comparable study of otitis media, with the weakness of only two data points in 1975 and 1990, also shows a line intersecting the baseline in this time frame [2]. *Something*, or *somethings*, happened to trigger the increases during the 1960s. There are lots of possibilities, but when you see comparable increases in both infectious and the allergic problems, it tends to limit those possibilities and focuses on commonalities. The only commonalities between allergic and infectious disorders in the airway center on the defenses.

## 3.2 The Body's Defenses

The body's defenses have largely been ignored in medicine. Back at the beginning of our microbial understanding, Louis Pasteur and Claude Bernard presented the two different mechanisms that determine clinical infection. Pasteur argued for a microbial reason, while Bernard focused on host defenses. Pasteur's germ theory won the day and defenses were forgotten. *Indeed, when defenses are bothersome, as they often are, we are more likely to look for ways to treat them.*

A. H. Jones (✉)
Common Sense Medicine, 4502 Horseshoe Bend, Plainview, TX 79072, USA
e-mail: drjones@commonsensemedicine.org

© Springer International Publishing AG, part of Springer Nature 2018
J. P. Sturmberg (ed.), *Putting Systems and Complexity Sciences Into Practice*,
https://doi.org/10.1007/978-3-319-73636-5_3

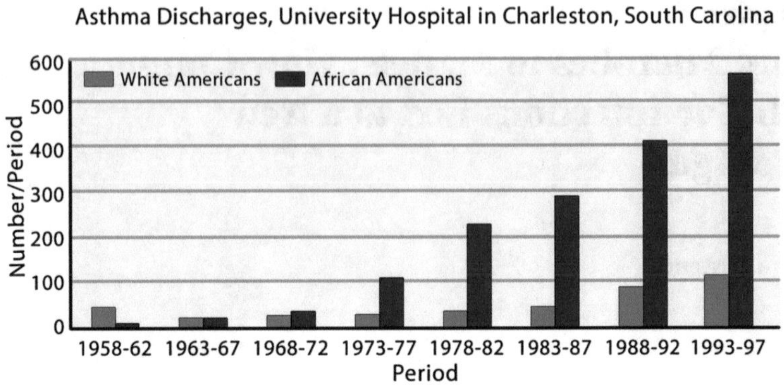

Asthma Discharges, University Hospital in Charleston, South Carolina

**Fig. 3.1** Asthma discharges from the University Hospital in Charleston, South Carolina between 1958 and 1997

Bothersome symptoms are seen as imbalances in our homeostasis, and the biomedical model teaches that such imbalances need to be corrected. We inherited that point of view from the humoral model which preceded it. In that model our humors—blood, phlegm, and yellow and black bile—needed to be in proper balance for us to be healthy. We no longer believe the humors to be important in our health, so we have replaced them with a variety of more scientific elements, but, just like the humors, they need to be in proper balance. Our fundamental thinking has not changed.

The allostatic model goes beyond this in recognizing that when stressed our systems can go out of balance in order to deal with the problem. Most of the explanation for the allostatic model looks at the hormonal or chemical markers that have replaced the humors, but others are pushing to expand it to include things like habituation and coping style [3]. One objective of the current paper is to expand this range even further to include our physiologic defenses.

These defenses are most robust where we are the most vulnerable: at the openings of our bodies—the gastrointestinal, respiratory, and genitourinary tracts. They are both primary and secondary. The primary defenses for all are composed of commensal bacteria along with a plethora of chemical defenses arising from their respective cellular environments. They work constantly to protect us from invaders, both infectious and toxic, and they do not bother us. Secondary defenses do bother us; we need to know we are being challenged because there are things we can do to help. Instead we have seen them as symptoms needing treatment, and the treatment is most often aimed at balancing the symptoms. That is a problem.

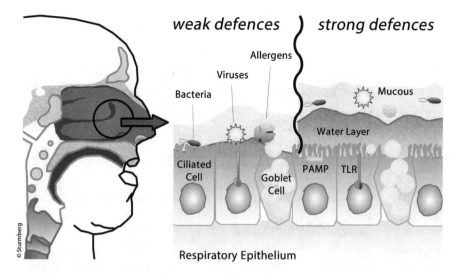

**Fig. 3.2** Nasal epithelial function. The left side illustrates too little fluid on top of the epithelium; the right side illustrates a proper amount of fluid to allow rapid clearance of undesirable agents entering the nostril

### 3.2.1  Airways Defenses

Our airways are kept clean by the combination of the mucus, which holds on to all of the garbage, and the cilia, the microscopic hairs which sweep it out. Both of these elements are dependent on the third element, which does not get much press— the airway surface fluid. The mucus is secreted by goblet cells interspersed among the ciliated cells that line the airway. But it is secreted in concentrated form; it needs lots of water to become the sticky stuff that holds on to the garbage and flows on top of the airway surface fluid. This fluid also provides a space in which the cilia can sweep. The water is critical for both. Things that effect this water are associated with increased problems. Adequate hydration is important but so is the moisture content of the air we breathe (Fig. 3.2).

### 3.2.2  The Role of "Ambient Humidity"

Ambient humidity is one such element. Arundel, in the following chart, showed how humidity is associated with a variety of respiratory problems (Fig. 3.3—edited for effect) [4]. Of note in this chart is the absence of data for respiratory infections when the humidity is high. Since allergens as well as both bacteria and viruses seem to thrive in higher humidity, this is only explained by enhanced defenses.

# Indirect Health Effects of Humidity in Indoor Environments

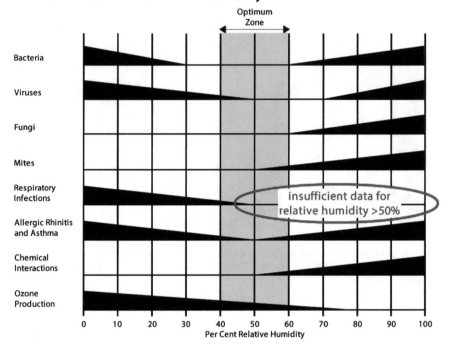

**Fig. 3.3** Optimum relative humidity range for minimizing adverse health effects [4]

Several things happened in the 1960s that effected our nasal defenses:

- the mid-1960s marked the time that half of all new homes constructed included central heating and air conditioning,
- the antihistamines and decongestants that were developed in the 1940s were made available without prescription,
- antihistamine and decongestant TV advertising began,
- pharmaceutical sampling at doctor's offices brought them free to many—and Medicaid brought more people to the doctor's offices.

Central heating and air conditioning both tend to decrease the ambient humidity, but increased insulation that goes along with these changes does indeed make our environments more comfortable. One of the best examples of this is provided by our Native American Alaskans. They have the highest incidence of chronic otitis in our country, and likely the world, but according to their elders—those old enough to remember—they did not have ear problems before they were "civilized." That happened in the 1950s when their traditional homes on the ice were replaced by prefabricated homes with central heat. Ambient humidity on the ice is close to 100% while that in their more comfortable homes during the heating season was between 10 and 20%, if not less. Adding a humidifier to central heating and air conditioning would resolve this problem, but it is an expensive option.

### 3.2.3   The Effects of Antihistamines and Decongestants

The miracle drugs of the 1940s are a different matter. These drugs were compounded when the industry realized that histamine was the trigger for the runny nose. No one likes to deal with a snotty nose, either their own or in their child, and the drugs that sanitized the snotty nose were indeed the wonder drugs of the 1940s. But when Christer Svensson looked at the microstructure of nasal tissue during and after a histamine challenge, his conclusion was that the process was a defense [5]. If you hobble the defense of your favorite football team, they will lose the game. It is the same with us.

They were removed from the US formulary for children under four in 2007 after some studies showed they were more harmful than beneficial, even causing some deaths. When I called the FDA and suggested that the reasons behind the problems were more bad thinking on the part of the manufacturers than bad actions on the part of the caregivers, they remarked it was an interesting idea.

### 3.2.4   The Role of Histamine

According to the *American Academy of Asthma, Allergy, and Immunology*, the actions of histamine in the nose are fourfold:

- it opens the vascular bed (to provide more water for the washing),
- it increases the mucus (to grab on to more garbage),
- it is an irritant (so we sneeze more and get rid of it all),
- it shuts down the airway ((as in asthma?) to protect the more vulnerable lungs from the garbage in the upper airway).

Histamine triggers the backup for when the normal cleaning defenses are not up to the task. Rather than crippling our defenses we ought to realize, in line with the allostatic model, that supporting their aberration is a better choice.

## 3.3   Strengthening our Defenses: The Prototype Model

We have seen the results of strengthening our defenses with the use of oral rehydration for diarrheal diseases. Researched in cholera epidemics in the 1950s and 1960s, it was put into practice by an NGO, BRAC, working with cholera epidemics in what is now Bangladesh. Women volunteers went into the communities and told the people to mix a handful of sugar, a pinch of salt, and a liter of water and try to drink twice what they lost. Millions of lives have been saved by this treatment. The editors of *The Lancet* pointed out that in 10 years it saved more lives than penicillin did in 40 and called it one of the greatest advances of medicine in the last century.

But few in the medical community have seen it for what it does in optimizing our GI tract's defensive washing [6].

Nausea, vomiting, and diarrhea, like rhinorrhea, are bothersome, and we have lots of drugs to cope with it.

In its most virulent form, cholera, it even kills us. It is not cholera that kills us but our physiologic defenses that see the toxin as a lethal threat that needs to be removed by any means possible. It is the dehydration that kills. But if a simple solution of salt, sugar, and water is given early on to people with cholera, many more of them survive. This combination works by activating the *sodium-glucose transport systems* in the upper GI tract, which with one molecule of glucose and two of sodium actively pumps 210 molecules of water into the body [7]. It is by far the easiest, most efficient, and safest way to get water into the body. And the benefits listed by *The Lancet* editors show what happens when we optimize a defense.

## 3.4   Strengthening Nasal Defenses

With this model in mind, it is similarly easy to see how nasal defenses should be optimized—use an osmotic agent like sugar that has an adverse action on bacteria that live there. That is not exactly the order of discovery, but it is close.

### 3.4.1   Initial Observations

Finnish research dentists, realizing that sugar promotes tooth decay, asked: what would happen to the rate of tooth decay if one switched to differing sweeteners?

In Turku they conducted a study to answer this question: a group was divided into three with differing sweeteners in their diets—sucrose (table sugar), fructose, and xylitol. Their tooth decay was evaluated at the beginning and after 2 years. The sugar eaters had the expected increases in decay. The fructose group had less. The xylitol group had none [8]. More than 20 studies have been done on this population to further identify the elements of cariogenesis [9]. The bottom line of these studies was that xylitol has an effect on the bacteria, *Streptococcus mutans*, that live in our dental plaque and make an acid from the sugars we eat. This acid then dissolves the enamel surfaces of our teeth and opens them to further decay. The results led to chewing gum made with xylitol and that was used throughout Finland. It even formed part of the school preventive dentistry programs.

In 1996 Matti Uhari, a pediatric infectious disease researcher from Oulu, Finland, observed that children using xylitol chewing gum had less ear infections. He conducted a study on the effectiveness of children using this gum five times a day and found that it reduced ear infections, and the need for prescribing antimicrobials, by about 40% even though it had no impact on the carriage rate of *S. pneumoniae* [10].

## 3.4.2  Xylitol Nasal Spray

My granddaughter was only 7 months old when I read this article and far too young to chew gum. The authors said the benefit came from how xylitol affected the bacteria that cause the infections, and since they live in the nose, I thought it simpler to put it there.

Xylitol had the osmotic effects I saw as needed to optimize her own defenses. Her infections stopped when mom, dad, and other caregivers at day care sprayed the solution my hospital pharmacy compounded[1] in her nose prior to every diaper change. Ten children in my practice with similar problems had their ear complaints reduced by more than 94% following the same protocol [11].

I called Dr. Uhari, and he told me of their as yet unpublished article that fleshed out the other side of the equation. In lab experiments his group showed that xylitol had an antiadherence property on the significant nasal pathogens *S. pneumoniae* and *H. influenzae* [12]. The first of these is the most common pathogen in upper respiratory and ear infections, and a 5% solution of xylitol reduced their adherence to the epithelium by 68%. These researchers have subsequently focused on the effect of xylitol on these bacteria when they ingest the xylitol. Lacking the enzyme pathways needed to utilize the xylitol, their metabolism is significantly disturbed. They consider this the reason for the benefits.

## 3.4.3  Bacterial Adherence in Infectious Disease

We feel that their study [12] is indicative of another mechanism. It consisted of using a variety of bacteria harvested from patients with otitis media and cultured respiratory epithelial cells. Half of the bacterial culture and half of the epithelial cells were exposed to a 2.5% solution of xylitol before being exposed to each other. They were incubated together and then washed again, and then the bacteria were counted on each epithelial cell. They saw the 68% reduction of *S. pneumoniae* when both the bacteria and the cells had been exposed to xylitol.

*What they did not comment on that persuades us to a different explanation is their finding that the reduction in adherence of the two middle pots, where either the cells or the bacteria were exposed to xylitol, but not both, were comparable. Exposing the cells to xylitol was just as effective in reducing adherence as exposing the bacteria* (Fig. 3.4).

Adherence to cell surfaces is important in our dealing with infectious diseases. One of the major defenses of the mucus in our airway is the rich variety of carbohydrates on the mucus chains. These sugar complexes provide a wide range of substances that can adhere to pollutants. As Knowles and Boucher point out:

---

[1] To make your own spray put one teaspoon of Xylotol in a 20 ml nasal spray or dropper bottle and fill with water.

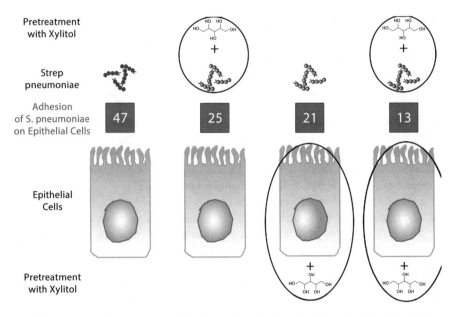

**Fig. 3.4** Antiadhesive effects of xylitol on otopathogenic bacteria. Figure based on descriptions in [12]

> ...they provide, in effect, a combinatorial library of carbohydrate sequences, mucins can bind to virtually all particles that land on airway epithelia and can thus clear them from the lung [13].

Xylitol, a five-carbon flexible sugar-like molecule, is able to conform to and fill many of these glycan seeking bacterial lectins and, by competitive inhibition, block their adherence to our host cells. It may not be exactly what they are looking for, but it seems an appropriate mime for this environment.

## 3.5  Bacterial Adherence and Infectious Disease: A New Model that Honors Complexity and Adaptation

Our search for the reasons behind the effect of xylitol linked with the ideas of Paul Ewald and Nathan Sharon. Ewald argues that we can shape bacterial adaptation by constraining their ability to get around [14]. In the context of public health, we use clean and chlorinated water, we adhere to handwashing regulations, and, in hospital practice, we use gowns and gloves in surgery. These methods prevent the bacteria from moving to a new host, so they must live with their current host, creating evolutionary pressure toward commensalism. Furthermore these methods mostly affect planktonic bacteria, so they are not likely even to register as a threat. If there is no threat, there is no resistance.

However, this is different with antibiotics where communities of bacteria are exposed to a real threat. Bacterial adaptation is most often a community affair; threatened bacteria release signaling molecules and when the community, in what has been described as "twitter like," senses the significance of the signal the community as the whole community shifts. A proportion, namely, those with the least neighbors [15], ramps up its rate of mutation to cope with the threat, and with a few billion bacteria doing this, it is not usually long before help is found. Another edge comes from the mutating bacteria's willingness to share their success, vertically by multiplying and horizontally in plasmids, with any other bacteria, with no concern at all for the profit or intellectual property rights that delay our human responses. We are not likely to win this war, and as with our own failing wars, it may be time to try negotiation; Ewald's argument begins that pathway.

A point that Ewald makes in the process of his explanation is one that fits all evolutionary models: if you threaten an adaptive agent, i.e., one that is alive, it will tend to adapt in *survival mode*, but if there is no threat, it is more likely to adapt toward in *diversity mode*. These two modes of evolution permeate all adaptive systems and provide a rich understanding of how best to guide their adaptation to insure a healthier environment. This is an approach that is far simpler than trying to gain predictability by analysis. Just as Ewald's public health measures apply pressure toward diversity, so does blocking adherence. We introduced this concept in 2003 [16] as a way out of our endless warfare with bacteria and despite some critics [17] others are picking up on the idea [18].

Nathan Sharon was one of the pioneers of bacterial adherence. He helped to identify the type I mannose lectin on the *E. coli* that is the cause of most urinary tract infections [19]. Bacterial lectins, Sharon found out, have a sweet tooth: they mostly attach to sugar complexes on our cell surfaces, like those Knowles and Boucher find in the nasal mucins. But he did not stop with just identifying it; through the rest of his life, he tried to get us to realize that by putting mannose in the environment of these bacteria we could remove them and do so without them developing resistance [20]. Unfortunately changing a paradigm is difficult—changing it with an unpatentable and therefore unprofitable sugar is well-nigh impossible.

Our warfare with bacteria has been ongoing ever since we discovered their presence and that they cause many of our illnesses, but as we are seeing with our growing problem of antimicrobial resistance, their adaptation is more effective than is our arms race. We win tactical battles, but are not likely to win this war unless we learn some lessons from other complex systems.

### 3.5.1 Support from Other Areas

International relations is a fruitful field in this regard. In medicine we make tactical decisions that help us win battles with infectious agents; it seldom registers that our decision is creating more antibiotic resistance. That larger view is the strategic one, and the difference in tactical versus strategic decisions is universally important. It was summed up very nicely some time ago by Moshe Yaalon, the Israeli Defense Minister who recently resigned in protest to the radical right government. Referring to Israel's problems with Palestine he said: "In our tactical decisions we are operating contrary to our strategic interests [21]."

His comments are just as appropriately applied to our problem with bacteria as they are to Israel's Palestinian problem. The desire to stop an infection is a tactical decision that does not usually consider the adaptation of the bacteria, and the adaptation of any threatened adapting organism is to resist—it is in survival mode. We need to think strategically instead of tactically.

One can also carry this analogue further by recognizing that chronic infections in humans most often come from communities of bacteria living in biofilms that protect them from threats, including antibiotics. In the absence of a threat planktonic bacteria will exit the biofilm in order to spread the infection, hence the chronic nature of these infections. These biofilm colonies can easily be seen as state actors in our human sphere. Like our friend Saudi Arabia, it is not the biofilm that is the threat, but the planktonic rebels it sprouts. This view suggests that infectious disease is better seen as an insurgency. Infections come from opportunistic planktonic bacteria invading a host with weakened defenses.

Kalev Sepp teaches history at the Naval Postgraduate Institute and wrote *Best Practices in Counterinsurgencies* [22]. In it he looks at the insurgencies of the last century to determine how best to win and concludes that if the empire—the side with dominant power—relies only on force, they tend to lose. If, instead, they address the issues that weaken the defenses or the resilience of the system or society they tend to win.

## 3.6   Conclusion

Living adapting organisms make up all complex adaptive systems. They all defy predictability, but as we see here, we can do things that affect how they adapt. Warfare or threats of any kind lead to resistance—a pathway leading to continued violence. Providing a safe environment in which to play and optimizing the toys that are available are the best foundation for producing novelty and diversity in any system, as anyone trained in early child education will tell you. And if you want to measure the *health of any adaptive system you **do not** look at survival, you look at its **diversity***.

These two modes—survival and diversity—also drew the attention of Steve Cole a researcher at UCLA interested in the foundations of health. He and his group identified a set of genes associated with good health—those needed to develop viral resistance—and a set that were associated with not so good health— chronic inflammation. Then they looked at behaviors that triggered the expression of these sets of genes. They found that survival mode behavior triggered more of the unhealthy inflammatory genes while working for the benefit of others—which we consider diversity mode—triggered the healthy genes [23].

In order to benefit from an understanding of complexity in both our healthcare and our world, we need to step beyond our reductionist view. Ever since the scientific revolution, analysis has been the source for our understanding. That is why the hard sciences are those dealing with the world around us. It is also why the sciences dealing with the living agents in our world so often fail to maintain the predictability seen in the hard sciences—adaptation cannot be computed, even with complex mathematics. But we can, using the principles based on the ideas outlined above, encourage healthier adaptations in all of the living systems in our environments, including the bacterial ones.

**Acknowledgements**   None of this would have happened without my wife, Jerry's input. Trained in early child education, special ed, and play therapy, she understands children. It was her panic, based on her experience trying to teach kids who had early problems with ear infections, that prompted our experimenting with xylitol. And it was her understanding of how children adapt that confirmed the idea of the modes of evolution. Children are in fact the archetype of complex adaptive systems, and we should all pay a lot more attention to the experts in this area as we try to cope with our problems in all other areas of our lives.

I would also like to thank Joachim Sturmberg for his excellent illustrations of mucociliary function and Kontiokari's adherence study.

# The Journey

I was raised in Los Angeles and had an early morning paper route that enabled me to witness, long-distance, many of the Nevada nuclear tests that so often lit up the early morning skies. My high school yearbook says I wanted to make bombs.

For 2 years of college, I studied the hard sciences and the math that went with them. But life events persuaded me that people were more important and history is the proper study of mankind.

I learned about Leopold von Ranke, the giant of history in the nineteenth century, but that history *wie es eigentlich gewesen war* was an illusion. I learned that the winners usually write the history; that paradigms, in Thomas Kuhn's sense, are just as important, if not more so, in history than they are in science. And I learned, from W.I. Thomas, that "If men define situations as real, they are real in their consequences." History, I saw, tried to make sense of the adaptations of the complex adaptive systems that are human beings by connecting what appeared to be the important dots. But all human dots are in turn made of numerous connections that defy analysis.

This view was strengthened after I completed my MA in the History of Science and Ideas. It was time to go to work, and it being midyear academia wasn't an option. A management development program at an AT&T regional was. I learned more about groups and how they work. And from groups I learned about systems and their mathematical representation from binary to complex and even complex adaptive systems. Binary systems can be figured out with a pencil and paper, but if you add more elements, you need a computer; if you add a lot more, you need a modeling program, like the one I was in charge of at the Boeing Company that figured out the windows for experiments on an orbiting space lab. If you add even more, you wind up with a complex system where you have basins of solutions called attractors, and with even more, you have strange attractors where the basins of solutions morph into new areas.

Then I was dragged into the delivery room to witness the birth of my third daughter, and my dread of things medical, which had been born years earlier by watching a bloody pneumonectomy designed to dissuade our group from smoking, evaporated. So it was back to school.

Osteopathic medical school was often difficult. It was based almost entirely on the reductionist ideas of the times. But I had read and thought about Jacques Monod's statement that "the cell is a machine, the animal is a machine. Man is a machine." And it did not fit. Living organisms, from bacteria to humans are not binary systems that can easily be figured out. We are much better described as strange attractors.

I saw evolution as similar to integral calculus; every time you integrate, you add a new constant, change the constants into variables, and increase the power of the variables by one. It is like creating the butterfly effect in reverse, and if the system is integrated repeatedly as had been done in evolution, the result is a well-integrated individual, both physically and physiologically, that has an element of choice and is beyond analysis.

I saw this as being true for our genetic evolution, but it is also true for our memetic evolution, except the latter, in dealing with human and cultural ideas, occurs orders of magnitude faster.

But this way of seeing does not support a legal system that demands accountability. For that we need a mechanical framework. Our pharmaceutical companies try to do that by looking for reactions that take place in the body that affect a process of interest. But in isolating that reaction, all of the other connections are pruned away and discarded, which is reflected in the subsequent withdrawal of so many of our drugs for unintended side effects.

I appreciated osteopathic medicine for its foundational principle that the body can heal itself if it is in proper order. But when A.T. Still, the founder of osteopathic medicine, said that he too was in the mechanical framework and looking only at the structure of the body. "Structure determines function," he said, but there was much more to it than that.

Everything that I had learned and experienced told me that humans are complex organisms with all of the integrated relationships that come along with an eon of evolution. Connecting the dots is an artificial and reductionist attempt to instill some sense of order into a chaotic system. It is short sighted.

A far better manner of dealing with the complexities of life, in whatever area we are working, is to try to frame the environment in a nonthreatening way in order to shift as much as possible the adaptation of the agent toward a response that fits into our strategic goals. I knew this from my work with people. It was clarified greatly by my wife's training as a play therapist. In this training she was taught to give language to the play that is a child's way of expressing him or herself. The primary rule of play therapy is that the playground be safe, caring, and controlled by the child and have lots of toys with which to play. This environment fosters healthy growth in children; therapists in doubt are told to "trust the process"—and it does work.

Our goal is to be healthy, in the broad terms of the WHO, as "a state of complete physical, mental, and social well-being." We have gained by adaptation and natural selection a large set of defenses that help us toward this goal, and significant among them are the two backup defenses that protect us where we are most vulnerable: at our two major openings. I saw my role as a physician as working with my patients in a safe and caring environment playing with ways to help them enhance their well-being. And the major complaints I dealt with as a family physician were associated with these two areas: gastrointestinal and upper respiratory problems.

Which brings us full circle, honoring and supporting these physiologic defenses is one of the best ways to help.

Take-Home Message
Trust the process:

- if it does not endanger or threaten anyone or any other living agent.
- if it is physiological.
- if it takes place in a caring and safe environment.

And, as my mother told me every day as she sent me off to school: "keep your nose clean."

# References

1. Crater DD, Heise S, Perzanowski M, Herbert R, Morse CG, Hulsey TC, Platts-Mills T. Asthma hospitalization trends in Charleston, South Carolina, 1956 to 1997: twenty-fold increase among black children during a 30-year period. Pediatrics. 2001;108(6):E97.
2. Schappert SM. Office visits for otitis media: United States. 1975–90. Adv Data. 1992;8(214):1–19.
3. Brindal E, Wittert G. The weight balancing act and allostasis: commentary on the homeostatic theory of obesity. Health Psychol Open. 2016;3(1):2055102916634363.
4. Arundel AV, Sterling EM, Biggin JH, Sterling TD. Indirect health effects of relative humidity in indoor environments. Environ Health Perspect. 1986;65:351–61.
5. Svensson C, Andersson M, Grieff L, Persson CG. Nasal mucosal endorgan hyperresponsiveness. Am J Rhinol. 1998;12(1):37–43.
6. Water with sugar and salt. Lancet. 1978;2(8084):300–1.
7. Meinild A, Klaerke DA, Loo DD, Wright EM, Zeuthen T. The human Na+-glucose cotransporter is a molecular water pump. J Physiol. 1998;508(Pt 1):15–21.
8. Scheinin A, Mäkinen KK, Ylitalo K, et al. Turku sugar studies. I. An intermediate report on the effect of sucrose, fructose and xylitol diets on the caries incidence in man. Acta Odontol Scand. 1974;32(6):383–412.

9. Scheinin A, Mäkinen KK. Turku sugar studies I-XXI. Acta Odontol Scand. 1975;33 Suppl 70:1–349.
10. Uhari M, Kontiokari T, Koskela M, Niemelä M. Xylitol chewing gum in prevention of otitis media. Br Med J. 1996; 313(7066):1180–84.
11. Jones AH. Intranasal xylitol, recurrent otitis media, and asthma: report of three cases. Clin Pract Altern Med. 2001;2(2):112–7. Available at http://commonsensemedicine.org/articles-of-interest/nasal-xylitol-from-clinical-practice-of-alternative-medicine/.
12. Kontiokari T, Uhari M, Koskela M. Antiadhesive effects of xylitol on otopathogenic bacteria. J Antimicrob Chemother. 1998;41(5):563–5.
13. Knowles MR, Boucher R. Mucus clearance as a primary innate defense mechanism for mammalian airways. J Clin Invest. 2002;109(5):571–7.
14. Ewald E. The evolution of infectious disease. Oxford: Oxford University Press; 1994.
15. Krašovec R, Belavkin RV, Aston JAD, Channon A, Aston E, Rash BM, Kadirvel M, Forbes S, Knight CG. Where antibiotic resistance mutations meet quorumsensing. Microb Cell. 2014;1(7):250–2.
16. Jones AH. The next step in infectious disease: taming bacteria. Med Hypotheses. 2003;60(2):171–4.
17. Zimmer C. Taming pathogens: an elegant idea. But does it work? Science. 2003;300(5624):1362–4.
18. Ferreira AS, Silva-Paes-Leme AF, Raposo NR, da Silva SS. By passing microbial resistance: xylitol controls microorganisms growth by means of its anti-adherence property. Curr Pharm Biotechnol. 2015;16(1):35–42.
19. Sharon N, Halina L. Carbohydrates in cell recognition. Sci Am. 1993;268(1):82–9.
20. Sharon N. Carbohydrates as future anti-adhesion drugs for infectious disease. Biochim Biophys Acta. 2006;1760(4):527–37.
21. Moore M. Washington Post, 2003 October 31. P.AO1. Ms. Moore is quoting Nahum Barnea, columnist for the Yedioth Aharonoth.
22. Sepp K. Best practices in counterinsurgency. Mil Rev. 2005:8–12.
23. Cole SW, Hawkley LC, Arevalo JM, Sung CY, Rose RM, Cacioppo JT. Social regulation of gene expression in human leukocytes. Genome Biol. 2007;8:R189.

# Chapter 4
# Suspending Hierarchy, Liberating Innovation: Personal Reflections on the Triple Chronotherapy Journey

**Diane Hurd, Nicholas Coombs, Cara Fairbanks, Heather Landon, Andrea Macdonald, Kyle Luraas, and Keri Cross**

## 4.1 Introduction

At the 2016 Conference, *Putting Systems and Complexity into Practice*, Dr. Eric Arzubi and I presented a 5- min mini-talk on the role that collaborative inquiry and team dynamics played in our current research on the use of triple chronotherapy (Box 1) in the treatment of depression here at Billings Clinic. We presented the intersecting journeys of the first adolescent treated with triple chronotherapy, a severely depressed 17-year-old boy with extreme self-harm behaviors who refused all medications, and a loosely organized team of caregivers who were willing to try something new. These interactions created an unprecedented momentum which ultimately resulted in the formation of an interdisciplinary team of caregivers, further trials, formal research, and a dynamic culture of inquiry, learning, and innovation.

We asserted that the informal co-learning structure of our team and its inclusion of the patient as both catalyst and a central member of the research team were essential to the successful journey from the treatment of a single patient to innovative research in the treatment of adolescent depression. During the breakout sessions, one of our nurse colleagues, Rebecca Kitzmiller, approached us with a wonderful article entitled *Learning from Samples of One or Fewer* [1]. I believe March et al. very aptly describe so much of what has gone right with the triple chronotherapy team's approach to frontline research.

Very simply, one patient, one anomaly, and one variation can profoundly affect the journey of individual caregivers, departments, organizations, and even what we define as evidence-based practice. Identifying opportunities to learn from

D. Hurd (✉) · N. Coombs · C. Fairbanks · H. Landon · A. Macdonald · K. Luraas · K. Cross
Billings Clinic, Psychiatric Center, 2800 Tenth Avenue North, Billings, MT 59101, USA
e-mail: dhurd@billingsclinic.org

© Springer International Publishing AG, part of Springer Nature 2018
J. P. Sturmberg (ed.), *Putting Systems and Complexity Sciences Into Practice*,
https://doi.org/10.1007/978-3-319-73636-5_4

43

hypothetical and single occurrences is such an integral idea to patient safety and healthcare improvement. Yet in research, we look instead to large samples to define phenomena and to establish evidence-based practices. However, viewed through the lens of complexity science, both the micro and macro views are essential, and the significant relationships between cause and effect are nonlinear. Our ability as caregivers to capitalize on and learn from clinical occurrences, whether accidental, intentional, or spontaneous, is at the heart of putting complexity science into practice. I believe good organizations find ways to learn from samples of one or fewer.

## 4.2   Reflections

What follows are the personal reflections of several members of the triple chronotherapy team at Billings Clinic, each sharing how the journey of this one patient has influenced their own journey.

---

**Summary of Triple Chronotherapy**

The triple chronotherapy procedure is a structured manipulation of sleep-wake cycles and exposure to bright light. Nurses partner with patients to complete the 5-day intervention. The first 24 h are spent with 1:1 nursing care for provision of comfort measures, to stimulate wakefulness and to encourage successful completion of the intervention.

- Day 0: One night of total sleep deprivation
- Day 1–3: Sleep phase advancement

  - Day 1: Sleep occurs from 6 PM to 1 AM
  - Day 2: Sleep occurs from 8 PM to 3 AM
  - Day 3: Sleep occurs from 10 PM and 5AM

- After Day 3 sleep occurs from 10 PM to 6 AM and continues on this schedule.
- Every morning from 0700 to 0730, patients receive bright light therapy using a 10,000 lux light box which should be continued at home on a daily basis (Fig. 4.1).

---

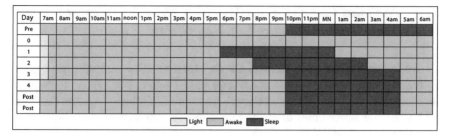

**Fig. 4.1** Triple chronotherapy protocol

## 4.2.1 Diane Hurd, Co-principal Investigator - Triple Chronotherapy Research, Charge Nurse, Billings Clinic

I still find it extraordinary that one patient, a brave and vulnerable teenage boy, could be such a powerful agent of change in the lives of so many caregivers and in the culture of an organization. This patient did a very bold and simple thing. He challenged our assumptions about the necessity of delivering the standard of care as usual. His refusal was absolute—*I've already had seen what you're offering. I've tried it. And I don't want any more of it.*

It might have ended there. A defiant and "noncompliant" teenager, discharged to a higher level of care. Yet that is not what happened. His caregivers rose to his challenge. The physician went to the literature and found an innovative evidence-based treatment. Frontline staff weary of the heartbreaking landscape of less than happy endings rallied around the chance to try something new. Members of leadership who might have blocked this treatment for a number of administrative reasons took a leap of faith to pursue something that might make a difference. This is where I always ask myself—*what if this treatment had failed?* We were very fortunate. The results of the treatment were astounding, and success has been duplicated with many other patients since.

Our story has a journey of its own. Like the treatment itself, the reception it receives among caregivers both within and outside our organization is always exceptional. Psychiatry has no corner on disappointing patient outcomes, broken systems, and the frustration of individual caregivers. Our story speaks to an untapped potential that resides in individuals (both caregivers and patients). It describes the homegrown impetus which can create dynamic evidence-based practice and real changes in patient care.

### 4.2.2 Nicholas Coombs, Data Analyst, Center for Clinical Translational Research, Billings Clinic

My work relationship with Billings Clinic began in 2015 almost a year after the original case report. I was immediately pulled into a work group to discuss something called "Triple Chronotherapy,", a treatment of which I was not familiar, and it was there where I met the champions who were just beginning to pioneer this new innovative research into healthcare.

The passion that resonated off each of them was incredible; it still is to that effect. What this 17-year-old boy did for this department and this organization is beyond noteworthy. My original presence was the product of a group of clinical professionals who wanted to make a difference but did not have all the tools to do so on their own. Once brought up to speed, I engaged the group on the research methodology, data analysis, and statistical considerations for the pilot study we were designing.

From a statistician's lens, clinical professionals are generally either extremely pro-research or extremely anti-research due to something decided well before I meet them, and their minds do not seem to change unless they possess a dog in the fight. Implementing triple chronotherapy treatment on a whim and having it continue into one of Billings Clinic's most successful case reports led the Psychiatry team to develop that unconditional appreciation and desire to seek new knowledge, and I was fortunate enough to experience the result of that first hand.

### 4.2.3 Cara Fairbanks, Registered Nurse, Psychiatric Center, Billings Clinic

I am extremely lucky to be involved in triple chronotherapy at Billings Clinic. At the time of our first patient's treatment, I was a very new nurse and believe that this experience helped shape who I am today as a psychiatric nurse, as well as the quality of care that I provide to my patients. This patient's acuity level was like none that I had seen before. He presented with an unimaginable number of severe, self-inflicted cuts and a level of hopelessness that I have not seen again in the 4 years that I have worked in the inpatient psychiatric setting. This patient was truly ready to give up on life. He refused to take further medications as he had been on a myriad throughout his life, all of which he reported made him feel "numb." As a unique, multidisciplinary team was formed based on clinical research, this patient began to express a new found hope. Triple chronotherapy was extremely successful in treating this patient's distress, and he has, since, gone on to live a productive life in the community. Previously, it appeared that the only option was a high acuity residential facility.

We as a team are extremely fortunate and thankful to have widespread support for our efforts to continue the implementation of this protocol. Numerous adolescents in our youth psychiatric unit have undergone this procedure, often with extremely successful outcomes. Our physicians, nursing staff, management, and hospital-wide personnel have been enormously supportive and instrumental in our work. Triple chronotherapy is a truly unique and successful nonpharmacological approach to adolescent depression, and we are excited to see many more positive results.

### 4.2.4  Heather Landon, Nurse Clinician, Psychiatric Center, Billings Clinic

At first, watching this young man's struggle was very discouraging. I wondered if there was any treatment which could help him. After the triple chronotherapy protocol was initiated, we witnessed something which dramatically restored our hope. As a team, we celebrated his first smiles, renewed energy, and even the day the patient played a prank on one of the staff. It was a remarkable feeling, to be boldly hopeful again, and to be part of a team with a common goal.

With this patient in the forefront of our minds, we led with our hearts. The desire to help others continues to inspire this team to develop protocols and guidelines so that triple chronotherapy can be used to treat other patients with depression in the inpatient youth psychiatric setting. A team so united in its purpose is unstoppable. We have shared our story throughout our organization and at several national conferences. With current research being conducted on the youth inpatient unit, the team continues to thrive and is able to tell many other stories, stories with positive and powerful endings.

### 4.2.5  Andrea Macdonald, Charge Nurse, Psychiatric Center, Billings Clinic

The work we do as a healthcare team can be mentally and physically draining. It can leave us weary and discouraged. No one knew when we walked into work that day that it would be the day that changed everything. Once Tim, a depressed and helpless youth, was placed in our care, we knew that we had to do something. Due to past failed attempts on medications, his physician was willing to try something new. Without hesitation, the staff followed eagerly and would do anything to help save the life of a teen who had essentially reached his rock bottom. Over the next week, the triple chronotherapy protocol was started, and Tim changed. He learned to appreciate himself, look around at what the world had to offer, and have the ability to smile again. Watching his transformation was amazing and profound to all of us who witnessed it.

This one patient, this one deviation in our everyday work week, and this chance to do something different helped change me too. It made us all realize that there is value in each encounter that we have every day with our patients. It made us more open-minded to try new things in order to help others. It also gave us hope—that no matter how depressed or hopeless a patient is, they still have a chance to get better, and they still deserve our help to put the pieces back together and create a life worth living. This patient has helped the development of a protocol that could potentially help hundreds, if not thousands of adolescents across the country. This hope is why we as healthcare providers continue to come to work, in the hope that we can change just one life.

### 4.2.6  Kyle Luraas, Mental Health Worker, Psychiatric Center, Billings Clinic

When I first started working with this patient, I had never seen anyone more motivated to end his own life. There were cuts all over his arms and his body. I worried that being on one-to-one staffing with this patient would be extremely difficult. What was I to do? What was I to say? How was I going to keep this patient safe from himself? As I came on shift, I asked myself all of these questions, but forgot to ask myself one very important question—*If I were him, what would I need to hear?*

Working with this patient taught me that it is not always hearing what we want to hear, but instead hearing what we need to hear that can make a difference. As I worked with him during the triple chronotherapy process, I saw an incredibly sad and flat young man become brighter and brighter. His response at first was "Well, I really have nothing left to lose." During the protocol, I saw that his determination and drive to succeed gave him what he needed to get better and return home. This patient showed me on both a personal and professional level that I can make a difference no matter how small by simply saying what needs to be said. He is one patient that I will never forget. He showed me what my career path really is, and let me see the difference that I can make in the lives of others along the way.

### 4.2.7  Keri Cross, Nurse Manager, Psychiatric Services, Billings Clinic

I have never been as proud of our psychiatric team as I was when I saw how our first patient responded to the treatment. It was miraculous. To know that our team adapted an adult treatment to be effective for adolescents is astonishing.

I played a very small part in the triple chronotherapy process. I was presented with a challenge, to make a new process in our environment accessible for a patient when all others had failed or to say no. Many questions ran through my mind that day, but the main concern was for our patient. If everything else we had access to had been tried and failed, what can we do to help? Other immediate questions were: What is in the patient's best interest? What are the risks and expected outcomes? Is it safe? Once these questions were answered according to the information we had, how could I say no?

We had key staff who led the initiative in developing our processes. This was the best way to get buy-in from other staff to make this process successful. They assisted me in showing our team members the changes that were occurring with the patient and how much better the patient was as his ive and suicidal symptoms diminished. I recall the first time I saw the patient smile. It made me remember why I became a nurse, why I became a psychiatric nurse, and why I went into a leadership role.

Take-Home Message

- Evidence-based practice is a process of collaborative inquiry.
- Collaborative inquiry employs an informal co-learning style and includes the patient as catalyst and central member of the research team.
- The complexity lens allows us to capitalize on occurrences of one or fewer, learning from unique and hypothetical occurrences.
- One patient, one anomaly, or one variation can profoundly affect the journey of individual caregivers, departments, organizations, and even what is defined as evidence-based practice.

# Reference

1. March JG, Sproull, LS, Tamuz M. Learning from samples of one or fewer. Organ Sci. 1991;2(1):1–13.

# Chapter 5
# Supporting Complex Dynamic Health Journeys Using Conversation to Avert Hospital Readmissions from the Community: An Ecological Perspective Incorporating Interoception

Carmel Martin, Joachim P. Sturmberg, Keith Stockman, Donald Campbell, Lucy Hederman, Carl Vogel, and Kevin Smith

## 5.1 Background

The 80/20 or Pareto rule [1] applies to the health and disease distribution and the need for healthcare across communities: 20% of the population incurs 80% of all healthcare costs, particularly through hospital admissions and readmissions [2]. Rising costs of emergency department (ED) visits and avoidable hospitalizations in an aging population with multimorbidity and frailty have increased in parallel with

C. Martin (✉) · K. Stockman · D. Campbell
Monash Medical Centre, General Medicine Offices, Level 2, 246 Clayton Road,
Clayton, VIC 3168, Australia
e-mail: carmelmarymartin@gmail.com; Keith.Stockman@monashhealth.org;
donald.campbell@monashhealth.org

J. P. Sturmberg
School of Medicine and Public Health, University of Newcastle, PO Box 3010,
Newcastle, NSW 2260, Australia

Foundation President, International Society for Systems and Complexity Sciences for Health,
Newcastle, NSW, Australia
e-mail: jp.sturmberg@gmail.com

L. Hederman
Centre for Health Informatics (CHI), Trinity College Dublin, The University of Dublin,
College Green, Dublin 2, Ireland
e-mail: lucy.hederman@scss.tcd.ie

C. Vogel
Trinity Centre for Computing and Language Studies, Trinity College Dublin,
The University of Dublin, College Green, Dublin 2, Ireland
e-mail: carl.vogel@scss.tcd.ie

K. Smith
Research Computing Centre Level 5, The University of Queensland,
Axon Building (Bldg 47), St Lucia, QLD 4072, Australia
e-mail: kevinallansmith@gmail.com

© Springer International Publishing AG, part of Springer Nature 2018
J. P. Sturmberg (ed.), *Putting Systems and Complexity Sciences Into Practice*,
https://doi.org/10.1007/978-3-319-73636-5_5

51

family and community network disruption. Increasing health inequalities related
to housing, welfare, and environmental challenges all compound the burden of ill-
health on the healthcare system.

### 5.1.1  The Changing Role of Hospitals and the Health and Welfare System

Societies around the world are confronted with a rising burden of ill-health arising
from the increase in preventable conditions like obesity as well as the increase in
conditions associated with aging and frailty.

Not only does the healthcare system bear the brunt of acute, chronic, and acute-
on-chronic medically recognized systemic conditions, but it also encounters the
effects of the nonmedical *social determinants* of health, which extend into the
purview of other jurisdictions including welfare, housing, transport, and justice.

Historically, the hospital was a place of support and healing. Hospitals have been
described in very early texts as

> ...houses for dispensing charity and medicine. All the poor and destitute in the country,
> orphans, widowers, and childless men, maimed people and cripples, and all who are
> diseased, go to those houses, and are provided with every kind of help, and doctors examine
> their diseases. They get the food and medicines which their cases require, and are made to
> feel at ease; and when they are better, they go away of themselves.
> A record of Buddhistic kingdoms; being an account by the Chinese monk Fâ-Hien of his
> travels in India and Ceylon, A.D. 399-414, in search of the Buddhist books of discipline
> J. Legge [3]

The modern hospital emergency department (ED) is a cross between a refuge for
disadvantaged, "MASH" for the traumatized, and a gateway to "modern technology
palace" for biomedical diseases.

> The appeal of the modern ED is undeniable - it is in some ways all things to all people.
> To the uninsured, it is a refuge. To the community physician, it is a valuable practice asset.
> To the patient, it is convenient, one-stop shopping. To the hospital itself, it is an escape valve
> for strained inpatient capacity. The demands being placed on emergency care, however, are
> overwhelming the system, and the result is a growing national crisis.
> The Evolving Role of Hospital-Based Emergency Care [4]

### 5.1.2  ED: At the Fuzzy Boundary Between "Medical Emergency" and "the Need for Social Support"

Hence the problem in preventable hospitalizations and emergency department
utilizations is related to the complex systems in which they operate and the fuzzy
rationale for their existence. Who should legitimately attend emergency departments
and be admitted on an *emergency basis* to a hospital bed and who should be

redirected to *social support-oriented healthcare networks* to avoid the need for crisis care in an anticipatory manner?

Currently the modern ED is struggling to cope with complex and ill-defined demands arising from:

- The social determinants of health
- The lack of health system responsiveness
- True medical emergencies

### 5.1.3   The Role of Primary Care

Has primary care organized itself to accommodate the deprived, the disadvantaged, and the diseased in a friendly nonjudgmental manner? Arguably a person-centered approach can support people to access timely care in primary care without reaching some personal crisis point that lead them to seek supportive care in emergency services.

There have been alternatives to ED delivered "primary care" in the communities in Ireland and Australia; these models have fluctuated and lack the historical legacy of the ED. Primary care "urgent care services" do not provide direct access to the reassurance of hospital-based technology and wider resources. Individuals with opioid problems or with alcohol intoxication are actively discouraged from attending primary care services (Fig. 5.1).

**Fig. 5.1** The emergency department—all things to all people. On one level, the ED dichotomizes people along the survival continuum into "life-threatening disease" and "minor illness." EDs also act as a "guiding source" to community care, temporary inpatient care, and/or organ-specific disease care. On another level, the ED is used to legitimize personal concern and act as a haven to address "psychosocial crises"

## 5.2    Health Journeys, Resilience, Interoception, and Anticipatory Systems

Individual life histories progress with episodic and/or cumulative loss of resilience causing an increased inability of an individual to respond to stressors—be they physical, psychosocial, and/or environmental—ultimately resulting in death. *Resilience* can be understood as the "capacity to bounce back" from stressors [5]. The inability to respond to stressors—internal or external—leads to greater tendencies toward unstable health states characterized by:

- More diagnosable diseases
- Greater severity of diseases
- Physical, social, and emotional dysfunction
- Disability

### 5.2.1    The Journey of Vulnerable People

The journeys of vulnerable individuals frequently include failures to detect triggers for instability that, if addressed in time, might avert avoidable emergency hospital utilization [5]. Emerging evidence indicates that unstable journeys with deteriorations over (2–3 days) occur usually in the home. Signposts of increasing instability include:

- Changes in illness experience
- Increase in pain
- Deterioration in mental state
- Deterioration in coping
- The emergence of "high-risk symptoms"
- Medication issues
- Carer stress and/or loss of carer
- Withdrawal of social support (perceived or real)
- Home challenges

Contact with health service providers may not flag the impending crisis or evoke adequate responses to ameliorate the situation or tipping point.

### 5.2.2    Anticipating Tipping Points in the Journeys of Vulnerable People

*Anticipation of such tipping points*, early warnings, and transitions in community journeys is considered the "holy grail" of prevention.

> An anticipatory system is a natural system that contains an internal predictive model of itself and of its environment, which allows it to change state at an instant in accord with the model's predictions pertaining to a later instant.
>
> Rosen [6]

There is much activity in this area. Human healthcare systems are increasingly learning from natural systems and seek to develop anticipatory systems to both improve individuals' and communities' health outcomes and manage health services more effectively.

Early warning systems to identify health deterioration are gaining scientific rigor and currency in healthcare, particularly in critical and frailty care [7, 8]. There are very few publications related to critical transitions and tipping points in emergency hospital utilization.

Biomarkers, biometrics, and patient-reported outcome measures increasingly can predict death, dependency, and disability [9]. Nevertheless, markers and metrics are not necessarily person-centered and orientated to personal health experiences and quality of daily life. Solutions abound with smartphones and sensors with self-monitoring or passive monitoring, and much work is needed to make these useful [10].

But very vulnerable individuals who are most at risk of hospitalization may have triggers which are not related to specific disease process or psychosocial and environmental crises. It is very difficult for standard "objective" population-based approaches to ascertain the meaning of a situation or conversely the situatedness of meaning of a potential health crisis [11, 12].

## 5.3  Conversations Provide Insights

Humans appear to have—at a deep intuitive level—evolved "the capacity to *know* their physiology and its trajectory" that otherwise is difficult to categorize—a phenomenon known as interoception [13]. Our human capacity for interoception is reflected in our "self-rated health perceptions." *Self-rated health* appears to account for physiology, meaning and situatedness, and has predictive power related to predicting mortality, hospital admission, and service utilization [14].

Regular conversations may tap into interoception of personal health states (self-rated health) but also provide information about the meaning and chronology of the experiences so that potential crises might be averted.

Conversations and narrative-based support over time help people make sense of their interoception in the context of their journey, as evidenced by the comments of this patient:

> You are a wonderful sounding board for how sick I really am. I can tell you my symptoms without necessarily knowing how sick I am and you can put in in perspective of whether I should be seeking further help and with whom. When I'm in a lot of pain or having breathing difficulties, I'm so focused on coping with that that I don't always have the foresight to work out what my next move should be - this is something that Monash Watch are really good at. Mick Dolan (pseudonym) in conversation with Sue W (Care Guide) in the MonashWatch service.

Potentially avoidable hospital (PAH) emergency attendances/admissions occur as a result of complex adaptive system (CAS) interactions in personal journeys influenced by:

- Internal biology, disease
- Personal sensemaking, strongly linked to feeling ill/pain or anxiety
- External healthcare, social, and environment

Self-care support in PAH improvement requires increasing, but varying, levels of clinical, personal, appraisal, informational, and practical support as illness becomes unstable.

## 5.4  Implementing the Patient Journey Record System (PaJR) in Ireland and Australia

The Patient Journey Record System (PaJR) applies a complex adaptive person-centered approach to understand and manage potentially avoidable hospitalizations (PAH). Telecare guides (TCG) regularly converse with "at risk" individuals to track their concerns and self-perceived health.

PaJR was initially piloted in a rural Irish cohort who were deemed to have had 1 PAH in the last year.

The framework is now being trialled by MonashWatch (MW), an Australian deprived inner-city cohort, who are predicted to have 3 PAH/year using hospital analytics following an index event.

### 5.4.1  Irish and Australian General Practice Systems

Both Australia and Ireland have a "British" model of general practice with some differences.

The Irish system is a blended capitation and private model with a well-organized out-of-hours primary care system with GPs contracted to provide 24/7 care for their capitated patients. This has led to a centralized "safety net" system with nurse triage and local GP and nursing teams working with community GPs providing consultations and home visits for many with at risk of potentially avoidable hospitalizations.

The Australian system has a fee-for-service model with ad hoc after-hours arrangements, including home doctor visiting which in many cases can be competitive with clinic-based services that are open for a wide variety of hours.

There is no centralized round-the-clock organization in Australia, while in Ireland a database of OOH utilization is available for quality improvement and research. The Irish system provides a traditional model for GP patients still predominantly retaining a non-corporate model, particularly for acute minor illness and subacute potentially serious illness with OOH "homes" for crises.

Emergency departments tend to operate on similar principles in both countries. The Irish system had an adjusted health expenditure (%GDP) of 14.2% compared with Australia 10.2%. Per 1000 population Ireland versus Australian reports: 17.5 vs 11.5 nurses, 4.2 vs 3.5 physicians, 3.5 vs 3.8 acute beds, and 157.2 vs 172.9 hip replacements [15].

### 5.4.2  Irish Primary Care Cohort (IPCC)

The PaJR Ireland IPCC pilot study was conducted in 2009–2013 [16, 17] aimed to reduced avoidable hospital attendances in 198 patients (+90 controls) in three settings (Fig. 5.2).

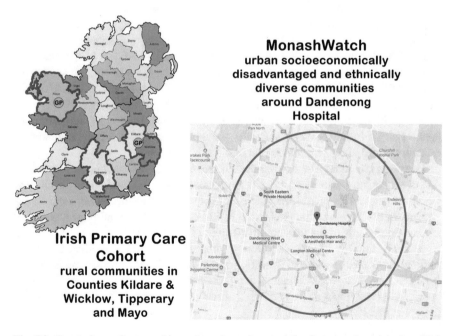

**Fig. 5.2** Comparison of geographic and services characteristics between the trial sites. Irish cohort: GP out-of-hours service (County Kildare and western part of County Wicklow), GP practices around Castlebar (County Mayo), and patients discharged from Nenagh Hospital (County Tipperary). MonashWatch cohort: patients who can be visited within 10 min drive from Dandenong Hospital

Recruitment criteria were:

- Having been admitted to a ward with at least one overnight stay
- Having one serious chronic disease—congestive health failure, chronic lung disease, diabetes, and other serious conditions such as cancer (in remission) and inflammatory bowel disease
- Likely to be socially isolated

Patients and controls were recruited consecutively: on hospital discharge—Co. Kildare & western Co. Wicklow, and recruited through GP practices based in Co. Mayo. The ratio of intervention:control was 2:1.

### 5.4.3   MonashWatch (MW)

MonashWatch is a scalable small locally based team approach beyond traditional silos of services that aims to be a holistic, proactive, intensive, and timely approach to avert potentially preventable admissions.

Based on DHHS Chronic Care Links (HLCC) (Box) algorithms, the eligible Monash Health cohort was identified. Predictive analytics based on hospital datasets identified a cohort with predicted 3+ overnight stays and/or hospital ward admissions. Patients predicted to have 3 PAH in the next 12 months were entered into the MW program after an index event, either admission or ED attendance.

The MW program is an outreach service of Monash Health, the largest public health service in Melbourne, Australia, providing services to almost a quarter of metropolitan Melbourne's population of 4.4 million people.

Hospitals including Monash Medical Centre Clayton, Moorabbin Hospital, Dandenong Hospital, Casey Hospital, Kingston Centre and the Cranbourne Centre, and Community Services provide an extensive array of allied health services supporting patients in recovery and the prevention of ill-health. MW's initial pilot takes place in Dandenong, one of the most deprived areas of Melbourne.

Monash Health's 15,000 staff work at more than 40 sites, providing over three million occasions of service, admitting more than 238,000 hospital patients, and handling more than 206,000 emergency presentations.

Monash Health was an early adopter of readmission prevention programs. These programs include:

- Complex continuing care (CCC) program—this program has reduced avoidable admissions from chronic disease such as cardiac failure and psychosocial health issues by providing self-management and supportive programs[1]

---

[1] http://www.monashhealth.org/page/Chronic_disease_services_HARP_CDM—last accessed: 31-Aug-2017.

- Hospital in the Home (HITH) program—this program has reduced admissions for management of common infections like cellulitis and pneumonias by administering iv antibiotics in the patient's home
- Community services link with care planning, team care referrals (EPC) available to GPs and primary care through Medicare funding
- In some settings, telehealth programs were provided for patients with complex conditions such as renal disease

**HealthLinks** Chronic Care (HLCC) is a funding pilot that forms part of the Victorian Department of Health and Human Services' approach to public hospital funding reform and its objective of delivering person-centered and integrated care.

It is generally well accepted that integrated community-based care and active management can result in better outcomes for people living with chronic conditions and may help reduce their need for inpatient care. However, the overlapping role and responsibility of ambulatory and inpatient care services, separate funding streams and models of care, as well as activity-based funding for acute care, can create a barrier to integrated care.

The HLCC funding model has been designed as a first step in removing the funding barriers to delivering alternate models of care for patients with complex chronic care needs. Health services will be given the flexibility to use projected inpatient activity-based funding to design packages of care around the needs of these highly complex patients. Packages will be inclusive of inpatient care and can include services that reach beyond the traditional hospital walls, therefore delivering a more comprehensive and integrated mix of services.

This approach, which uses a capitation funding model, is designed to promote innovative models of care that produce better outcomes for patients, at no additional total cost to the public health service system. Health services will benefit from any cost savings achieved through service innovation and efficiency.

Overtime, it is anticipated that patients at high risk of readmission to hospital will be more accurately identified and provided with targeted active management, thus reducing their use of unplanned inpatient care. It is recognized that in delivering this new model, enrollees may consume more planned and community-based care. This shift will not increase the overall cost of the individual patient's care if their use of unplanned inpatient services can be reduced.

Independent, external evaluators will be engaged for the duration of the trial and will assess the impact of the trial at the system level. Health services may seek to engage external evaluators to assess the impact of the interventions/changes they deploy at the local level.

In the first phase, Monash Health is only one of a small number of selected health services invited to consider participation.

## 5.5 Falling Between the Silos of "Evidence-based" Care

Why does Monash Health (and possibly Ireland) have so many patients falling between the silos of "evidence-based" disease care, necessitating the need to attend ED with potentially avoidable hospitalizations?

The following clusters of patient characteristics have emerged as possible reasons for avoidable ED use:

- Unstable journeys with a wide variety of stresses and tipping points
- Poor social support including partner, family, and/or community
- Poor engagement with supportive services
- Historical patterns of seeing ED/hospital as the place for primary care
- 24-h universal access to ED
- Younger people with substance abuse and medical consequences
- Older people with a combination of multiple morbidities, frailty, and/or social isolation
- Those struggling with self-management and the ability to anticipate and plan ahead
- Poor access to healthcare due to lack of transport, poor housing and limited finances, and cultural and linguistic barriers

## 5.6 PaJR: The Principles

PaJR Care Guide conversations (*outbound and inbound*)—mainly by telephone— are recorded and analyzed using predictive analytics. Conversation sensemaking takes place on a real-time basis. Clinician coaches provide mobile, anticipatory care and initiate home visits and care coordination in response to the current conversations and alerts generated by the PaJR algorithm. This is a learning system that adapts as the service develops.

PaJR developed its technologies to improve care management with providers who offer outbound calls to support patients after they have been discharged from hospitals or who have been identified as being at risk of hospitalization (Fig. 5.3).

Funding for the Irish study was initially through the National Digital Research Centre to develop a person-centered information technology approach to avoidable admissions based on a complex adaptive chronic care conceptual framework developed previously [18]. A team comprising a clinician, two academic computer scientists, a project manager, two postdoctoral students, and two industrial partners developed and tested clinical algorithms on summarized outbound conversations with the potential to apply machine learning to these conversations. The intention

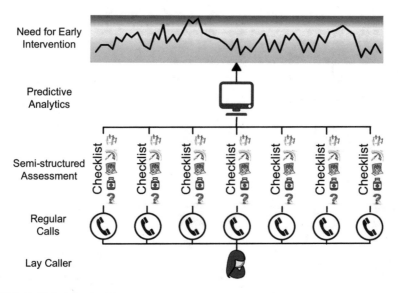

**Fig. 5.3** PaJR design principles

was to identify patterns in the conversations which would predict deterioration leading to hospital admission.[2]

The MW innovation connects "big data" with "personal data." MW identifies eligible adult (>18 years old) patients via a predictive analytics model allowing innovative use of hospital inpatient funds. Patient care profiles from routine care—primary and community care, social care, and hospital data (with addition of other big data over time)—are linked into the MW data system (Fig. 5.4). These almost real-time data are used in the context of conversations to stabilize journeys where possible and anticipate future risks.

### 5.6.1 Clinicians in IPCC and MW

Both IPCC and MW utilized care guides to listen, converse, and use these conversations to "predict deteriorations." The IPCC clinicians/nurses and allied health professionals triaged and guided patients to appropriate services. Monash-Watch Health Coaches, who are clinicians including nursing, physiotherapy, and occupational therapy located inside the Monash Health hospital system, provide this role in an innovative and adaptive manner. They provide home visits, accompany patients to hospitals or GPs, and facilitate transport, financial, and housing support

---

[2]https://www.siliconrepublic.com/start-ups/patient-journey-record-taps-into-global-health-tech-demand—last accessed 31-Aug-2017.

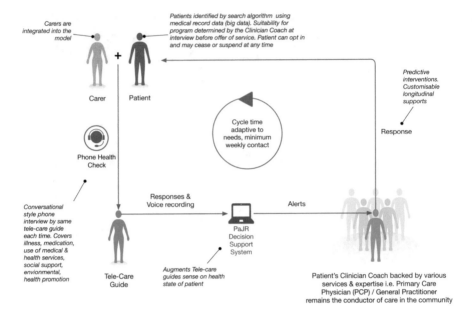

**Fig. 5.4** MonashWatch incorporating PaJR system—customized patient service. Connecting "big hospital data" with "personal health experience data." These almost real-time data are used in the context of conversations to stabilize journeys where possible and anticipate future risks

in an open-ended responsive manner. Care guides are supervised by coaches to help patients planning with their "next step." In addition MW Health Coaches provide essential communications especially when prompt advice is needed from within the hospital system which is hard for GPs, let alone, for patients to obtain. The leading brokerage role of coaches aims to connect GPs, hospitals, and community care in an anticipatory manner well in advance of patients reaching a tipping point.

## 5.7 Complex Adaptive Care and Feedback Loops: Preliminary Analysis from Pilot Studies

This analysis aimed to compare the first data (616 calls) from the IPCC and MW pilots and to provide feedback to adjust the processes for the MW rollout.

A complex adaptive systems intervention recognizes that continuous adaptation is needed based on ongoing feedback. In particular, we aimed to adapt the intervention based on the following questions:

- What profiles emerged from the PaJR conversations?
- How do MW patients compare with IPCC in their concerns, their expressed significant symptoms, and their perceived urgency of problems (translated into alerts)?
- Are different dynamics emerging? What do they tell us about the PaJR system and the different groups? How might these influence the likely responses and interventions?

## 5.7.1  Using Qualitative and Quantitative Data of IPCC and MW PaJR Calls

The first 616 calls from MW and IPCC pilots were analyzed using descriptive statistics. Variables included self-rated health (SRH), disease symptoms of concern, and psychosocial and environment concerns. Which combination of variables was associated with triggering red or pink alerts?

Red alerts are those that require clinical assessment either immediately or within a specified time within 24 h. Features that trigger a red alerts include chest pain, severe pain of any nature, a fall, a mental health or housing crisis, and recent attendance at the ED.

Pink alerts are those that do not require prompt attention; features that trigger a pink alert include persistent diagnosed pain, other chronic symptoms, ongoing concerns about sleep and mobility, ongoing need of social support, and financial and housing issues.

### 5.7.1.1  Findings

The IPCC group were older from a rural environment but had similar frailty levels to the MW group. Care guides making calls in the IPCC were all local Irish women.

The participating MW cohort were all English-speaking but had a very diverse ethnic background coming from Asian, West and East European, and Middle Eastern countries. The MW care guides and coaches were all from the local community, but did not mirror the diversity of the MW cohort.

Reported concerns and self-rated health reports were similar between the two groups with no significant differences. Symptom patterns were different with significantly more pain and depression reported in the MW group. Statistically more psychosocial and environmental alerts were reported per call in the MW group compared to the IPCC group (Table 5.1).

Particularly striking was the preponderance of "not coping," pain, and depression in calls to the MW group. In the first 3 months, none of the IPCC patients reported "non-coping." The rate of problems reported per call in "MW non-coping calls" were ($n = 48$):

**Table 5.1** Comparing PaJR Profiles in IPCC and MW cohorts at 3 months

|  | IPCC | MW |
|---|---|---|
| No of participants | 52 | 48 |
| Recruitment | GP invitation | Outreach by hospital |
| Profile difference | ≥1 ward admission in the last 12 months | Prediction of ≥3 ED or ward admissions in the next 12 months |
| Uptake rate | 90% | 60% |
| Dropout rate | 5% | 3% |
| Number of calls | 616 | 616 |
| Time | 5 months | 4.5 months |
| Age | 76 (67–85) | 65 (31–91) |
| Self-rated health average | Fair-good | Fair-good |
| Alerts per call (problems identified) | Mean 0.45, median 0, SD 1.06 var. 1.12, skewness 2.24 range 0–4 | Mean 2.70, median 1, SD 3.62 var. 13.09 skewness 1.84 range 0–21 |
| Red alerts 0–4 h⇒24 | 28% of calls | 25% of calls |
| Requiring attention |  |  |
| Most common "symptoms of concern" reported | Breathlessness and fever/feeling ill | Pain and depression |
| Calls reporting "Not coping" | none | 48/616 calls (8%) |
| Patients reporting "Not coping" in 1 or more calls | none | 19 out of 48 patients (40%) |

- Medication problems 23/48
- Healthcare access/use problems 21/48
- Social support and social services 57/48
- Environmental—housing, finances, and transport 24/48
- Self-care and functional problems such as nutrition, sleep, etc. 66/48

The following two cases illustrate the different "type" of patient in the IPCC and MW groups.

**Kevin**[3] (see Table 5.2). Kevin is a 79-year-old bachelor who lives next door to his sister Mary who is 81 and a caregiver to Kevin and her husband who has dementia (but she is quite fit). Kevin is a retired farm worker in County Kildare. He has chronic lung disease, diabetes, heart disease and peripheral vascular disease, sciatica, and recurrent chest infections. Kevin at times forgets about his treatment and appointments. His GP has a very large rural practice but has been Kevin's GP for 50 years.

---

[3]The names of the patients and timelines of their journeys have been altered to conceal their identities.

**Table 5.2** "Kevin": a "typical" Irish patient's conversational journey

| | |
|---|---|
| 15/06/12 | My breathing has improved since stay in hospital |
| 16/06/12 | My throat feels better and generally feels better than yesterday |
| 17/06/12 | I feel 2–3 out of 5 today and will never be 100% |
| 20/06/12 | Breathlessness will be more or less the same. Not likely to get much better than is at the moment |
| 21/06/12 | My chest is reasonably today 80%; says as 3/5 is as good as it gets |
| 22/06/12 | Ankles are better today than yesterday, 0 swelling, didn't go to or ring the GP as asked; Kevin's sister seemed to think P was confused that he may have missed an appointment. That was why I had asked him to speak to the GP |
| 28/06/12 | Kevin didn't feel great on Thursday. My chest can change very quickly, I didn't want to take another antibiotic but have to. Stomach is beginning to settle down and I went for a short stroll today |
| 29/06/12 | I still have pain in the ankle when walking, but pain relief is working at night; I am more breathless in the morning and this improves as the day goes on |
| 30/06/12 | My health will remain at 80% |
| 01/07/12 | Fine today and I went to town |
| 04/07/12 | Legs are sore today especially when walking. Back to the hospital tomorrow for a follow-up and hopefully will get them sorted |
| 06/07/12 | Consultant was happy with my chest yesterday and prescribed pain relief for his leg and a scan in 6 weeks time |
| 08/07/12 | Chesty this morning, but the leg has improved not as sore when walking |
| 12/07/12 | Chest is still the same |
| 14/07/12 | Legs are 3, and chest is fine today |
| 18/07/12 | Pains in the leg when walking |
| 20/07/12 | Chest is "middling" today as he puts it. Going to the GP this afternoon to get a prescription and have a listen to the chest |
| 25/07/12 | A bit of a cough, not too breathless, my GP put me on steroids and antibiotics |

Kevin's health journey demonstrates an ongoing unstable dynamic of managing his conditions. Kevin, in the first 3 months of the study despite many fluctuations in his health, remained cheerful and accepting of his health condition.

**Mick** (see Table 5.3). Mick is a 59-year-old, of British descent who lives with his wife in a rented apartment in an estate in inner-city Dandenong, one of the most deprived areas in Melbourne. Some major industries have collapsed leaving a very high rate of unemployment with an influx of refugees and immigrants with low socioeconomic backgrounds. Mick began drinking when he lost his job 15 years ago and has relapsed on many occasions. His relationship with Betty is strained by his drinking and her cancer makes him feel very guilty. His chronic pain is related to pancreatitis, gastritis, liver disease, back pain, and depression. Mick has many fluctuations in his health related to drinking and decompensated depression. His GP is part of a large corporate primary care practice which has been set up within the past 12 years.[4]

---

[4]Corporatization is becoming a dominant model of Australian medical practice.

**Table 5.3** "Mick": a "typical" MW Australian patient's conversational journey

| | |
|---|---|
| 30/12/16 | I really like to know what's going on with me and what's causing all my pain. The doctors aren't telling me anything |
| 03/01/17 | My pain taking relief is holding at 3 to 4 |
| 06/01/17 | I was concerned about tummy neck pain and headache last Sat |
| 10/01/17 | Worried about why and the fact that I didn't eat at all last Sat |
| 11/01/17 | "I'm in trouble I want a drink" (Mick is an alcoholic and had a drink last night for the first time in some months) |
| 10/01/17 | "Can I tell you something—I've had enough. Enough of the pain and everything." "B tries to help but doesn't understand." "I can't eat a big meal I'm not even hungry." Mick is worried about B who is a breast cancer patient who had a mastectomy and is currently having a skin test |
| 13/01/17 | Sat. Tummy sore but not sick. I couldn't help myself and started drinking again |
| 17/01/17 | Got drunk again |
| 25/01/17 | Crisis took him to hospital |
| 02/02/17 | Released from hospital yesterday and didn't feel well. I thought I was in for detox and to start medication. I was in for pancreatitis, but they didn't address alcohol issue. Drug and alcohol appoint on 14/2, but I may be in any state by then. Drug and alcohol said if Mick could get him to present to the hospital then they would start detox and meds. MB confused as to why they released him. Mick took a taxi home by himself |

## 5.8  Discussion

Despite very different settings and risk profiles, self-rated health and red alerts that require attention (mostly GP care) were very similar in the MW and Irish cohorts. Pink alerts were statistically more numerous in the MW cohort with psychosocial/environmental comorbidities and more frequent in the IPCC cohort affected by disease multimorbidity.

The two communities in which PaJR has been implemented are very different but have some surprising similarities. Recruiting patients from a general practice setting might select a more socially stable group, while patients with pain and alcoholism may present more readily to hospital emergency departments.

Despite poverty in rural Ireland, there may be more social cohesion within the community which provides a social safety net, but this may not exist in the inner city with a highly fluctuating population structure. As our recruiting occurred through primary care, we may not have tapped into the cohort with different needs presenting to ED of a hospital.

The use of ED for short-term crises related to a cluster of pain, depression, and drug problems in MW—as illustrated by Mick's case—is evident in the pattern of admissions and length of stay. The MW cohort has a distinct pattern of repeated ED short stays. The predominant reason for these short stays is "pain" in the cluster of cluster of "pain, depression, and alcohol/drug problems." Figure 5.5 illustrates the persistence of a pattern of frequent 1-day admissions (known as ED short stay admissions) in the progress of MW at 6 months related to the cluster described.

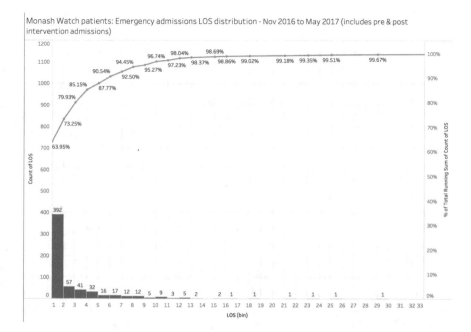

**Fig. 5.5** Length of stay and number of admissions in MonashWatch patients. Length of stay and number of admissions in MonashWatch patients ($\geq 1$ overnight stay in hospital either in the ED department or admitted to a ward). Admissions are frequently for ED short stay at 6 months of MonashWatch. 33/148 patients had 33 admissions. Not all admissions are avoidable and indeed may reflect optimal care

Nevertheless, MW also had older patients similar to the IPCC with longer LOS, who presented with typical patterns of breathlessness and poor health.

Because PaJR is a practical system, not a research instrument per se, its value lies in identifying the unmet needs of patients. The patterns described in the IPCC and MW patients are different, which raises hypotheses for further research and investigations. As a complex adaptive systems tool, it does adapt to different populations in different contexts. The findings reported here confirm PaJR's utility and adaptability; there is sufficient evidence support continuing implementation of PaJR type approaches.

Conversations that tap into interoception and support resilience are the cornerstone of "helping." Trust in care guides is essential, and potential limitations relate to the use of a common language and perhaps culture.

The use of care guides who are trained to use the system under supervision, but are not health professionals, has worked in both locations. However, some authorities are cautious about the risks of employing a nonprofessional "lay" workforce, in particular legal implications if serious problems are missed.

However, the PaJR system is an outreach system beyond existing formal health services. It exists where there is a vacuum in unstable complex patient journeys.

The central intervention is conversations and self-report, not the diagnostics of new complaints. Lay care guides are supervised by professionals, and the PaJR system has "embedded" expert knowledge and decision support. The low dropout rate suggests that conversations tap into interoception and support resilience—the cornerstone of "helping." Trust in care guides appears to be achievable where there are a common language and cultural sensitivity.

The role of coaches in MonashWatch in a supervisory role and the transparency of audiotaped calls addresses these risks. The coaches are the first line of the response arm and make it possible for the lay persons to be care guides. The brokerage role of the coaches while not unique is highly innovative and adaptive. The use of informatics and almost real-time analytics allows for rapid feedback loops and anticipatory activities.

Ultimately the success of any service utilizing PaJR approaches to identify need depends on what resources and services are available to meet these needs.

Providing adaptive medical care for chronic disease in the face of an aging population is challenging, yet compared to addressing broader psychosocial and economic health determinants, health and aged care services are able to manage these challenges. MW has identified considerable unmet needs in the care of younger- and middle-aged adults in pain, depression, and substance use clusters which are linked to unemployment, poverty, and poor social cohesion.

## 5.9  Conclusions

The PaJR system identifies needs that benefit from being met in a timely fashion. In deprived diverse communities, interventions in particular need to address the social determinants of health beyond "disease management."

Hospital avoidance schemes using a complex adaptive and resilience-focused systems approach such as PaJR are demonstrably appropriate in at least two different settings, provided they are highly adaptive in their responses. Self-care support in PAH improvement requires varying levels of clinical, personal, appraisal, informational, and practical support as illness becomes unstable.

Operationalizing the biopsychosocial model in two different settings, we found two distinct profiles. A younger, more depressed urban cohort suffering from pain and social and environmental problems, and an older rural population affected by social isolation and typical chronic disease morbidity.

Increased utilization of a dynamic systems understanding through conversations recognizes the importance of personal health perceptions in critical health state transitions [19]. Talking to individuals about their health and actively understanding their meanings of signs and symptoms in the context of their personal family, social, and health networks would seem to be a core activity in improving preventable admissions.

**Acknowledgements** Deirdre Grady, Laurence Gaughan, Brendan O'Shea, John Kellett, Narelle Hinkley, Damian Byrne, John-Paul Smith, Michael Jaurigue, Basem Youry, and all the wonderful care guides in Ireland and Melbourne.

# The Journey

The journey to MonashWatch has evolved from the networking among multiple actors with the emergence and confluence of different streams of experience, data, knowledge, and, hopefully, the "getting of wisdom." This journey is a response to the changing nature of population aging, health and illness, societal changes, and the dynamics in the political economy of healthcare.

Carmel's Journey. I first came to the nature of chronic illness because of the almost fatal consequences of the medical management of my healthcare. I experienced the effects of lack of time and effort taken to understand my condition by one group of medical practitioners, the exemplary care by another group, and (perceived) lack of support from general practitioners, to serious illness. As a practicing general practitioner, in much better health, I returned to this topic, because I found that chronic care was difficult and time-consuming with intense personal demands. This forced me to question the processes and directions of my and health systems efforts. I began a 25-year journey to understand and improve the care of chronic illness using complex systems theories, because the linear disease-based evidence did not fit my experiences. Complex systems theories have developed from insights with respect to human behavior, human values, evolutionary biological systems, and statistical physics of the early complex systems theorists. These seemed more relevant to chronic illness.

This drive for innovation with new clinical approaches inspired by complex adaptive systems (CAS) theories found synergies with my collaborators at various junctures: Joachim Sturmberg in improving primary care as complex systems, Keith Stockman and Donald Campbell from Monash Health with their wealth of experience in user-centric design and health service innovation in hospitals, and Carl Vogel, Lucy Hederman, and Kevin Smith from the perspective of information theories, natural language processing, and computer science. Taking a broad view of health and healthcare related to human systems innovations in nonlinear CAS requires a range of "complex bundles" of innovation from a widely distributed knowledge base based on information from individuals, families and communities, services, and populations.

My journey through complexity continues to encounter the reductionist analyses and simplistic (off-the-shelf) solutions that are always attractive to funders and managers as mechanisms to "control" uncertainties. Accounting for the human dimension (experience) of health and systems requires three overarching principles: a fundamental commitment to emancipation through practical action, critical awareness rather than conventional "wisdom," and methodological pluralism. Systems thinking in general seeks to understand an issue as a "gestalt of its parts". During my career, there has been a gradual widening of understanding and application of these principles in health; however, political expediency and reductionism continue to undermine progress.

*Life is Precious Because it is Precarious:*
*Individuality, Mortality and the Problem of Meaning*
Tom Froese [20]

Take-Home Message
Supporting complex health journeys through conversations using lay care guides and an adaptive systems approach is feasible in at least two very different settings and patient groups. This approach identifies problems that are amenable to intervention but also some that may be challenging to solve with existing resources.

# References

1. Robertson TM, Lofgren RP. Where population health misses the mark: breaking the 80/20 rule. Acad Med. 2015;90(3):277–8.
2. Robinson RL, Grabner M, Palli SR, Faries D, Stephenson JJ. Covariates of depression and high utilizers of healthcare: impact on resource use and costs. J Psychosom Res. 2016;85:35–43.
3. Legge J. A record of Buddhistic kingdoms: being an account by the Chinese monk Fâ-Hien of his travels in India and Ceylon (399-414 CE) in: search of the Buddhist books of discipline, 1886. Translated and annotated with a Corean recension of the Chinese text by Fâ-Hien, ca. 337-ca. 422. https://archive.org/details/recordofbuddhist00fahsuoft.
4. Institute of Medicine. The evolving role of hospital-based emergency care. In: Hospital-based emergency care: at the breaking point. Washington, DC: The National Academies Press; 2007. p. 37–40.
5. D'Souza S, Guptha S. Preventing admission of older people to hospital. BMJ. 2013;346:f3186.
6. Rosen R. Life itself: a comprehensive inquiry into the nature, origin, and fabrication of life. New York: Columbia University Press; 1991.
7. Li X, Dunn J, Salins D, Zhou G, Zhou W, Schüssler-Fiorenza Rose, SM, Perelman D, Elizabeth Colbert E, Runge R, Rego S, Sonecha R, Datta S, McLaughlin T, Snyder, MP. Digital health: tracking physiomes and activity using wearable biosensors reveals useful health-related information. PLoS Biol. 2017;15(1):e2001402.
8. Olde Rikkert MG, Dakos V, Buchman TG, Boer R, Glass L, Cramer AO, Levin S, van Nes E, Sugihara G, Ferrari MD, Tolner EA, van de Leemput I, Lagro J, Melis R, Scheffer M. Slowing down of recovery as generic risk marker for acute severity transitions in chronic diseases. Crit Care Med. 2016;44(3):601–6.
9. Scheffer M. Critical transitions in nature and society. Princeton: Princeton University Press; 2009.
10. Bloss CS, Wineinger NE, Peters M, Boeldt DL, Ariniello L, Kim JY, Sheard J, Komatireddy R, Barrett P, Topol, EJ. A prospective randomized trial examining health care utilization in individuals using multiple smartphone-enabled biosensors. PeerJ. 2016;4:e1554.
11. Lyon ML. Psychoneuroimmunology: the problem of the situatedness of illness and the conceptualization of healing. Cult Med Psychiatry 1993;17(1):77–97.

12. Shubin S, Rapport F, Seagrove A. Complex and dynamic times of being chronically ill: beyond disease trajectories of patients with ulcerative colitis. Soc Sci Med. 2015;147:105–12.
13. Craig AD. Interoception: the sense of the physiological condition of the body. Curr Opin Neurobiol. 2013;13(4):500–5.
14. Jylhä M. What is self-rated health and why does it predict mortality? Towards a unified conceptual model. Soc Sci Med. 2009;69(3): 307–16.
15. Public Policy.IE. Expenditure and outputs in the Irish health system: a cross country comparison, 2012. http://www.publicpolicy.ie/expenditure-and-outputs-in-the-irish-health-system-a-cross-country-comparison/.
16. Martin CM, Grady D, Deaconking S, McMahon C, Zarabzadeh A, O'Shea B. Complex adaptive chronic care - typologies of patient journey: a case study. J Eval Clin Pract. 2011;17(3):520–4.
17. Martin CM, Vogel C, Grady D, Zarabzadeh A, Hederman L, Kellett J, Smith K, O'Shea B. Implementation of complex adaptive chronic care: the patient journey record system (PaJR). J Eval Clin Pract. 2012;18(6):1226–34.
18. Martin CM, Biswas R, Joshi A, Sturmberg JP. Patient journey record systems (PaJR): the development of a conceptual framework for a patient journey system. In: Biswas R, Martin CM, editors. User-driven healthcare and narrative medicine: utilizing collaborative social networks and technologies, vol 1. Hershey, PA: IGI Global; 2010. p. 75–92.
19. Martin CM. What matters in "multimorbidity"? Arguably resilience and personal health experience are central to quality of life and optimizing survival. J Eval Clin Pract. 2016;https://doi.org/10.1111/jep.12644.
20. Froese T. Life is precious because it is precarious: individuality, mortality and the problem of meaning. In: Dodig-Crnkovic G, Giovagnoli R, editors. Representation and reality in humans, other living organisms and intelligent machines. Studies in applied philosophy, epistemology and rational ethics, vol 28. Cham: Springer; 2017. p. 33–50. https://doi.org/10.1007/978-3-319-43784-2_3.

# Chapter 6
# Transforming Monitoring and Improving Care with Variability-Derived Clinical Decision Support

Christophe L. Herry, Nathan B. Scales, Kimberley D. Newman, and Andrew J. E. Seely

## 6.1 Introduction

Monitoring of patients with existing or impending critical illness routinely involves the recording of multiple waveforms, including electrocardiography, oxygen saturation, capnography, chest impedance and arterial blood pressure, with continuous display of vital signs such as heart rate, oxygen saturation, respiratory rate and systolic/diastolic blood pressure. Although waveform data is sampled hundreds of times per second, vital signs are commonly charted once per hour, as changes in vital signs are meaningfully evaluated over hours to track response to interventions or gauge clinical trajectory. Clinical improvement or deterioration is evaluated by change in vital signs over hours to days; infection is detected with fever or laboratory tests, and clinical intuition plays a significant role.

Utilizing the currently untapped information contained in waveform data has the potential to reduce the diagnostic and prognostic uncertainty inherent in critical care, even when patients are managed by trained intensivists. This uncertainty results in delayed diagnosis, unnecessary or inappropriate therapy and increased complications, mortality and cost of care. In fact, studies have shown that the most expensive patients are those with indeterminate outcomes [1, 2]. For example, late diagnosis of infection and the cost of treating sepsis represent a large burden on the healthcare system [3]. Similarly, uncertainty in determining optimal timing of extubation in mechanically ventilated patients can harm patients and waste resources [4]. The care of patients with serious acute illness and the demand for ICU services are expected to increase by 40% in the year 2026 compared to 2011 [5, 6].

C. L. Herry (✉) · N. B. Scales · K. D. Newman · A. J. E. Seely
The Ottawa Hospital Research Institute, Clinical Epidemiology Program, 501 Smyth Road, Box 708, Ottawa, ON, Canada K1H 8L6
e-mail: cherry@ohri.ca; nscales@ohri.ca; knewman@ohri.ca; aseely@ohri.ca

© Springer International Publishing AG, part of Springer Nature 2018
J. P. Sturmberg (ed.), *Putting Systems and Complexity Sciences Into Practice*,
https://doi.org/10.1007/978-3-319-73636-5_6

Heart rate variability (HRV) and respiratory rate variability (RRV) time series derived from the continuous physiological waveforms help characterize the degree and complexity of the patterns of the inter-beat and inter-breath interval time series. Decreased variability is associated with age and illness and correlates with illness severity, indicating reduced adaptability and/or increased stress. Alterations in HRV have been associated with sepsis and septic shock [7–9]. HRV monitoring provides early detection of infection in neutropenic patients and determines severity of illness in critically ill patients [10, 11]. Respiratory rate variability (RRV) is also altered in association with critical illness, with a reduction in RRV during organ failure [12] and restrictive lung disease [13]. Reduced RRV has also been evaluated as a marker of increased stress during weaning from mechanical ventilation [14]. Reduced RRV is also statistically associated with and predictive of extubation failure [15, 16].

In the following, we outline our current approach to utilize information buried in the variability of inter-beat and inter-breath intervals routinely monitored at the bedside, transforming the information into clinical decision support that reduces uncertainty, standardizes approach and improves quality and efficiency of care.

## 6.2   Our Approach

Combining waveform-based variability analysis with predictive modelling, we can enhance timely clinical decision-making at the bedside by providing probabilistic prediction of upcoming clinical events. In order to produce a practical, useable and clinically relevant decision support, we focus on unsolved clinical problems, where altered variability is associated with a well-defined clinical outcome, tied to a decision that the healthcare team has to make. Conditions are then optimal to utilize variability analysis and predictive modelling.

### 6.2.1   Data Collection

The vital signs of patients are often monitored continuously and used to derive alarms and run predictive analytics or simply to get a quick feedback on patients' status. On the other hand, while routinely displayed, physiologic waveform data such as ECG is rarely recorded for more than a few days or made available for additional offline analyses. Collected waveforms may be used to track vital signs precisely and continuously but also enable the derivation of predictive analytics based on patterns of variation in heart rate, respiratory rate or blood pressure, which in turn can help identify patients at higher risk of a negative outcome. At present, there is no standard method to extract waveform data from bedside monitors or ambulatory physiological devices. Waveform capture solutions depend on the brand and model of the equipment and have varied technical requirements and costs. Setting up waveform data acquisition at clinical institutions is usually not trivial and requires a diverse range of clinical and technical stakeholders.

Research studies involving multiple sites face the additional challenge of harmonizing the waveform data coming from very different systems. The choice of data repository, database and file formats as well as developing software for easily reviewing large amounts of clinical data and physiological recordings should be considered carefully for each study.

## 6.2.2 Variability/Complexity Assessment

Physiological waveforms acquired from a patient are processed through a software engine, which we have termed Continuous Individualized Multiorgan Variability Analysis (CIMVA). CIMVA performs a series of automated algorithms that process the waveform files into a comprehensive multivariate characterization of the quality of the waveform and the event time series (i.e. consecutive inter-beat and inter-breath intervals over time) and the calculated measures of degree and complexity of variability.

The first step is to translate the waveform into a time series of physiological events. For example, individual heartbeats are identified from an ECG waveform, using commonly used algorithms and fiducial points (e.g. peaks of the P, R or T waves). We form time series of time intervals, such as R-peak to R-peak intervals (RRI). Similarly, a time series of inter-breath intervals (IBI) can be derived from a capnogram ($CO_2$ waveform). A thorough automated assessment is performed on the quality of the underlying physiological waveform signal and derived physiological events time series. Movement artefacts, noise, disconnections and saturations are identified on the waveforms. A signal quality index is determined on a beat-by-beat or breath-by-breath basis, using continuity and morphology analyses. In addition, the times series of physiological events (RRI, IBI) are filtered to exclude non-sinus beats, abnormally shaped breaths and nonphysiologically plausible data.

Using the cleaned time series of events, the signal complexity and degree of variability are assessed. This is performed through a moving window analysis, whereby a window of fixed duration (or fixed number of events) is shifted in time across the entire duration of the event time series. A comprehensive set of variability metrics are calculated within each window. Variability measures include measures characterizing the statistical properties (e.g. standard deviation, RMSSD), the informational complexity (e.g. entropy measures), the pattern variations across time scales (e.g. fractal measures, power law exponents) or the energy contained in the signal (e.g. spectral measures). Each technique provides a unique perspective on the data; no single technique offers a definitive characterization of biologic signals, and thus investigators agree a plurality of techniques offers the most complete evaluation [17–19]. This analysis is performed iteratively and repetitively, measuring variability over time intervals (e.g. 5 min for HRV, 15 min for RRV), then tracked over time. Nonstationarities (i.e. rapid underlying trends, spikes) are assessed and removed. Only high-quality variability estimates are used in subsequent processing steps. This automated high-quality comprehensive variability analysis forms a multivariate representation of variability and signal complexity tracked over time.

## 6.2.3  Predictive Modelling

Predictive modelling is ideally suited to translate multivariate variability into clinically relevant information. To do so, we identify clinical outcomes statistically associated with altered variability and perform observational clinical research measuring variability and outcomes for multiple patients. Outcomes are categorized, such as extubation outcomes (e.g. failed extubation requiring re-intubation vs. successful), the presence or absence of infection or rapid vs. slow death after withdrawal of life-sustaining therapy (which determines eligibility for donation of organs after cardiac death); and the dataset is typically separated into patients who develop the outcome and patients who do not.

Several strategies are available to develop a prediction tool that estimates the likelihood of a patient developing the outcome of interest. First, a set of relevant features is determined that will be fed to one of the several possible multivariate statistical techniques such as logistic regression, k-nearest neighbour analysis, decision trees, support vector machines, neural networks and so on. Relevant input features are determined through a priori expert knowledge or a feature selection process whereby the discriminative power of each feature is assessed on a subset of patients (training set), based on a predetermined performance metric (e.g. prediction accuracy). Considered features include the set of variability measures as well as relevant clinical parameters (e.g. tidal volume, gender, comorbidities, risks scores, etc.) and/or laboratory data. In addition, separate predictive models can be derived for variability measures and clinical or laboratory parameters and the models later combined, through fusion or decision scores via appropriate weighting or using a Bayesian framework. This may result in a more efficient model and improved prediction when features are recorded at different time intervals (e.g. daily scores).

The development and performance assessment of the multivariate statistical techniques is carried out with a cross-validation scheme, whereby the dataset is separated into training and validation sets for model and feature selection, and an unseen testing set for an unbiased estimate of the performance and generalizability on future datasets. Finally, performance evaluation of predictive models is based on receiver operating characteristic (ROC)-derived metrics (i.e. area under the curve, sensitivity, specificity, and positive predictive value and negative predictive value), as well as time-dependent metrics (i.e. time-stamped endpoints) for tracking patient improvement or deterioration prior to or post-outcome. The output of the predictive model is a probability of developing the outcome and can, for example, be presented to clinicians in the form of a continuously updated fold increase in risk to facilitate timely clinical decision-making.

## 6.3 Example of a Clinical Application: Weaning and Variability Evaluation (WAVE)

Expeditious, safe extubation is vitally important in the care of intensive care unit (ICU) patients as prolonged mechanical ventilation harms patients, and failed extubation (i.e. re-intubation within 48 h) is associated with increased morbidity, mortality and costs [4, 20–22]. Absence of elevation of the respiratory frequency to tidal volume ratio (f/VT) or rapid shallow breathing index (RSBI<105) during a spontaneous breathing trial (SBT) is the current standard indicator that extubation will be successful [23, 24]. Despite this practice, several studies document an extubation failure rate of 15% [23, 25, 26], suggesting that the RSBI, the most objective measurement available, has only limited value in predicting successful extubation after an SBT [24].

Several small studies have demonstrated that reduced heart or respiratory rate variability (HRV or RRV) during SBTs is associated with extubation failure [27–30]. In a large, multicentre (12 sites), prospective observational study, we enrolled 721 patients and collected information during spontaneous breathing trials including physiologic measures, ECG, capnograms and extubation outcomes [15].

A large set of HRV and RRV metrics were derived using CIMVA software. Repeated randomized subsampling with training, validation and testing sets were used to derive and compare an ensemble of logistic regression models. An optimal predictive model utilizing five RRV metrics during the last SBT prior to extubation was derived, which outperformed other commonly used measures such as RSBI and vital signs or clinical judgement. The output from this model was a probability of extubation failure (WAVE score) or equivalently a fold increase in risk, which in turn could help physicians stratify patients more efficiently.

The previous work of the WAVE study was seminal to the development of the clinical decision support software, Extubation Advisor™. Extubation Advisor™ was developed to deliver a comprehensive assessment of the risk of extubation failure to clinicians at the bedside. A key set of clinically relevant information is gathered from the respiratory therapist at the bedside via an electronic form, and a report is generated, which summarizes the patient condition during an SBT as well as his/her risk of extubation failure. The components of this standardized report were determined via a mixture of best clinical practices available in the literature as well as feedback from targeted clinical users and include patient information, SBT information and parameters, vitals, extubation readiness checklist, respiratory therapist impression and risk of extubation failure.

Great care must be taken to ensure that a clinical prediction tool does not negatively disrupt the established clinical workflow. The identification of all stake-holders that are anticipated to be impacted by the tool is critical at an early stage. Furthermore, actively engaging healthcare staff, technical and research teams and patients/family can greatly help identifying a relevant, impactful clinical problem, focusing on metrics relevant to the problem as well as providing feedback on user interface and efficient deployment of the predictive tool.

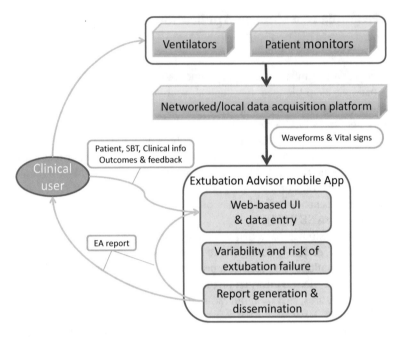

**Fig. 6.1** High-level flow diagram of Extubation Advisor™

Figure 6.1 shows an example of integration of the extubation failure prediction tool based on the WAVE study.

A typical workflow for Extubation Advisor™ would be as follows:

- An intubated and mechanically ventilated patient is scheduled for a spontaneous breathing trial (SBT). The patient is connected to a bedside monitor displaying ECG, CO2 and other relevant waveforms. A respiratory therapist (RT) logs on to the Extubation Advisor™ application on a tablet or mobile device. The RT inputs patient/admission information, completes an SBT checklist and starts the trial. During the SBT, the waveform data is continuously acquired via the bedside monitor or the ventilator using a hospital-based data acquisition platform or mobile data acquisition device attached to the ventilator.
- After the SBT is complete, Extubation Advisor™ requests the portions of waveforms and vital signs data (if available) corresponding to the SBT, proceeds to clean and assess the quality of the data, computes variability metrics and generates a score summarizing the risk of extubation failure. Extubation Advisor™ also generates an interactive report for the RT to view on a mobile platform and a PDF version that can be dispatched to interested parties. The attending physician and RT examine the report along with other clinical information and determine whether to proceed with extubation or not.

- Finally, the extubation information and outcome are entered via the EA user interface 48 h post-extubation for post-analysis of the performance of the model and future improvements.

## 6.4   Conclusions

In this paper, we presented a systematic approach to highlight how to systematically derive relevant decision support tools from well-defined clinical questions to bedside implementation. Focusing on the weaning process in mechanically ventilated ICU patients as an example, we showed that by assessing the complexity and variability of often unused physiological waveforms commonly acquired at the bedside, combined with easily obtainable clinical data, we could provide a timely standardized report of the risk of extubation failure. A possible integration of this Extubation Advisor™ tool in clinical processes and workflow was also highlighted.

Stemming from a desire to extract useful information from physiological signals as surrogate "sensors" of the human body, we quickly realized that often used single summary parameters were inadequate for making timely decisions on complex health problems. Instead, we noted that complex behaviours similar to what could be observed in health systems have been addressed in other fields such as chaos theory, network theory, fluid dynamics, etc. with a range of tools and methods, each tool presenting a slightly different insight into the complex problem.

We believe it is also important to view our understanding of physiological signal complexity in the wider context of cellular, metabolic, macroscopic and population interactions, where complex interactions similarly occur. The complexity science umbrella of methods and applications is broad, and valuable insights can be gained by sharing and pooling knowledge from its various subdisciplines.

## The Journey

The framework presented in this paper offers a practical approach for utilizing variability as a window into the integrity of the complex system that is the human body.

Major challenges in critical care are related to complex illnesses such as multiple organ dysfunction syndrome, yet until two decades ago, most approaches relied on analytical approaches, focusing on individual immunologic mechanisms and assuming linear relationships. The failures of these reductionist models prompted us, and others, to reframe the host response to major insults as a complex nonlinear system, whereby nonlinear interactions between interconnected organ systems contribute to the emergence of complex properties, which individual parts of the system do not otherwise exhibit. This represented a profound shift in our approach but also opened the door to a great amount of new and exciting techniques from nonlinear dynamics, including variability analysis.

We embraced variability analysis as a natural toolkit to characterize the emergent properties of a complex system, following earlier works from Glass and Mackey [31] and Goldberger and West [32], among others. We embarked on a comprehensive exploration of a wide range of linear and nonlinear variability metrics, working on physiological signals from multiple organ systems (ECG, $CO_2$, ABP, etc.), in an effort to characterize different aspects of the underlying system dynamics of the systemic host response.

After many years using this rich complex science toolkit, we are slowly working towards individualized variability directed intervention, where therapeutic approaches are tailored to a patient based on his/her own patterns of variability and systemic host response.

Take-Home Message

- There is much untapped potential in routinely collected yet discarded clinical waveform data (e.g. electrocardiogram, capnography)
- The complexity and degree of variability of heart and respiratory rate measured from waveforms and their changes over time are linked to a variety of ill health states
- Predictive models using clinical data and variability of physiological signals can provide key decision insights to the clinical team
- A systematic approach is described to ensure that the clinical problem answered by a decision support tool is well-defined and relevant to clinical practice and that its development and implementation is beneficial to clinicians and integrates with clinical workflows

# References

1. Detsky AS, Stricker SC, Mulley AG, Thibault GE. Prognosis, survival, and the expenditure of hospital resources for patients in an intensive-care unit. N Engl J Med. 1981;305(12):667–72.
2. Luce JM, Rubenfeld GD. Can health care costs be reduced by limiting intensive care at the end of life? Am J Respir Crit Care Med. 2002;165(6):750–4.
3. Burchardi H, Schneider H. Economic aspects of severe sepsis: a review of intensive care unit costs, cost of illness and cost effectiveness of therapy. Pharmacoeconomics 2004;22(12): 793–813.
4. Epstein SK. Extubation failure: an outcome to be avoided. Crit Care 2004;8(5):310–2.
5. Needham DM, Bronskill SE, Calinawan JR, Sibbald WJ, Pronovost PJ, Laupacis A. Projected incidence of mechanical ventilation in Ontario to 2026: preparing for the aging baby boomers. Crit Care Med. 2005;33(3):574–9.

6. Wunsch H, Linde-Zwirble WT, Angus DC, Hartman ME, Milbrandt EB, Kahn JM. The epidemiology of mechanical ventilation use in the United States. Crit Care Med. 2010;38(10):1947–53.
7. Barnaby D, Ferrick K, Kaplan DT, Shah S, Bijur P, Gallagher EJ. Heart rate variability in emergency department patients with sepsis. Acad Emerg Med Off J Soc Acad Emerg Med. 2002;9(7):661–70.
8. Garrard CS, Kontoyannis DA, Piepoli M. Spectral analysis of heart rate variability in the sepsis syndrome. Clin Auton Res Off J Clin Auton Res Soc. 1993;3(1):5–13.
9. Korach M, Sharsha T, Jarrin I, Fouillot JP, Raphaël JC, Gajdos P. Cardiac variability in critically ill adults: influence of sepsis. Crit Care Med. 2001;29(7):1380–5.
10. Ahmad S, Ramsay T, Huebsch L, Flanagan S, McDiarmid S, Batkin I, McIntyre L, Sundaresan SR, Maziak DE, Shamji FM, Hebert P, Fergusson D, Tinmouth A, Seely AJ. Continuous multi-parameter heart rate variability analysis heralds onset of sepsis in adults. PloS One 2009;4(8):e6642.
11. Bravi A, Green G, Longtin A, Seely AJE. Monitoring and identification of sepsis development through a composite measure of heart rate variability. PloS One 2012;7(9):e45666.
12. Green GC, Bradley B, Bravi A, Seely AJE. Continuous multiorgan variability analysis to track severity of organ failure in critically ill patients. J Crit Care 2013;28(5):879.e1–11.
13. Brack T, Jubran A, Tobin MJ. Dyspnea and decreased variability of breathing in patients with restrictive lung disease. Am J Respir Crit Care Med. 2002;165(9):1260–4.
14. Papaioannou VE, Chouvarda I, Maglaveras N, Dragoumanis C, Pneumatikos I. Changes of heart and respiratory rate dynamics during weaning from mechanical ventilation: a study of physiologic complexity in surgical critically ill patients. J Crit Care 2011;26(3):262–72.
15. Seely AJE, Bravi A, Herry C, Green G, Longtin A, Ramsay T, Fergusson D, McIntyre L, Kubelik D, Maziak DE, Ferguson N, Brown SM, Mehta S, Martin C, Rubenfeld G, Jacono FJ, Clifford G, Fazekas A, Marshall J, Canadian Critical Care Trials Group (CCCTG). Do heart and respiratory rate variability improve prediction of extubation outcomes in critically ill patients? Crit Care Lond Engl. 2014;18(2):R65.
16. Segal LN, Oei E, Oppenheimer BW, Goldring RM, Bustami RT, Ruggiero S, Berger KI, Fiel SB. Evolution of pattern of breathing during a spontaneous breathing trial predicts successful extubation. Intensive Care Med. 2010;36(3):487–95.
17. Bravi A, et al. Towards the identification of independent measures of heart rate variability. J Crit Care 2013;28(1):e16.
18. Bravi A, Longtin A, Seely AJE. Review and classification of variability analysis techniques with clinical applications. Biomed Eng Online 2011;10:90.
19. Goldberger AL, Peng C-K, Lipsitz LA. What is physiologic complexity and how does it change with aging and disease? Neurobiol Aging 2002;23(1):23–6.
20. Boles J-M, et al. Weaning from mechanical ventilation. Eur Respir J. 2007;29(5):1033–56.
21. Seymour CW, Martinez A, Christie JD, Fuchs BD. The outcome of extubation failure in a community hospital intensive care unit: a cohort study. Crit Care Lond Engl. 2004;8(5): R322–7.
22. Rello J, Ollendorf DA, Oster G, Vera-Llonch M, Bellm L, Redman R, Kollef MH; VAP Outcomes Scientific Advisory Group. Epidemiology and outcomes of ventilator-associated pneumonia in a large US database. Chest 2002;122(6):2115–21.
23. Yang KL, Tobin MJ. A prospective study of indexes predicting the outcome of trials of weaning from mechanical ventilation. N Engl J Med. 1991;324(21):1445–50.
24. Meade M, Guyatt G, Cook D, Griffith L, Sinuff T, Kergl C, Mancebo J, Esteban A, Epstein S. Predicting success in weaning from mechanical ventilation. Chest 2001;120 Suppl 6:400S-24S.
25. Esteban A, Alía I, Tobin MJ, Gil A, Gordo F, Vallverdú I, Blanch L, Bonet A, Vázquez A, de Pablo R, Torres A, de La Cal MA, Macías S. Effect of spontaneous breathing trial duration on outcome of attempts to discontinue mechanical ventilation. Am J Respir Crit Care Med. 1999;159(2):512–8.

26. Esteban A, Frutos F, Tobin MJ, Alía I, Solsona JF, Valverdu V, Fernández R, de la Cal MA, Benito S, Tomás R, Carriedo D, Macías S, Blanco J, for the Spanish Lung Failure Collaborative Group. A comparison of four methods of weaning patients from mechanical ventilation. N Engl J Med. 1995;332(6):345–50.
27. Shen H-N, Lin LY, Chen KY, Kuo PH, Yu CJ, Wu HD, Yang PC. Changes of heart rate variability during ventilator weaning. Chest 2003;123(4):1222–8.
28. Wysocki M, Cracco C, Teixeira A, Mercat A, Diehl JL, Lefort Y, Derenne JP, Similowski T. Reduced breathing variability as a predictor of unsuccessful patient separation from mechanical ventilation. Crit Care Med. 2006;34(8):2076–83.
29. Engoren M, Blum JM. A comparison of the rapid shallow breathing index and complexity measures during spontaneous breathing trials after cardiac surgery. J Crit Care 2013;28(1):69–76.
30. Huang C-T, Tsai Y-J, Lin J-W, Ruan S-Y, Wu H-D, Yu C-J. Application of heart-rate variability in patients undergoing weaning from mechanical ventilation. Crit. Care Lond Engl. 2014;18(1):R21.
31. Glass L, Mackey MC. From clocks to chaos: the rhythms of life. Princeton: Princeton University Press; 1988.
32. Goldberger AL, West BJ. Chaos in physiology: health or disease? In: Chaos in biological systems. New York: Plenum Press; 1987.

# Chapter 7
# Linking Gulf War Illness to Genome Instability, Somatic Evolution, and Complex Adaptive Systems

Henry H. Heng, Guo Liu, Sarah Regan, and Christine J. Ye

## 7.1 Introduction

Gulf War illness (GWI) impacts nearly one-third of Gulf War veterans in the United States [1]. The complex etiology and diverse symptoms of GWI lead to difficulties both for diagnosis and treatment, which also slows down the acceptance of this clinical condition within the medical community [2]. Recently, an increasing number of symptoms, exposures, and molecular defects have been identified for GWI [3–7]. However, the general mechanism of GWI remains elusive, which prevents further developments of common biomarkers and treatment options. By considering GWI as a common and complex illness, we have searched for the somatic evolutionary mechanism of GWI. Because many different initial trigger factors of GWI occurred over 26 years ago, it is logical to study GWI in the context of complex adaptive systems that follows the principles of somatic evolution. In particular, based on the recently introduced genome theory [8–10], which suggests that the karyotype or chromosome sets (the physical relationship of genes) encode the blueprint of the bio-system by defining system inheritance, and genome-level

H. H. Heng (✉)
Center for Molecular Medicine and Genetics, and Department of Pathology, Wayne State University School of Medicine, 3226 Scott Hall, 540 E. Canfield, Detroit, MI 48201, USA
e-mail: hheng@med.wayne.edu

G. Liu · S. Regan
Center for Molecular Medicine and Genetics, Wayne State University School of Medicine, 3226 Scott Hall, 540 E. Canfield, Detroit, MI 48201, USA
e-mail: gliu@med.wayne.edu; saregan@bu.edu

C. J. Ye
The Division of Hematology/Oncology, Department of Internal Medicine, Comprehensive Cancer Center, University of Michigan, 1500 East Medical Drive, Ann Arbor, MI 48109, USA
e-mail: jchrisy@med.umich.edu

© Springer International Publishing AG, part of Springer Nature 2018
J. P. Sturmberg (ed.), *Putting Systems and Complexity Sciences Into Practice*,
https://doi.org/10.1007/978-3-319-73636-5_7

variations play an important role in both the initiation and progression of various diseases/illnesses, we have used our own finding that elevated genome instability is commonly observed from GWI patients to unify the diverse etiologies and symptoms of this illness. In this presentation, we share our journey of searching for the common mechanism of GWI by applying principles of complex adaptive systems into our synthesis. Furthermore, we introduce the framework of genome alteration-mediated somatic evolution to understand common and complex diseases and illnesses including GWI.

## 7.2  The Unexpected Journey of Studying GWI

Our journey to study GWI was unexpectedly initiated by a documentary production project of Discovery Channel back in 2007 [11]. At that time, we had just published a number of research articles that linked genome instability to cancer evolution, following years of reviewing by a number of journals [12–14]. One of the technologies we used to score stochastic chromosomal changes was spectral karyotyping or SKY, which can reliably measure cellular genome instability. SKY "paints" each pair of human chromosomes with a unique color, and any major chromosomal aberrations can be easily identified following SKY detection [15–17]. The TV show was interested in applying SKY to study GWI patients. The initial goal was to identify specific chromosomal changes associated with radiation (to establish a potential link of Gulf War syndrome to depleted uranium (DU)). Following further discussion about our novel concept of linking seemly random chromosomal aberrations to overall genome instability, they were highly interested in using our approach to examine five Gulf War veterans who displayed the mysterious illness. Back then, Gulf War syndrome was a rather sensitive and a highly controversial subject, as both the medical community and government agents were refusing to accept it as a legitimate illness due to how difficult it was to understand. In fact, many thought that GWI was imagined by patients, as there are no acceptable medical explanations. Knowing the sensitive nature of this subject, some of our colleagues have advised us not to be involved with this politically sensitive research, as the least thing a scientist wants is for their own research to be disrupted by politics. This was especially relevant for us given the fact that our genome-mediated cancer evolutionary research was already sharply in contrast to the main gene mutation centric cancer concept.

After some quick research, we were puzzled by how complicated GWI was: the duration of the Gulf War was obviously short, yet there is a large impacted patient population; there are some identifiable war factors that can be linked to GWI, but no uniformed exposure to all patients; there are diverse symptoms, and even the basic diagnosis is hard. Considering this, it becomes obvious that GWI likely represents a complex adaptive system based on many seemingly confusing factors within this medical mystery. We thought, "Why not check it from the genome perspective? We already know from our cancer research that the diverse molecular mechanisms of cancer can be unified by elevated genome instability, and many illnesses/conditions should be understood using the principles of evolution and complex adaptive systems." Of course, multiple levels of consultations within the school were necessary due to the politically sensitive nature of this project at that time, but finally, after given the green light, we started to test samples from GWI patients. The plan was straightforward: we would culture the lymphocyte cells from patients and examine the cells' chromosomes. Following SKY detection, all karyotype changes would be recorded to see if there were radiation exposure-related chromosomal aberrations (such as dicentric chromosomes). At that time, one of the dominating viewpoints was the potential linkage between DU exposure and GWI. We anticipated that we would finish this project in 2–3 weeks.

To our surprise, after examining the chromosomal aberrations for these GWI patients, we observed that the majority of them did not display dicentric chromosomes. However, all of them displayed highly elevated levels of diverse chromosomal aberrations, including many novel types, some of which had never been reported in the literature. Based on our experience in cancer research, a high level of non-clonal chromosome aberrations (NCCAs) often indicates increased genome instability, and various stress conditions are linked to elevated NCCAs [9, 12–14, 18–22]. As it turns out, these five GWI patients represented different Gulf War exposure types, and not all of them had been exposed to DU. (To avoid any bias in our analyses, we only accessed patient profiles after we had presented our findings.) This made sense of our finding that most patients did not display radiation-specific chromosomal aberrations. In addition to elevated chromosomal aberrations across all patients, the most surprising discovery was the level of NCCAs. Many of them displayed a higher rate than many cancer patients!

Despite the fact that the exact mechanisms were unclear to us, we were convinced that the linkage between the unstable genome and GWI was real and could serve as a common feature among all tested patients. This observation supports the view that GWI has a physical or pathological basis, as patients' imaginations should not change the status of their genome instability. Therefore, this discovery could play an important role in understanding GWI and legitimizing GWI research and care.

Following the airing of the Discovery program in 2007, we received a large number of phone calls and emails from the veteran community. Many personal stories from GWI patients deeply touched us. We decided to make more efforts to study GWI based on our newly established genome theory, as the evolutionary framework of genome theory suits studies of complex adaptive systems. Since then, teamed up with Dr. Chowdhury from the Detroit VA hospital, we have applied for a research grant from DOD to link genome instability to GWI, the first key characterizations of the complexity of GWI.

## 7.3 The Complex Features of Chromosomal Aberrations in GWI Patients

Prior to our studies, there were limited chromosomal analyses examining the relationship between chromosomal abnormalities and exposure to DU in Gulf War veterans. A significant increase in the frequency of dicentric chromosomes (dic) and centric ring chromosomes (cR) was observed from 16 individuals, reflecting a possible previous exposure to DU [23]. However, our initial studies pointed in a different direction, as the majority of observed chromosomal aberrations differed from dicentric chromosomes and ring chromosomes. Another study of 35 DU-exposed veterans failed to exhibit a significant relationship between any cytogenetic endpoint and log [urine uranium] levels, smoking, or log [lifetime X-rays] [24], which further complicated the case. On the surface, this study even seemed to disagree with our observations that there is a significant elevation in overall chromosomal instability in GWI. But a brief analysis can easily reconcile the key differences. Despite using a similar cytogenetic-based platform, our chromosomal analyses have examined different aspects of GWI with advanced tools [7, 15–17, 25]. First, our correlation study has focused on GWI patients rather than types of exposure, such as DU exposure. Not all individuals with exposure will develop GWI, and, importantly, medical examination after longer periods of time (over 26 years) might not capture the initial response of the system. In contrast, as explained by our model, when somatic evolution is involved, the general feature of genome instability should be detected regardless of the different types of initial factors. Second, we have performed more systematic analysis by scoring different types of chromosomal and nuclear abnormalities rather than just chromosomal translocations. Using all different NCCAs to monitor genome instability has proven to be the most effective strategy compared to using translocations alone [26]. Some GWI patients displayed a high frequency of other types of chromosome aberrations, including DMFs and sticky chromosomes, without exhibiting a high level of translocations. These aberrations represent examples that likely would have been missed by previous studies [7]. Even for the detection of chromosomal translocations, the 24-color SKY method is much more effective than 3-color FISH used by previous reports due to its coverage and sensitivity. Third, the detection of multiple chromosome aberrations in a single cell is of special importance, as these "outliers" strongly suggest genome instability. In fact, it is rare to detect them in normal individuals. Interestingly, Bakhmutsky et al. have also observed such outliers even using interphase detection with limited probes (unfortunately, they did not pay enough attention to these important outliers) [27]. If SKY is performed to examine these individuals, a high level of genome instability will likely be observed. Finally, prior to the establishment of the genome theory, the meaning of many seemingly stochastic chromosomal aberrations was not clear, and many researchers have considered them as genetic "noise" [9, 22, 28]. Our synthesis, that different karyotypes represent different systems, has called to change the practice of ignoring them. As illustrated by our expression studies, these long-ignored NCCAs represent evolutionary potential and have defined the transcriptome dynamics of cancer cells [29–31]. Increased attention is now being paid to multiple chromosomal translocations [27, 32]. Further analyses have unexpectedly revealed many novel types of chromosomal/nuclear abnormalities including sticky chromosomes and defective mitotic figures (DMFs) [7, 25, 32], suggesting that diverse molecular mechanisms can be linked to GWI, as stochastic chromosomal alteration has been linked to various molecular pathways in our cancer research [29, 30]. Furthermore, cellular stress has also been linked to GWI, explaining the relationship among stress, elevated genome instability, and the diverse phenotypes observed in GWI patients.

Obviously, even for studying chromosomal aberrations in GWI, a new approach is needed to understand seemly stochastic genome alterations. The fact that a high level of genome instability is observed in the cells of GWI patients also reflects the reality that GWI represents a complex clinical condition, which requires the action of treating it as a complex adaptive system.

## 7.4 GWI: A Case Study of Somatic Evolution and Complex Adaptive Systems

In our previous cancer research, elevated genome instability has been identified as a common key driver for cancer evolution [12, 21]. Of equal importance, we have proposed using the evolutionary mechanism of cancer to unify cancer's diverse molecular pathways [9, 18, 19]. The recent large-scale cancer genome sequencing data forcefully confirmed our genome theory of cancer evolution by revealing both punctuated cancer evolution and unmanageably high levels of genetic heterogeneity. Cancer is no longer a gene disease but a complex adaptive system featuring genome-mediated macro-cellular evolution. This realization calls for a new approach of using complex system-based thinking to study other disease conditions.

As most common and complex diseases/illnesses involve the cellular evolution process and constant multiple genotype-environment interactions, it is logical to consider them as various complex and adaptive systems [33–37]. Under such a framework, the multiple genetic variants and cellular/tissue/organ structural components of patients represent various "agents"; the initial Gulf War-specific environments and the patients' involved cellular environments following the Gulf War's original impact function as environments, and the diverse symptoms represent "emergent features." Due to the high level of genome instability present in GWI patients, all of these genetic alterations are different, leading to increased unpredictability. Furthermore, the mind/body/treatment interactions within an individual, and individual-society interactions, as well as over 26 years of cellular evolution, make GWI a highly complex illness featuring the clear involvement of somatic evolution.

Defining GWI as a complex adaptive system is thus of particular importance, since a portion of the current medical community still doubts the legitimacy of considering GWI as an illness condition, due to the very nature of complex adaptive systems. For example, different from many infectious diseases and single-gene Mendelian diseases, there seems to be no fixed dominant causative relationship between specific environmental or genetic factors and the diverse symptoms of GWI. This fact represents a major rationale for some to question if GWI is real. By accepting GWI as a complex adaptive system, most of the confusion should be resolved. Clearly, it is not suitable to use a reductionist approach to define GWI, as there is no dominant linear causation for either the etiology of the illness or its symptoms. In contrast, the observation of the generally unstable genome in GWI patients fits well with key features of somatic evolution and complex adaptive systems.

Interestingly, using evolution and complex adaptive systems to study GWI can also generate useful information to illustrate the relationship between bio-evolution and how complex adaptive systems work. For example, in the field of complex adaptive systems, evolution was thought by some to be a result of an adaptive biological system, while others use evolution and complex adaptive systems in an overlapping description. Thinking of GWI, we realized that evolutionary and genomic mechanisms, such as fuzzy inheritance [9, 20], selection acts on the genome [8], and genome alteration-mediated macro-cellular evolution, serve as effective means for the bio-system to adapt [12, 19], supporting the notion that bio-evolution also serves as a strategy for bio-complex adaptive systems. Furthermore, the details of how genome level change has an impact on the macroevolution of cancer (while gene mutation impacts microevolution) provide new insight for differentiating stepwise system adaptation and the emergent punctuated system of genome reorganization [20]. Genome reorganization can significantly alter the status of agents, which raises the issue of the emergence of new systems based on altered agents, further complicating the systems under investigation. The increased heterogeneity among agents will further complicate a system, which makes some complex adaptive systems more complicated than others. While the somatic cell evolution pattern of GWI is less clear compared to the two phases of cancer evolution, GWI can nevertheless be considered as stress-induced, genome instability-mediated evolution, which can be used to define some key characteristics of complex adaptive systems.

For example, unlike many cancer cases and some genetic diseases, in which clonal chromosomal aberrations can be observed, GWI patients often display high levels of non-clonal chromosome aberrations or NCCAs. The linkage between GWI and NCCAs is rather interesting when considering how the heterogeneity of lower level agents can have an impact on emergent properties. To explain how elevated NCCAs can lead to GWI, we hypothesize that NCCAs contribute to the degree of heterogeneity among individual cells, which alters emergent properties above the level of individual cells, such as immune response, tissue/organ function, or overall health status of individuals. Due to the different degree and types of altered genomes, the emergent properties (symptoms) could be highly diverse due

**Fig. 7.1** The illustration of how the heterogeneity of agents (the cell population of tissues) impacts the emergent properties of tissue/organ functions. Circles represent cells with normal karyotypes, and triangles represent cells with altered genomes. These variable properties are the potential basis for diseases/illnesses

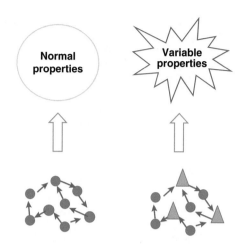

to cellular-environmental interaction. Our hypothesis is illustrated in Fig. 7.1, where the degree of genome heterogeneity itself leads to emergent variable properties at tissue or organ level, which can be considered as potential for abnormal system response. According to our definition that diseases are genotype/environment-induced variants that are not compatible with a current environment, the relationship between genetic heterogeneity and illness becomes obvious [2]. Note that the recently introduced concept of "fuzzy inheritance" likely plays an important role in these emergent properties based on the heterogeneity of agents [9], as how these agents pass the genetic information among somatic cells can influence the emergent properties as well. Clearly, further studies are needed to address this issue.

## 7.5 Search for the General Model for Common and Complex Diseases/Illnesses

By linking cellular stress, genome instability, and diverse molecular mechanisms to GWI in the context of complex adaptive systems [2, 35], we might have solved some key mysterious features of GWI. Stress-induced genome alterations, and their facilitative role in cellular evolution, have provided the mechanistic basis for understanding GWI, which also suggests that GWI is real and that a patient's imagination cannot significantly alter the genome (Fig. 7.2). Moreover, both GWI diagnosis and treatment could benefit from this finding. For example, treatment strategies should not further destabilize the genome of patients. Of equal importance, our research on GWI has further suggested that stress-induced, genome alteration-mediated cellular evolution might be used to explain other common and complex diseases as well.

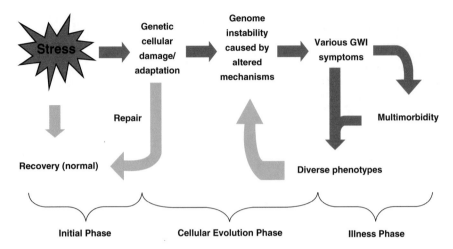

**Fig. 7.2** The model of the stress-induced genome instability and GWI phenotypes. During the initial phase, Gulf War-specific stress can generate genetic or cellular damages. The unrepaired bio-damage can trigger cellular evolution, which is driven by genome instability. Importantly, genome alterations can stochastically activate different molecular pathways. Together, this somatic evolution will lead to diverse symptoms. Note that the three phases interact closely with each other through different feedback loops. This model is adapted from [2].

The linkage between elevated genome instability and somatic evolution was initially observed in our cancer research. In particular, we have established a strong link between stochastic genome alteration and large numbers of individual molecular mechanisms. We later proposed the evolutionary mechanism of cancer, which can be explained by three key components (system stress, increased frequencies of non-clonal chromosome aberrations, and genome-mediated macro-cellular evolution). Paradoxically, such a simple evolutionary principle can lead to a large number of individual molecular mechanisms and their combinations. Our prediction has recently been confirmed by the cancer genome sequencing project, as most of the cancer cases do not share the same gene mutations, and cancer heterogeneity is overwhelming.

Since cancer belongs to the category of common and complex diseases, we have proposed that genome instability should also be shared by other common and complex diseases [35, 37, 38]. However, most researchers consider cancer as a special case due to its invasiveness, and it is hard for them to accept our viewpoint. Our arguments are the following: Despite that all diseases have unique phenotypic characteristics, most of them involve somatic evolution and system adaptation, and the invasiveness of cancer, even though it is unique, still represents an abnormal feature, emergent from a cellular population with unstable genomes. In fact, out-of-control growth and invasiveness also mean that the constraint of normal tissue function is lost. Fortunately, increased studies have revealed that increased genome instability can be observed from many disease types as well as normal tissues [39–43].

Following GWI data analysis, we proposed a general model for common and complex diseases to unify stress, genome instability, diverse molecular pathways, and diverse symptoms. This model states:

1. Stress and/or the requirement of cellular adaptation can trigger genome alterations, which initiate genome alteration-mediated somatic evolution [44]. NCCAs are eliminated as the dead end of the evolution. With extremely low likelihood, some CCAs (clonal chromosome aberrations) will form. Usually, a number of NCCA/CCA cycles are needed to bring about disease conditions. It is also possible that a high level of NCCAs alone (without dominant CCAs) can lead to phenotype abnormalities.

2. Some rare outliers become successful to form the dominant population. The altered genome can stochastically be linked to different molecular pathways [29, 30], or different emergent properties, which reduces the normal function or response of specific organs or tissues. Unlike cancer, although there likely is no homogenously altered genome, significant genome heterogeneity will change the emergent function of the cellular population, leading to different symptoms.

3. Moreover, some responses can come from different levels of the system [8]. For example, the heterogeneous cell population can simply reduce normal function, or produce cellular stress, leading to altered functions at high levels of system organization. Combining this process with infection, immune reaction, the aging process, and medical intervention, the emergent properties can further change, leading to more complications or even multimorbidity [45], in a stochastic fashion.

## 7.6   Conclusions

Our journey of studying GWI has been both exciting and rewarding, especially since we adapted the concept of somatic evolution and complex adaptive systems. It is worth noting that the concepts of somatic evolution and complex adaptive systems have been largely ignored by the medical research community, despite the fact that complexity sciences have been around for decades and there has recently been a new push to bring them into mainstream medical care [46]. For example, the cancer research field has started to pay more attention to evolutionary analyses, based on the increased realization that the somatic cell evolutionary mechanism of cancer can unify large numbers of devised molecular mechanisms, but such a realization has yet to become popular in the field of medicine. It is interesting to point out that evolutionary medicine has also been around for decades [47]. However, possibly influenced by the popularity of molecular medicine, the bio-determinist has promised predictive power based on advanced molecular medical research. Now, there is an increased call to question the reductionist's approach of current medicine, as not appreciating the uncertainty of bio-systems during evolution leaves us with increased confusion [48–50]. To change the status quo, which not only wastes research resources but also delays the search for new conceptual frameworks and compromises the needed care for patients, a new attitude and strategy is needed to consider many common and complex diseases/illnesses as complex adaptive systems, wherein somatic cell evolution plays a key role [8, 9]. Our GWI research likely will serve as such an example.

**Acknowledgements** This article is part of a series of studies entitled "The mechanisms of somatic cell and organismal evolution." This work was supported by a grant from the DOD (GW093028).

## The Journey

Our appreciation of the concept of complexity was paradoxically enhanced by the progress of our knowledge of the gene's function. As a graduate student (at the golden age of molecular cloning, and mentored by a leading gene hunter, Lap Chee Tsui, who cloned the cystic fibrosis gene), the power of the individual gene seemed obvious. However, increased data has clearly illustrated the nonlinear correlation between genes and their phenotypes. Some common explanations were: "Well, there is more than one gene responsible for a given phenotype; there exist modifiers and even modifiers of the modifiers ...." Clearly, life was complicated. Nevertheless, it was thought the reductionist approach should be able to solve this issue (if we just worked harder).

The overwhelming genomic heterogeneity in cancer has forced us to question our knowledge, from the gene mutation theory of cancer to how to define genetic information. In the past 20 years, we have reevaluated many important questions through the lens of complexity, including the function of sex (to ensure the genome system identity rather than simply increasing genetic diversity); the pattern of evolution ("punctuated" often in macroevolution and "stepwise" frequently in microevolution); the chromosomal coding which defines the "system inheritance" or blueprint (while a gene encodes only "parts inheritance"); and the concept that genetic information is rather fuzzy, representing a spectrum of potential phenotype variants (and should not be simply explained as either dominant or recessive without the consideration of continuous environmental-influenced variants). These realizations have provided new frameworks for us to understand many common and complex diseases.

We specifically benefit from learning and interacting with scholars in the community of complexity. Despite the relatively small number of members, we see the hope that comes from this collaboration, as we believe in the power of outliers during emergence. The new phase of our journey is to use unique features of biological systems (heterogeneity-mediated bio-evolution) to understand the principles of complexity.

Take-Home Message

- GWI (Gulf War illness) is a real illness condition which can be classified as an environmental illness
- The common mechanism of GWI is high stress-induced, genome instability-mediated somatic evolution. Cellular heterogeneity is likely responsible for the diverse abnormal properties observed
- Many common and complex diseases/illnesses should be considered as common adaptive systems

# References

1. Research Advisory Committee. Gulf War illness and the health of Gulf War veterans: scientific findings and recommendations. Washington, DC: U.S. Government Printing Office; 2008.
2. Heng HH. Challenges and new strategies for Gulf War illness research. Environ Dis. 2016;1:118–25.
3. Koslik HJ, Hamilton G, Golomb BA. Mitochondrial dysfunction in Gulf War illness revealed by 31Phosphorus Magnetic Resonance Spectroscopy: a case-control study. PloS One 2014;9:e92887.
4. Craddock TJ, Harvey JM, Nathanson L, Barnes ZM, Klimas NG, Fletcher MA, Broderick G. Using gene expression signatures to identify novel treatment strategies in Gulf War illness. BMC Med Genomics 2015;8:36.
5. Parihar VK, Hattiangady B, Shuai B, Shetty AK. Mood and memory deficits in a model of Gulf War illness are linked with reduced neurogenesis, partial neuron loss, and mild inflammation in the hippocampus. Neuropsychopharmacology 2013;38(12):2348–62.
6. White RF, Steele L, O'Callaghan JP, Sullivan K, Binns JH, Golomb BA, Bloom FE, Bunker JA, Crawford F, Graves JC, Hardie A, Klimas N, Knox M, Meggs WJ, Melling J, Philbert MA, Grashow R. Recent research on Gulf War illness and other health problems in veterans of the 1991 Gulf War: effects of toxicant exposures during deployment. Cortex 2016;74:449–75.
7. Liu G, Ye CJ, Chowdhury SK, Abdallah BY, Horne SD, Nichols D, Heng HH. Detecting chromosome condensation defects in Gulf War illness patients. Cur Genomics 2018 (in press).
8. Heng HH. The genome-centric concept: resynthesis of evolutionary theory. Bioessays 2009;31(5):512–25.
9. Heng HH. Debating cancer: the paradox in cancer research. Hackensack, NJ: World Scientific; 2015.
10. Heng HH, Liu G, Stevens JB, Bremer SW, Ye KJ, Abdallah BY, Horne SD, Ye CJ. Decoding the genome beyond sequencing: the new phase of genomic research. Genomics 2011;98:242–52.
11. Discovery Channel. Discovery channel in 2007: Gulf War illness-conspiracy test. https://www.youtube.com/watch?v=jhvdkdMFVJQ.
12. Heng HH, Stevens JB, Liu G, Bremer SW, Ye KJ, Reddy PV, Wu GS, Wang YA, Tainsky MA, Ye CJ. Stochastic cancer progression driven by non-clonal chromosome aberrations. J Cell Physiol. 2006;208(2):461–72.
13. Heng HH, Bremer SW, Stevens J, Ye KJ, Miller F, Liu G, Ye CJ. Cancer progression by non-clonal chromosome aberrations. J Cell Biochem. 2006;98(6):1424–35.
14. Heng HH, Liu G, Bremer S, Ye KJ, Stevens J, Ye CJ. Clonal and non-clonal chromosome aberrations and genome variation and aberration. Genome 2006;49(3):195–204.

15. Ye CJ, Lu W, Liu G, Bremer SW, Wang YA, Moens P, Hughes M, Krawetz SA, Heng HH. The combination of SKY and specific loci detection with FISH or immunostaining. Cytogenet Cell Genet. 2001;93(3–4):195–202.
16. Heng HH, Ye CJ, Yang F, Ebrahim S, Liu G, Bremer SW, Thomas CM, Ye J, Chen TJ, Tuck-Miller C, Yu JW, Krawetz SA, Johnson A. Analysis of marker or complex chromosomal rearrangements present in pre- and post-natal karyotypes utilizing a combination of G-banding, spectral karyotyping and fluorescence in situ hybridization. Clin Genet. 2003;63(5):358–67.
17. Ye CJ, Stevens JB, Liu G, Ye KJ, Yang F, Bremer SW, Heng HH. Combined multicolor-FISH and immunostaining. Cytogenet Genome Res. 2006;114(3–4):227–34.
18. Ye CJ, Stevens JB, Liu G, Bremer SW, Jaiswal AS, Ye KJ, Lin MF, Lawrenson L, Lancaster WD, Kurkinen M, Liao JD, Gairola CG, Shekhar MP, Narayan S, Miller FR, Heng HH. Genome based cell population heterogeneity promotes tumorigenicity: the evolutionary mechanism of cancer. J Cell Physiol. 2009;219(2):288–300.
19. Horne SD, Pollick SA, Heng HH. Evolutionary mechanism unifies the hallmarks of cancer. Int J Cancer 2015;136(9):2012–21.
20. Horne SD, Ye CJ, Heng HH. Chromosomal instability (CIN) in cancer. eLS 2015;1–9.
21. Heng HH, Bremer SW, Stevens JB, Horne SD, Liu G, Abdallah BY, Ye KJ, Ye CJ. Chromosomal Instability (CIN): what it is and why it is crucial to cancer evolution. Cancer Met Rev. 2013;32:325–40.
22. Heng HH, Regan SM, Liu G, Ye CJ. Why it is crucial to analyze non clonal chromosome aberrations or NCCAs? Mol Cytogenet. 2016;9:15.
23. Schröder H, Heimers A, Frentzel-Beyme R, Schott A, Hoffmann W. Chromosome aberration analysis in peripheral lymphocytes of Gulf War and Balkans War veterans. Radiat Prot Dosimetry 2003;103(3):211–9.
24. Bakhmutsky MV, Squibb K, McDiarmid M, Oliver M, Tucker JD. Long-term exposure to depleted uranium in Gulf-War veterans does not induce chromosome aberrations in peripheral blood lymphocytes. Mutat Res. 2013;757(2):132–9.
25. Heng HH, Stevens JB, Liu G, Bremer SW, Ye CJ. Imaging genome abnormalities in cancer research. Cell Chromosome 2004;3:1.
26. Heng HH, Stevens JB, Bremer SW, Liu G, Abdallah BY, Ye CJ. Evolutionary mechanisms and diversity in cancer. Adv Cancer Res. 2011;112:217–53.
27. Poot M, Haaf T. Mechanisms of origin, phenotypic effects and diagnostic implications of complex chromosome rearrangements. Mol Syndromol. 2015;6(3):110–34.
28. Abdallah BY, Horne SD, Stevens JB, Liu G, Ying AY, Vanderhyden B, Krawetz SA, Gorelick R, Heng HH. Single cell heterogeneity: why unstable genomes are incompatible with average profiles. Cell Cycle 2013;12(23):3640–49.
29. Stevens JB, Horne SD, Abdallah BY, Ye CJ, Heng HH. Chromosomal instability and transcriptome dynamics in cancer. Cancer Metastasis Rev. 2013;32(3–4):391–402.
30. Stevens JB, Liu G, Abdallah BY, Horne SD, Ye KJ, Bremer SW, Ye CJ, Krawetz SA, Heng HH. Unstable genomes elevate transcriptome dynamics. Int J Cancer 2014;134(9):2074–87.
31. Liu G, Stevens JB, Horne SD, Abdallah BY, Ye KJ, Bremer SW, Ye CJ, Chen DJ, Heng HH. Genome chaos: survival strategy during crisis. Cell Cycle 2014;13(4):528–37.
32. Heng HH, Liu G, Stevens JB, Abdallah BY, Horne SD, Ye KJ, Bremer SW, Chowdhury SK, Ye CJ. Karyotype heterogeneity and unclassified chromosomal abnormalities. Cytogen Genome Res. 2013;139:144–57.
33. Heng HH. The conflict between complex systems and reductionism. JAMA 2008;300(13):1580–1.
34. Heng HH. Bio-complexity: challenging reductionism. In: Sturmberg JP, Martin CM, editors. Handbook on systems and complexity in health. New York: Springer; 2013. p. 193–208.
35. Heng HH, Horne SD, Stevens JB, Abdallah BY, Liu G, Chowdhury SK, Bremer SW, Zhang K, Ye CJ. Heterogeneity mediated system complexity: the ultimate challenge for studying common and complex diseases. In: Sturmberg JP, editor. The value of systems and complexity sciences for healthcare. Cham: Springer; 2016. p. 107–20.

36. Heng HH, Regan S, Ye CJ. Genotype, environment, and evolutionary mechanism of diseases. Environ Dis. 2016;1:14–23.
37. Heng HH. Heterogeneity-mediated cellular adaptation and its trade-off: searching for the general principles of diseases. J Eval Clin Pract. 2017;23(1):233–237.
38. Heng HH. Missing heritability and stochastic genome alterations. Nat Rev Genet. 2010;11(11):813.
39. Hultén MA, Jonasson J, Iwarsson E, Uppal P, Vorsanova SG, Yurov YB, Iourov IY. Trisomy 21 mosaicism: we may all have a touch of Down syndrome. Cytogenet Genome Res. 2013;139(3):189–92.
40. Iourov IY, Vorsanova SG, Yurov YB. Chromsomal mosaicism goes global. Mol Cytogenet. 2008;1:26.
41. Yurov YB, Vorsanova SG, Liehr T, Kolotii AD, Iourov IY. X chromosome aneuploidy in the Alzheimer's disease brain. Mol Cytogenet. 2014;7(1):20.
42. Biesterfeld S, Gerres K, Fischer-Wein G, Böcking A. Polyploidy in non-neoplastic tissues. J Clin Pathol. 1994;47(1):38–42.
43. Duncan AW, Taylor MH, Hickey RD, Hanlon Newell AE, Lenzi ML, Olson SB, Olson SB, Finegold MJ, Grompe M. The ploidy conveyor of mature hepatocytes as a source of genetic variation. Nature 2010;467:707–10.
44. Horne SD, Chowdhury SK, Heng HH. Stress, genomic adaptation, and the evolutionary trade-off. Front Genet. 2014;5:92.
45. Sturmberg JP, Bennett JM, Martin CM, Picard M. "Multimorbidity" as the manifestation of network disturbances. J Eval Clin Pract. 2017;23(1):199–208.
46. Sturmberg JP, Martin CP. Complexity in health: an introduction. In: Sturmberg JP, Martin CM, editors. Handbook on systems and complexity in health. New York: Springer; 2013. p. 1–17.
47. Nesse RM. Evolution: medicine's most basic science. Lancet 2008;372(S1):S21–7.
48. Evans JP, Meslin EM, Marteau TM, Caulfield T. Genomics. Deflating the genomic bubble. Science 2011;331:861–2.
49. Heng HH, Regan S. A systems biology perspective on molecular cytogenetics. Curr Bioinfom. 2016;12(1):4–10.
50. Noble D. Physiology in rocking the foundation of evolutionary biology. Exp Physiol. 2013;98:1235–43.

# Chapter 8
# The Key to Implementing an Accessible Information Standard Across Complex Adaptive Health and Social Care Organisations

**Beverley Ellis, John Howard, and Howard Leicester**

## 8.1  Introduction

Digitising health and care is now a strategic priority within the English NHS, coupled with establishing and developing sustainability and transformation partnerships [1, 2]. This means greater partnership working between the NHS, local government, patient groups and community, voluntary and faith organisations. These partnerships aim to work together to improve outcomes and care for local people, reduce pressures on services and make best use of resources, building on what works to help people to stay healthy and well and exploring how technology can be used effectively to support those with the greatest needs.

In the UK, under the 1998 Data Protection Act, everyone has a legal right to ask to see their NHS or private health records, using a subject access request [3]. Access may be denied if it is considered that it would cause serious harm to the patient [4]. At the end of July 2015, the NHS Accessible Information Standard (AIS) was implemented throughout England (see Box 1 for a short history on the AIS). This means that any organisation providing NHS care or adult social care is now legally obliged to provide information in accessible formats, so that people with a disability or impairment (those who may not be able to access or read text and information in the traditional form) have the same access to health information as any other NHS user. This includes an obligation for organisations to provide alternative information formats to meet individuals' requirements, including Braille, electronic and audio formats.

B. Ellis (✉) · J. Howard · H. Leicester
Health Informatics Team, School of Health Sciences, UCLan, Preston, UK
e-mail: BSEllis@uclan.ac.uk; JHoward1@uclan.ac.uk; howard@accessible-info.co.uk

© Springer International Publishing AG, part of Springer Nature 2018
J. P. Sturmberg (ed.), *Putting Systems and Complexity Sciences Into Practice*,
https://doi.org/10.1007/978-3-319-73636-5_8

The specification of the AIS highlights the Equality Act 2010 as the legal basis for implementation (alongside a "compelling moral and ethical imperative"). The AIS is "unashamedly ambitious" in its overall aim of providing "clear direction for a dramatic improvement in the ability of the NHS and adult social care system to meet the information and communication support needs of disabled people". This is clearly a much-needed and positive step forwards in terms of providing everyone with accessible information [5].

---

**Box 1: A short history of the Accessible Information Standard (AIS)**

The AIS journey began with a draft standard on "Disability Needs & Personal Requirements" within NHS Scotland. That was made "legacy" in 2010 but revisited in 2012 when the English Department of Health received a legal challenge specifically on the inaccessibility of documents from health organisations for those with visual impairments.

AIS followed as the way to avoid a "judicial review" (the health secretary in a court case). Whilst not as wide-ranging as the earlier Scottish work, AIS went well beyond the legal challenge. It focuses on information and communication needs for all with difficulties arising from "disability, impairment or sensory loss" in any area of health and social care.

The new standard has five stages which all providers should follow. They should ask about needs, record those needs, flag those needs in records, share those needs with other providers and act, or deliver, on those needs.

Connections with GP records are clear. The AIS recording component should be part of GP, and all other, record systems. Patients with records access should be able to review their record of needs and have any information, within the record or connected websites, provided in formats that match the patient's needs. They should also be able to see if face-to-face support, such as sign language, can be booked. GP records are also a repository of documents coming from other health and care providers. So GP records are a test case for primary care also connecting with other health and care sectors.

AIS has recently undergone a review. It is widely seen as "fit for purpose", with only minor changes to the specification and guidance. AIS is also moving into other sectors: it is often quoted in consultations in education, and a Member of Parliament has agreed to encourage adoption across constituencies.

The progress and continuing success of AIS are largely due to much hard work by NHS England and the advisory group. Dr Howard Leicester received a related MBE in 2017 on behalf of all those colleagues and friends.

---

### 8.1.1 Our Approach

The authors' comprehension of complex adaptive systems (CAS) suggests a move away from simple objective observation to understand humans as participants in systems, which allows for the flow of energy (motivation, information and innovation) and networked interactions that enable change in an adaptive organisation. CAS theories assist thinking about the nature of health and social care digital programmes with a focus on the people involved and their responses to sustainable and transformational problem-solving.

We believe that innovation comes through assistive technologies, building on what works to help people to stay healthy and well. Healthcare informatics is recognised as a major contributor to care delivery, and although this is less developed in social care, the two will need to evolve in parallel.

Exploring accessible information issues shows what may well be possible through technology for those with the greatest needs. In the UK, older and disabled people not only have most to gain through innovative use of communications technology, but they also form the largest user group. For example, Fig. 8.1 shows how this influences what we are doing in NW of England region, illustrating workshop participant involvement in informing and shaping Lancashire Digital Health Strategy 2015–2020 and accessible information for all.

Electronic care record access, supported by AIS, is an opportunity to improve access for patients, especially those with disabilities [6]. For example, those with visual impairments can use assistive technology to help read their records. Those with hearing problems can go back and see what has been recorded [7]. People with English as a second language can check the details of their care with English speakers and use translation software if necessary.

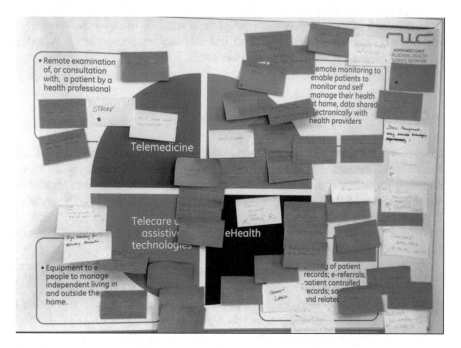

**Fig. 8.1** Lancashire Digital Health Strategy Workshop—delegate suggestions

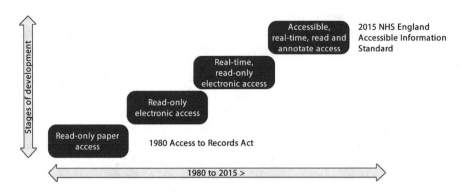

**Fig. 8.2** Accessible Information Standard—NHS England patient online access to care record context. Acknowledgement to: Record Access Collaborative. *Enabling patients to access electronic health records. Guidance for Health Professionals.* London: RCGP, 2010. www.rcgp.org.uk. Patient Information Forum (PIF) and Professor Iain Buchan, June 2012 [personal communication]. *The power of information: putting all of us in control of the health and care information we need.* Department of Health, 2012. http://informationstrategy.dh.gov.uk

NHS England's patient online access to care record context is shown in Fig. 8.2. Figure 8.3 shows Dr Howard Leicester, MBE, co-author of this chapter, who suggests that "The right tools in the right hands can help everyone".

This paper provides practical examples and describes the complex, non-linear, innovative and adaptive network of relationships and flow of information (energy) that support the delivery of care, which includes implementation of the AIS that supports those with special communication needs.

### 8.1.2   The Epidemiology of Disability

Goodley [8] suggests that "second wave" writers are questioning the assumptions that underpin the social model of disability [9], "refocusing epistemological attention onto impairment, alongside an alliance with the social model and disability movement, re-socialises impairment" whilst acknowledging that "disability remains a social problem to be eradicated by societal change through reconstruction of current systems and by deconstruction through revolutionising direct action". Goodley reflects a clear social perspective:

- Firstly, "society creates disablement and is the arbiter of disciplinary powers that (re)produce pathological understandings of different bodies and minds".
- Secondly, "disabled activists point to the need for social change in which all social members—disabled and non-disabled—are to be involved".

**Fig. 8.3** The power of assistive technologies: "The right tools in the right hands can help everyone". Dr Howard Leicester, MBE (image taken from http://www.tech4goodawards.com/)

AIS was co-produced with a range of voluntary organisations and with disabled people themselves and has been called a "step change" in disabled people's access to health and social care. An environment results in which learning processes, end-user and other stakeholder involvement, continuous feedback and a willingness to foster innovation and diversity are facilitated. Changes in behaviours emerge that include listening, whole-system learning, evaluation and reflection, focused on making informed choices that leads to quality improvement, characteristics associated with complex adaptive systems. The content that follows describes the complex, non-linear, innovative and adaptive network of relationships and flow of information (energy), which includes implementation of the AIS that supports those with special communication needs.

### 8.1.3   The Aim of NHS England's Accessible Information Standard (AIS)

The AIS standard aims to ensure that disabled patients, service users and carers with particular information or communication support needs have those needs met.

This means that any organisation providing NHS care or adult social care is now legally obliged to provide information in accessible formats, so that people with a disability or impairment (those who may not be able to access or read text and information in the traditional form) have the same access to health information as any other NHS user. This includes an obligation for organisations to provide alternative information formats to meet individuals' requirements, including Braille, electronic and audio formats.

### 8.1.4  Impairment Prevalence

NHS England recognises that numbers of those people who may require particular information or communication support needs, within any setting, are likely to be high. This follows because "29% of the population have impairments" (like chronic pain, dexterity problems, memory challenges as well as sensory and cognition difficulties), according to the Life Opportunities Survey [10]. Figure 8.4 illustrates the impairment prevalence across Great Britain extracted from the Office of National Statistics (http://www.ons.gov.uk/ons/datasets-and-tables/index.html? pageSize=50&sortBy=none&sortDirection=none&newquery=impairment).

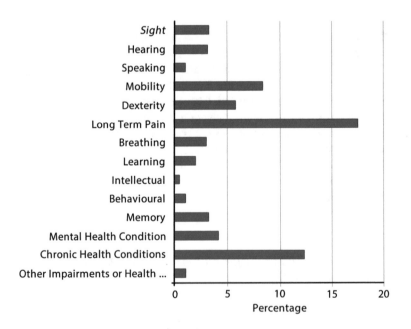

**Fig. 8.4** Impairment prevalence rates across Great Britain (http://www.ons.gov.uk/ons/datasets-and-tables/index.html?pageSize=50&sortBy=none&sortDirection=none&newquery=impairment)

## 8.2   Study Context

### 8.2.1   The Population of the Lancashire Region

The region of Lancashire, in the North West of England (14-authority areas), has an older population structure than the national average with greater proportions aged over 45. The subregions display diversity: in Blackburn with Darwen, Lancaster and Preston, at least two out of five residents are aged under 30 years, whilst in Fylde and Wyre, half of the population are aged over 45. Local authority fertility rates vary quite noticeably across the subregion, and demographic projections indicate changes in the population structure with fewer young people and greater proportions of older people by 2033. Overall, the population is expected to grow by around 7.8%, well below the national growth rate of 18%. There will be an additional 112,000 people in Lancashire, two thirds of whom will be aged 60 or over, whilst there will be 12,000 fewer children aged 0–19 years.

An ageing population brings a range of considerations for health and social care services. Treatment of disease becomes much costlier, and prevention becomes more important as a way of managing the health of the population.

### 8.2.2   Ethnic and Social Diversity

Lancashire's population is less ethnically diverse than the national average, although large Pakistani and Indian communities are present in the subregion. Between 2001 and 2007, there has been population growth, albeit at levels below the national level. Whilst white groups have remained stable, black and minority ethnic populations increased between 2001 and 2007.

National Insurance Number Registrations suggest that new migrant numbers are reducing. However, the younger population of black and minority groups and higher birth rates will mean continued increases in the populations in future years. Specific health risks within South Asian populations mean that numbers of diabetes sufferers are likely to increase in the future.

More detailed patient profiles compiled by Clinical Commissioning Groups (CCGs), the Health and Wellbeing Board and population data of Lancashire as a whole are available online from the Lancashire Joint Strategic Needs Assessments website (http://www.lancashire.gov.uk/lancashire-insight.aspx).

### 8.2.3   What Are the Local Issues for Implementing the AIS?

A need for a small-scale proof of concept (POC) study was identified and supported by the Digital Health Lead and Head of Lancashire's Patient Record Exchange Service (LPRES) (http://www.northwestsis.nhs.uk/lpres/lpres-process). The aim was to determine a set of document design principles that support the Accessible Information Standard (AIS) and to inform the Lancashire Digital Health Strategy 2015–2020. It also allowed an exploration of the potentials of RoboBraille®[11]. A further objective was to explore the possibility to automatically generate accessible formats from existing care documents. The overall purpose of the study has been to reveal the scale of adjustments necessary to automatically convert a representative sample of the most frequently used care documents. This POC should be seen in the context of increasing patient access to their health records as required by relevant European Union and subsequent UK initiatives such as the EU Digital Agenda (https://ec.europa.eu/digital-single-market/en/europe-2020-strategy) which establishes "the right of individuals to have their personal health information safely stored within a healthcare system accessible online". This right is clearly not limited by an individual's needs regarding accessibility of such information.

## 8.3  Methods

Data collection included a workshop and user evaluation of the exemplar electronic health record, illustrated in Fig. 8.5. The workshop focused on a series of specific points of the latest Web Accessibility Initiative (WAI) standard (https://www.w3.org/WAI/). Electronically available documents such as referral letters were downloaded and fed through RoboBraille®, a free online service, to evaluate the outputs from this accessibility tool.

## 8.4  Ethics

The proof of concept study was approved by the University's Ethics Committee.

### 8.4.1  Contributors Including Workshop Attendees

Workshop participants who provided the source information underpinning this report included:

- Members of the Professional Records Standards Body (PRSB)
- Members of the Accessible Information Standard advisory group
- Dr Howard Leicester MBE, http://www.onevoiceict.org/node/136
- Bruce Elliott, Programme Manager, Developing Informatics Skills and Capability (DISC), Health and Social Care Information Centre (HSCIC)
- Software providers of alternative formats and communication support: RoboBraille®
- Members of UCLan's Health Informatics Project Team

**Fig. 8.5** Screenshots of the electronic medical record (reproduced with kind permission of *EMIS Health*) and RoboBraille® file conversation software (reproduced with kind permission of RoboBraille®)

## 8.5   Results from the Workshop Sessions

A central aspect of the approach used was to involve patients identified with the help of COMENSUS, UCLan's user involvement unit. These individuals were given remote access to the patient portal using the dummy patient record provided for the use of the project and the Patient Access to Electronic Record Systems (PAERS) (https://patient.emisaccess.co.uk/).

The workshop utilised a series of points based on the Web Accessibility Initiative (WAI) standard (https://www.w3.org/WAI/). The accessibility issues under this standard are grouped in categories:

- Perception
- Operation
- Understanding
- Robustness
- Patient Priorities

The workshop primarily focused on the patient accessibility portal of the main primary care system supplier in the North West of England as illustrated in Fig. 8.5. The outputs of RoboBraille® are illustrated in Fig. 8.6.

MRS R STUBINGTON, CONSULTANT UROLOGICAL SURGEON, Leighton
Hospital, Middlewich Road, Crewe, Cheshire, CW14QJ.
DIRECT DIAL NO 01270-612010
FAX NO: 01270-250168
Our Ref: WILA / 7313621 ETel: 01270255141
Recipient details:
Dr Kerslake, Willow Wood Surgery, Wharton Phc, Crook Lane, Wharton,
Winsford, Cheshire, CW7 3GY.
Fax: 01270 587696
Your Ref: 11J81123/4786845817
Referral details:
Registered GP:Dr J.Kerslake
Referred By: Dr J.C.Kerslake, Willow Wood Surgery
Dear Dr Kerslake,
Date of Clinic:
Monday 1st October 2015
Reason for referral:
Microscopic haematuria.
History:
Two-week cancer fax for asymptomatic microscopic haematuria.
Multiple presentations with symptoms of cystitis but no infection on MSU.
Ultrasound surveillance for 4 em right ovarian cyst containing daughter cyst
-believed to be benign.
Past medical, surgical and mental health history: Left choroidal naevus April
2012.
Page1 of 2

Investigations results: Multiple MSUs back to August 2010 - often pyuria but
not a single proven UTI.MSU dip today: red cells and white cells but no nitrites.
Management plan: She requires and ultrasound scan, plain abdominal x-ray,
renal function tests, stone metabolites and flexible cystoscopy.
Advice, recommendations and future plan:
Although you are perfectly entitled to refer such patients on the two week
cancer fax, we are then obliged to see them within two weeks which means
that they end up attending the hospital anywhere between two and three
times, whereas a standard referral letter for asymptomatic microscopic
haematuria will allow us to arrange all the appropriate investigations in a
single visit saving time, energy and money for everybody.
Next appointment details:
Flexible cystoscopy ideally with linked radiology, but this has now been
dissociated from the standard microscopic haematuria service so may well
not occur on the same day.
Information given to patient: Copy of this letter.
Flexible cystoscopy version 9.1(c) SRS 090109
Yours sincerely
Mr S R Stubington

Page 2 of 2

**Fig. 8.6** RoboBraille®output file suitable for screen readers

The participants evaluated the patient view of an electronic health record (demonstration system), in terms of the following categories and subcategories based on the Web Accessibility Initiative (WAI) standard with the following results:

## 8.5.1   Perception

User feedback on the overall design and layout was positive, but there were some suggestions and concerns:

- *It was a bit of a shock when I logged onto this site, but it works well. There is one thing my browser initially and worryingly picked up on. The security measures certificate was not recognised by the browser for the site.*
- *All the sections worked and it was easy for me to access them and to send messages, book appointments, order drugs etc.*
- *Overall, a very good site which works well.*
- *Make the font and work areas a little bigger.*

*Create content that can be presented in different ways (e.g. simpler layout) without losing information or structure.*

Structure and content appear logical and easy to follow for users without accessibility issues; however it became clear that the lack of standardised structure to the "linked" content providing further information was not always easy for those with impairments to handle.

*Make it easier for users to see and hear content including separating foreground from background.*

This was not a particular issue for sighted users; however there was no obvious way of adjusting text or background styles to improve usability.

## 8.5.2   Operation

*Make all functionality available from a keyboard.*

The ability to tab between sections of the screens was available but not signposted to the user. For example, in order to sign in to the system, a user needs to tab through:

- Patient access logo
- Home button
- Help button

- Register button
- Sign-in help
- Get my user id link
- User ID entry field
- Password entry field
- Forgot user ID link
- Forgot Password link
- Remember my User ID checkbox
- Remember my User ID help/explanation
- Sign in

This is followed by several further tab-able options, but a visually impaired user, even after successfully setting up the webpage to remember them, would need to tab through 13 controls before being able to sign in. This problem continues throughout the site, e.g. to view repeat prescriptions requires further 14 tabs to reach the appropriate control at which point the user is required to revert to their screen reader to access their prescription detail.

*Provide users enough time to read and use content. Each screen is static so it requires user input to move forwards.*

Do not design content in a way that is known to cause seizures. Not tested but static nature of content minimises this risk.

*Provide ways to help users navigate, find content and determine where they are.*

As outlined above this is acceptable for users with full visual capacity but problematic if user is visually impaired.

### 8.5.3   Understanding

*Make text content readable and understandable.*

Content that was provided was felt to be appropriate; however it is worth mentioning the "experienced" user level of all those participating in the workshop.

*Make Web pages appear and operate in predictable ways.*

Content that was provided was felt to be appropriate; however it is worth mentioning the "experienced" user level of all those participating in the workshop.

*Help users avoid and correct mistakes.*

This appears adequate for sighted users; however the convoluted tabbing characteristics required for keyboard navigation were not felt particularly helpful for users requiring keyboard control.

## 8.5.4   Robustness

*Maximise compatibility with current and future user agents, including assistive technologies.*

There appears little evidence of consideration of assistive technologies being used in the patient portal tested.

## 8.5.5   Patient Priorities

*Up-to-date information*

As the data was the patient's own record (a dummy record in this case), all information within the patient portal was clearly as up to date as that held in the clinical system. When users followed the "i" link to further information, as this was addressing an external commercial site, the currency of such information could be variable and was unconfirmed. It may be appropriate for the "i" link to be made to either NHS held generic material or more closely focused additional information which is more clearly and closely related to the patients' actual diagnosis.

*Use of pictures*

There appeared no use of images, either photographic or diagrammatic. It was felt there was scope for helpful use of such material.

*Use of colours*

Colour use was consistent and simple; however there was no obvious way to alter this to allow users to customise background and font colours to maximise readability.

*Appropriate font*

Font size and style use was consistent and simple; however there was no obvious way to alter this to allow users to customise font size and style to maximise readability.

*Easy to understand language*

No problems observed.

*User Experience*

There was agreement that the provision of additional information to help the patient understand their record and health generally was a very positive aspect of the system. There was concern that not all links seemed to work or that

**Table 8.1** Accessibility principles

| Accessibility | Design principles that allow as many people as possible to use digital solutions |
|---|---|
| Universal design principles | Need to fit diverse environments |
| Comply with relevant regulation and national legislation including | • Equality Act 2010<br>• World Wide Web Consortium (W3C)<br>• ISO standard, EU regulation, national legislation including Accessible Information Standard (AIS)<br>• Web Content Accessibility Guidelines 2 (WCAG 2)<br>• Guidance on Applying WCAG 2.0 to Non-Web Information and Communications Technologies (WCAG2ICT) |

the information was actually relevant to the specific patient. It was felt that more targeted and therefore relevant "additional" information would be highly desirable.

- "A map linking information by disease, event or date will be highly desirable".
- "There are information options on diagnosis and test results that lead to websites accordingly. Also, some leaflets are available for physiological tests".

## 8.6 Recommendations

Lancashire's Digital Health Strategy 2015–2020 should incorporate:

1. Documents that describe *accessibility principles* (Table 8.1)
2. *Accessibility standards*
3. Documents that outline *best practices* (Table 8.2)

## 8.7 Achievements so Far

The following extracts from NHS England, with a contribution from Dr Clare Mander, Clinical Lead for Accessible Information at Solent NHS Trust, provide an outline of progress with the implementation of the Accessible Information Standard (AIS) to date:

As with any new, national initiative, the speed and effectiveness of implementation will vary. We are aware of fantastic work going on (for example, East Lancashire Hospitals NHS Trust has made significant progress in implementing the Standard) and have seen an increase in requests for large-print formats and audio, as well as via email, text and British Sign Language interpreter.

**Table 8.2** Sources of accessibility standards and best practices documentation

| |
|---|
| The World Wide Web Consortium (W3C) is the global authority on accessible design standards; http://www.w3c.org |
| The web contents accessibility guidelines (ISO/W3C WCAG 2.0) also apply to document accessibility; http://www.w3.org/TR/WCAG20/ |
| British Standards Institute have published Web Accessibility Code of Practice BS 8878:2010; https://www.access8878.co.uk/ |
| Information and updates about the Accessible Information Standard (AIS); http://www.england.nhs.uk/accessibleinfo |
| Abilitynet have produced a guide that complements the British Standards, BS8878, which is the de facto code of practise for commissioning and designing accessible websites; https://www.access8878.co.uk/bs8878-overview.aspx |
| RoboBraille®have authored various sets of guidelines and educational presentations for how to best prepare documents to meet the accessibility requirements (some of the information is written in English); http://www.robobraille.com/resources/guides-and-best-practices |

We welcomed the opportunity to contribute to the development and implementation of the national standard. The legal requirements have galvanised a decade of local developments, which include qualitative research, service evaluations and innovation projects. Implementation of the standard across a Community and Mental Health Trust, with over 100 clinical sites, is no easy task. In 2015, we began a project to develop a tiered model of accessible information training that was co-produced with patients living with communication and information needs. Our awareness DVD has now been rolled out across the Trust, an interactive accessible information learning platform is in development, and a programme of specialist training has been piloted with ten services. Through this specialist training, champions were identified and formed a new accessible information network that will link with our patient leads. The network aims to facilitate collective intelligence and social learning to improve accessible information practice across the Trust. We still have a long way to go, but together we have the opportunities to make a real difference.

Resources to support the implementation of the AIS are available on the NHS England website: https://www.england.nhs.uk/ourwork/accessibleinfo/resources/.

## 8.7.1 AIS Review

A largely questionnaire-based review led by Sarah Marsay looked at the impact of the AIS so far and found that it is "fit for purpose".

The full AIS review report (published in Spring 2017) will be the first Information Standards Notice (ISN) issued under the new DCB system (https://www.england.nhs.uk/ourwork/accessibleinfo/).

Dr Howard Leicester MBE and others are pressed to extend its content to include the widest spread of digital accessibility issues as a springboard for wider action in healthcare.

### *8.7.2   Standards Development in the UK, Europe and the USA*

Leading on UK activities are the British Standards Institution's (BSI's) committee ICT6 (ICT Accessibility).

The UK is trying to update its own web standard (BS8878) to a full, international standard. ICT6k is also responsible for inputs from:

- An EU Directive on Web and Mobile Accessibility
- W3C/WAI's underpinning and ongoing work to take WCAG to the next level

Information about key US laws pertinent to web accessibility and online resources, including conditions under which web content can be created to ensure accessible content to individuals with disabilities under US law, is available via www.webaim.org/articles/laws/usa/.

## 8.8   Conclusion

The UK government's vision focuses on access to good information as the basis for genuine decision-making for all who need it. Local policies relate to services centred on patients, and increased use of networked, digital health and social care systems focused on improving outcomes by giving individuals greater control to access their health data in a variety of ways to make informed choices. Innovation comes through apps and assistive technologies, building on what works to help people to stay healthy and well. Exploring AIS shows what may well be possible through technology for those with the greatest needs. Older and disabled people not only have most to gain through innovative use of communications technology, but they also form the largest user group.

## The Journey

The author's journey into networked theories began almost two decades ago whilst working and researching in a UK primary care organisation during a time of change and flux. Based on personal experience, underpinning positivist and ontologically objective approaches seemed inadequate in providing insight into the relational networks that emerged following challenges brought about by new NHS organisational structures and quality improvement policies. It was felt that our thinking needed to be supplemented and our attention was drawn initially to social network analysis (SNA) theories, its origins illustrated in the following figure:

Lineage of social network analysis (Ellis [12], based on Scott [13, p. 8])

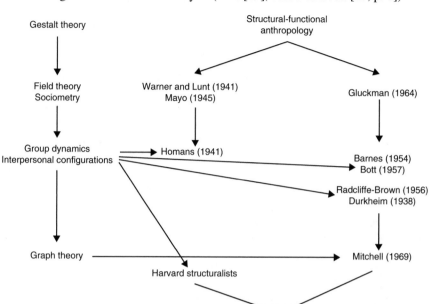

The figure above illustrates SNA theorists, for example, Boissevain [14] and Scott [13]; These two theorists have been influenced by the development of earlier theoretical positions by citing their work, which include the works of Manchester anthropologists Barnes [15] and Bott [16], attributed as some of the originators of the concepts underpinning SNA such as identifying agents and the structure of their links in a unit. Boissevain [14] is attributed as drawing attention to systematic interlinkages between units of analysis and linking these concepts to the potential offered by technology to support interdisciplinary activities. Such interlinkages may be outward links between individuals and between groups; they may also be inward links, setting out the interrelations between members of a group or other unit of analysis. By focusing systematically on the relations between units of analysis, SNA claims to support the study of interdependencies. This interdependency and its consequences for social action are assumptions underpinning the network approach. The configurations of interlinked, and therefore, interdependent, persons and groups are thus taken into account in trying to predict behaviour. By systematically tracing all interlinkages between units of analysis, it is claimed that certainty, predictability and control are challenged by flexibility, responsiveness and human condition. SNA thus claims to provide a systematic framework for analysing tension and asymmetry in social relations.

The figure above illustrates SNA theorists that drew attention to systematic attention to interlinkages between units of analysis and linked these concepts to the potential offered by technology to support interdisciplinary activities. Interdependency and its consequences for social action are assumptions underpinning the network approach. The configurations of interlinked, and therefore, interdependent, persons and groups are thus taken into account in trying to predict behaviour. The study of such patterns and their historical changing trajectories provides opportunities to reveal complex webs of relationships, interdependencies and consequences for social action to quantify patterns of decision-making. In this context, our experience suggested that the application of SNA theories would be limited to mapping a first outline of the network of relations that occurred during organisational restructure and implementation of clinical governance policies within NHS primary care organisations. The author's experience suggested SNA principles could be applied to provide a snapshot as it were, for further investigation into the content and experience of these relations, to improve our understanding of relations, interaction and dependencies. Our concerns focused on the extent that SNA theories focus on method, mathematical manipulations and classification rather than with the complexity, ambiguity and uncertainty of implementing clinical governance within PCOs.

Our attention was drawn to thinking about the emergent properties characteristic of complex adaptive systems (CAS) that lead to coevolution, a different way of acting and relating. A feature of CAS is that they constantly evolve over time and provide an emphasis on the whole system and behaviours emerge that cannot be predicted, which helped explain novel responses to change in local PCOs.

> Take-Home Message
> Innovation comes through assistive technologies, building on what works to help people to stay healthy and well. Exploring AIS shows what may well be possible through technology for those with the greatest needs. Older and disabled people not only have most to gain through innovative use of communications technology, but they also form the largest user group.

# References

1. Ellis B. An overview of complexity theory: understanding primary care as a complex adaptive system. In: Sturmberg JP, Martin CM, editors. Handbook of systems and complexity in health. New York: Springer; 2013. p. 485–94.
2. Ellis B. The value of systems and complexity thinking to enable change in adaptive healthcare organisations, supported by informatics. In: Sturmberg JP, editor. The value of systems and complexity sciences for healthcare. New York: Springer; 2016. p. 217–29.
3. NHS Choices. http://www.nhs.uk.
4. Confidentiality. London: General Medical Council. 2009. Endnotes, paragraph 16. http://www.gmc-uk.org.
5. E-Access Bulletin, section two: special report. The NHS Accessible Information Standard. December 2016: issue 185. http://www.headstar.com/eabulletin.
6. Record Access Collaborative. Enabling patients to access electronic health records. Guidance for health professionals. London: RCGP 2010. http://www.rcgp.org.uk.
7. Fisher B, Bhavani V, Winfield M. How patients use access to their full health records: a qualitative study of patients in general practice. J R Soc Med. 2009;102(12):539–44.
8. Goodley D. 'Learning Difficulties', the social model of disability and impairment: challenging epistemologies. Disabil Soc. 2001;16(2):207–31.

9. Barnes C. The social model of disability: a sociological phenomenon ignored by sociologists? In: Shakespeare T, editor. The disability reader: social sciences perspectives. London: Cassell; 1998.
10. Life Opportunities Survey. UK data service. (Free registration required. Product SN6653 (freely available). http://www.ukdataservice.ac.uk.
11. Robobraille®. http://www.robobraille.org/.
12. Ellis B. Managing governance programmes in primary healthcare: lessons from case studies of the implementation of clinical governance in two primary care trusts. PhD-thesis. 2008. University of Central Lancashire (UCLan).
13. Scott J. Social network analysis. A handbook, 2nd ed. Thousand Oaks, CA: Sage; 2000.
14. Boissevain J. Network analysis: a reappraisal. Curr Anthropol. 1979;20(2):392–394.
15. Barnes JA. Class and committees in a Norwegian island parish. Hum Rel. 1957;7:39–58.
16. Bott E. Family and social network. London: Tavistock; 1957.

# Part II
# Education and Healthcare Organisation

The seven contributions in the second part of *Putting Systems and Complexity Sciences into Practice* focus on the two domains of health professional education and the healthcare organisation.

*Health professional education* lays the foundations which shape as much the attitudes as the knowledge base of our aspiring future health professionals. It is of utmost importance to prepare them for the challenges arising in a constantly emerging complex adaptive healthcare environment.

- The Flexner reforms had their time; how to reform health professional programmes to enable future practitioners to manage in a complex adaptive environment?
- Implementing complexity sciences into a translational health science programme—how to overcome the challenges?
- Does the knowledge base of general practice show complex patterns, and are they assessed in postgraduate examinations?

*Healthcare organisations* are challenged to meet diverse needs from disparate stakeholders. Understanding the influential nodes and their influences on the organisation is critical to provide patients with seamlessly integrated care and healthcare experiences.

- Can one identify the ethically complex patient and provide him with "the right" care?
- While there is a general—nonlinear—relationship between health factors and health outcomes, what are the factors that "determine" better health outcomes?
- One disease, different outcomes. How do you get it right or wrong for that matter?
- How to optimise patient care in the emergency department? Can modelling help?

These papers reflect what Swiss psychiatrist and balloonist Bertrand Piccard describes as [The] *Pioneering spirit should continue, not to conquer the planet or space . . . but rather to improve the quality of life.*

# Chapter 9
# Transforming Health Education to Catalyze a Global Paradigm Shift: Systems Thinking, Complexity, and Design Thinking

**Chad Swanson and Matt Widmer**

## 9.1 Introduction

In 1910, the Flexner report accelerated a transformation in medical education that has had a profound impact on the way we as a global society approach health. Although the scientific method had begun to infiltrate medicine and public health since the sixteenth century, social and institutional resistance to change was still strong at the turn of the twentieth century. Abraham Flexner was an American educator commissioned by the Carnegie Foundation to survey medical schools in the United States [1]. His sweeping recommendations, along with a number of other related developments, had a profound impact, both immediately and long-term. Within 20 years of publishing his report, 38 medical schools in the United States closed their doors or merged with others [2]; much of what we still do in medicine and public health today is a direct result of the transformation catalyzed by his report and other activities with similar messages.

A major component of Flexner's recommendations was to link medical education to the scientific method. Neither he nor his contemporaries could have imagined what followed: antibiotics, heart catheterizations, transplants, and innumerable other effects extending well beyond medical practice and education. The biomedical reductionist paradigm—an approach to health concentrated on physiological minutia, professions working in silos, and a focus in episodic treatment—which surged

C. Swanson (✉)
Arizona State University School for the Science of Healthcare Delivery, Utah Valley Hospital, 1668 North 1590 West, Provo, UT 84604, USA
e-mail: swancitos@gmail.com

M. Widmer
Romney Institute of Public Management, Brigham Young University, 843 Wymount Terrace, Provo, UT 84604, USA
e-mail: matthewidmer@gmail.com

© Springer International Publishing AG, part of Springer Nature 2018
J. P. Sturmberg (ed.), *Putting Systems and Complexity Sciences Into Practice*,
https://doi.org/10.1007/978-3-319-73636-5_9

exponentially after Flexner's report continues to dominate every aspect of health today. Currently, 162 medical specialties and subspecialties [3] can bill for 155,000 different ICD-10 codes for diagnoses and procedures, and that number is still rising [4]. The slogan of the United States' National Institute of Health is "turning discovery into health." What that translates to in action looks more like "turning biomedical discovery into clinical treatment," at least while glancing at the NIH annual budget of over $30 billion dedicated almost entirely to researching 265 separate diseases or conditions [5]. The assumption, of course, is that the discovery and delivery of more science-based medicines and procedures for individual diseases is sufficient to improve population health. However, health improvement involves much more, including behavior change, community engagement, and organizational learning.

In this chapter, we will make the case that we need a change in mindset similar to what resulted from Flexner's report: a historical paradigm shift from biological reductionism toward more of a complex systems approach to health improvement. From an objective viewpoint, the need for change is increasingly apparent.[1] Population health outcomes are poor compared to what they could be, especially in vulnerable populations, and health improvement continues to prove costly, challenging, and controversial. The *law of diminishing returns* seems to govern our collective efforts at improving population health through biological reductionism. Consider the problems that plague our current efforts:

• Financial incentives reward volume over value
• Public health professionals compete for limited funds to deliver discrete programs
• Researchers largely engage in esoteric projects that are disconnected from social accountability

Figure 9.1 provides an illustration of the current health system's structure. Our current system has rigid boundaries for professionals and organizations, and for what counts as academically relevant. Meanwhile, the societal aims that we value most—population health, equity, efficiency, wellness, capacity, and satisfaction—are overlooked. In short, we have inherited an approach to health improvement that is fragmented, tribal, siloed, mired in invested interests, and woefully inadequate to meet the challenges and opportunities of our century. The surging opioid epidemic, pervasive obesity burden, neglected mental health challenges, and skyrocketing costs are just a few examples that highlight this inadequacy.

---

[1] A point already apparent some 20 years after the release of his report, Flexner himself observed: *...the very intensity with which scientific medicine is cultivated threatens to cost us at times the mellow judgement and broad culture of the older generation at its best. Osler, Janeway, and Halsted have not been replaced* [Flexner A. *Universities, American, English and German*. New York: Oxford University Press, 1930].

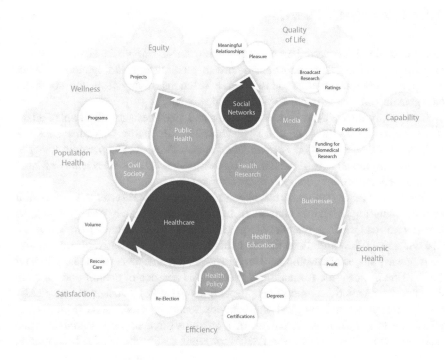

**Fig. 9.1** The "current" health system

## 9.2   A Systems Approach

The challenges we face today—like rising healthcare costs and obesity, as well as the tools we have to address them—are much different than they were in 1910. In this chapter, we introduce three overlapping and emerging perspectives that provide the theory, language, tools, and methods suitable for today's challenges: systems thinking, complexity thinking, and design thinking. We will also argue that some combination of these perspectives and approaches will provide the paradigm for the next century.

### 9.2.1   Systems Thinking

Systems thinking is a broad and diverse set of theories, constructs, concepts, tools, and methods used to understand and transform a system—a "regularly interacting or interdependent group of items forming a unified whole" [6]. Taken together, the various strands of systems thinking emphasize interrelationships between system parts, feedback loops, diverse perspectives, the definition of boundaries between subsystems, and methods for modeling systemic behavior over time [7].

## 9.2.2  Complexity Thinking

Complexity thinking describes a mental approach that appreciates the interconnected nature of problems and their nonlinear relationships and dynamics. When we apply a complex systems lens, we see solutions arising from the continual engagement and adaptation of a system's stakeholders.

Complexity theory describes the behavior and characteristics of complex adaptive systems (CAS). In Appendix B of Crossing the Quality Chasm, Paul Plsek defined a CAS as *a collection of individual agents that have the freedom to act in ways that are not always predictable and whose actions are interconnected such that one agent's actions changes the context for other agents* [8].

Complexity theory suggests that, in contrast to mechanical systems, CAS exhibit nonlinear and unpredictable patterns of behavior—inputs rarely equal outputs, so small inputs can produce relatively large changes in system behavior or vice versa. Likewise, in a CAS, initial conditions matter tremendously. Relatively small deviations in early stages of development tend to have monumental consequences in later stages. Emergence—the formation of order in the absence of central control from the ongoing interactions among simpler entities—is a key concept of complexity theory. Emergence in biological and complex social systems results from agents' adherence to simple rules in pursuit of a shared vision. Many researchers argue that complexity theory more accurately represents reality than our still-dominant, nineteenth century Newtonian clockwork view of the universe.

Complexity ideas are being increasingly considered by health practitioners as the interconnectedness and pace of the world heighten and are being used in diverse disciplines such as midwifery in developing settings [9] and in understanding the behavior of international health research systems [10].

## 9.2.3  Adaptive Design

Adaptive Design thinking is a problem-solving approach. It deliberately involves all affected stakeholders in an iterative problem-solving process. It combines insights from SCIENCE (finding similarities among things that are different), ART (finding differences among things that are similar), and DESIGN (creating feasible "wholes" from infeasible "parts") in ways that are best suited to find solutions to complex (*wicked*) problems [11] in the realm of uncertainty.

Adaptive design [12] is an emerging approach to managing change in complex environments. It synthesizes two vetted approaches to organizational practice: the austere, ruthlessly realistic *adaptive leadership* and the creative, optimistic *design thinking*. Adaptive design combines the political and social force of adaptive leadership with the innovation and inspiration of design thinking to provide a powerful tool capable of facilitating organizational improvement in complex environments.

The practice of adaptive design, as described by Bernstein and Linsky [12], involves four processes:

1. Empathy for and observation of organizational realities
2. Interpretation of those realities
3. Ideation of possible solutions
4. Prototyping interventions

### 9.2.3.1 Complex Systems Thinking

We define complex systems thinking—a conglomerate of concepts from systems thinking, complex adaptive systems, and adaptive design—as a way of approaching health challenges that considers interactions over time to better approximate the world we as a society really want [13].

Adopting this mindset leads to four changes:

1. The way we view the world
2. The questions we ask
3. The way we approach health challenges
4. The institutions and norms that enable or constrain our behavior

### 9.2.3.2 A CST Mindset Changes the Way We View the World

A biomedical reductionist mindset has dominated our global perspective in health over the previous 100 years. We conceive of diseases, patients, clinic visits, and public health programs at a single point in time, too often detached from history, relationships, patterns, and interdependencies. As a result, we tend to lose sight of the goals, such as population health, equity, and wellness, that we as a society really want. A CST mindset causes us to see patterns of interactions over time and the unintended consequences of reductionist interventions.

### 9.2.3.3 A CST Mindset Changes the Questions We Ask

Since the dawn of the twentieth century, we have thought about health improvement as a simple, linear process of cause and effect. Undernutrition—caused by a lack of nutrient intake or uptake—provides a representative example of how such an approach is unsuited for today's challenges. In a linear world, a perfect approach to ameliorating undernutrition would target increasing the intake of nutrients like protein or vitamins in a select population [14]. This kind of approach leads us to ask questions like:

- *What are the specific medical conditions (such as sepsis or dehydration) that are contributing to, or exacerbated by, this patient's undernutrition?*

- *How can we deliver food and supplements to starving children?*
- *How can we encourage mothers to breastfeed?*

However, like most of the health challenges we face today, undernutrition is a complex condition. Parental education, economic opportunity, agricultural productivity, environmental sustainability, clean water, political conflict, and the prevalence of infectious diseases are a few of the many interdependent factors associated with undernutrition. Practitioners with a CST mindset recognize these complex realities and, as a result, ask a different set of questions [15]:

- *How can we transform communities to support children's nutritional needs?*
- *What are this particular community's social, religious, and cultural barriers to a healthy diet?* [16]
- *What are the economic and political implications of an external organization delivering protein and supplements to this community?*
- *How will the implementation of this nutrition program affect the human resources, relationships, priorities, and other characteristics of the existing and future local system?*

### 9.2.3.4 A CST Mindset Changes the Way We Approach Health Problems

With a biomedical reductionist mindset, we insulate ourselves within our profession, specialty, discipline, clinic, or other "tribe." Healthcare providers treat one patient with a discrete condition at a given point of time. Health researchers engage in short-term, esoteric projects that are too often separated from social impact or accountability. Public health practice targets individual diseases in well-defined populations and then delivers discrete, logic-modeled programs dependent on competitive funding. With a complex systems lens, we challenge previous assumptions, focus on a shared vision of the future, cross boundaries between professions, and focus on creating an environment where locals can self-organize to create that future over time. But that approach is risky and challenging; it requires humility, empathy, and embracing uncertainty [17].

We propose that a CST approach includes these four essentials:

- Shared vision that truly involves all stakeholders
- Relentless, long-term focus on that vision
- Continuous challenging of mental models and assumptions
- Rapid cycle adaptation and learning organizations that fail often and fast

### 9.2.3.5 A CST Mindset Can Change Our Values and Institutions

Perhaps most importantly, CST can change our values and institutions. In our current world, we tend to value visible accomplishments over actual influence. For example, a physician with a degree from Johns Hopkins medical school, or an academic who publishes in the *New England Journal of Medicine*, or a researcher who receives a competitive grant from the National Institutes of Health is often esteemed solely on the basis of their degree, publication, or award without any consideration of impact on the community or world. Indeed, we may never question the impact of their work. Adopting a CST mindset shifts our focus toward what we actually want, which potentially changes what we value. For example, focusing on what we actually want from a doctor's visit—avoid unnecessary pain or risk and obtain relief from, or prevent, illness or injury, regardless of where the doctor attended medical school or whether she publishes in competitive journals—could lead us to rethink how we compensate physicians. This type of shift in thinking has recently spurred a transition in American healthcare from fee-for-service toward experimentation with value-based compensation.

Our current institutions—universities, nongovernmental organizations, public health departments, and hospitals—are conceptualized and structured in such a way as to resist adaptation. Within the current paradigm, these institutions do not reach their full potential. Fundamental assumptions remain unchallenged because an individual who questions "what has always been done" is often perceived as disloyal and dismissed, or even punished. Further, our institutions learn in a way that only reinforces current behavior and patterns of thought instead of encouraging innovative thought and challenging of fundamental assumptions. A CST approach to health enables institutions to constantly challenge basic assumptions, which in turn provides the environment necessary to improve institutions in transformational ways.

Figure 9.2 [18] represents the process of change that our health system could experience with a CST paradigm. Feedback, learning, and adaptation within and between organizations and institutions happen rapidly, frequently, and sometimes unexpectedly. A shared vision and aligned incentives maintain a relentless focus on societal goals. There seems to be a growing sense that complex systems thinking used broadly could provide the theory, language, tools, and methods to transform health.

## 9.3  Barriers to Change: We Are All Invested

Healthcare providers in the United States have been trained and are currently incentivized through fee-for-service reimbursement, to quickly address isolated conditions with inadequate consideration of history, patterns, relationships, capacity, or behavior change. For the most part, our medical education system maintains that status quo by training physicians and other care providers to be technically competent for episodic care, but ignorant of how the larger systems of care can also be improved. Similarly, researchers are incentivized to receive grants with short-term foci and publish esoteric papers, regardless of health impact. Funders want to demonstrate short-term gains. Finally, politicians are focused on policies that will get them reelected, regardless of long-term impact.

Given the current environment, many think that health education and research institutional reform are high leverage activities. A report by the Lancet Commission

## AN OPTIMAL HEALTH SYSTEM

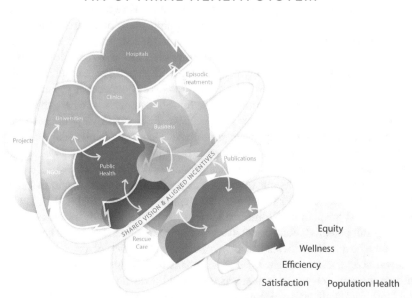

**Fig. 9.2** An "optimal" health system [18]

on health, *Health Professionals for a New Century*, explicitly called for a medical education "that should be systems based to improve the performance of health systems" [19]. There are a number of other groups that are also calling for transformational change with a focus on educational reform, including *Beyond Flexner* [20] and the *Next System Project* [21].

However, to our knowledge, these movements have not adequately embraced and mobilized around the theory and implications of a complex systems paradigm. While we cannot predict with certainty, or in detail, what a better health system might look like, there are some characteristics that we can hope for. A better system would not define health as merely "the absence of disease," but would be more expansive, incorporating wellness and the ability for individuals to achieve full potential. It would approach health improvement with an emphasis on prevention and early intervention and administer care on a coordinated continuum instead of discrete episodes [22]. Perhaps most importantly, a better system would have a relentless and primary focus on what we as a society ultimately aspire for.

Below we describe three current, innovative examples of CST principles applied to improve population health.

### 9.3.1   Arizona State University

Arizona State University, with President Michael Crow in the lead, has demonstrated an on-the-ground application of complex systems thinking principles and, as a result, is redefining higher education. By questioning fundamental assumptions underlying universities—particularly in the United States—such as the idea that a university's prestige or value is determined by its acceptance rate or that students who do not succeed in traditional university settings are not capable of learning complex concepts, ASU has evolved and challenged the higher-education status quo over the past 15 years. Figure 9.3 provides a simplified visualization of the current dominant university model: departments and colleges work largely independent of one another, with limited social impact.

Inclusion and collaboration are two of ASU's driving values. To increase inclusion and counter the trend of most twentieth-century American universities, ASU aims to break down the barriers between society and access to higher education—and not just in Arizona. So far, this has taken the shape of free online courses

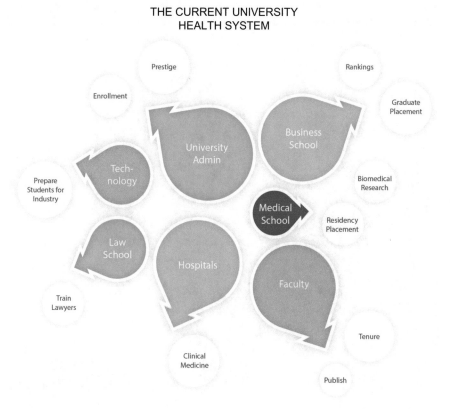

**Fig. 9.3** The current university model

taught by university faculty and accessed by people from around the world, online educational games that teach advanced linear mathematics, and a robust online degree-awarding program. An emphasis on collaboration led to a transformational restructuring of colleges and departments (including the establishment of over a dozen transdisciplinary schools within ASU and large research initiatives [23], the College of Health Solutions [24], and the School for the Science of Health Care Delivery[25]), an intentional shift of focus toward social embeddedness, and an interdisciplinary partnership with the Mayo Clinic campus in Arizona, among other novel developments. Figure 9.4 illustrates the new ASU model. ASU's progress over the past 15 years has been neither linear nor planned in detail. It was a learning process of experimentation, rapid failure, and relentless focus on achieving their shared vision of what higher education should be [26].

### 9.3.2   Jamkhed: A Comprehensive Rural Health Project

The Comprehensive Rural Health Project (CRHP), based in Jamkhed, India, provides a time-tested example of a successful systems-savvy approach to population health. CRHP was established by doctors Raj and Mabelle Arole in 1970 and has

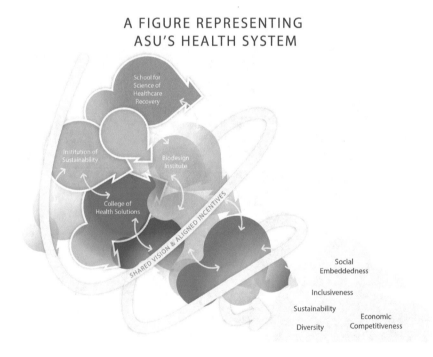

**Fig. 9.4**   ASU as new university model

had remarkable success in improving population health, perhaps some of the "best ever documented for a community health project" [27]. CRHP still provides health-related services for 500,000 people in the Maharashtra state in India. What makes CRHP successful is not the amount of money or external expertise delivered or even highly detailed interventions. What sets CRHP apart is the overall approach to health, which can be understood through a CST lens.

The central theme behind all CRHP activities is summarized in their vision: *We envision communities where families are healthy and enjoy fulfilling lives. The full human rights of every individual, especially women and children, are protected and uncompromised . . .* [28]. This vision is shared between stakeholders who, over time, have self-organized toward creating healthy communities. CRHP activities go well beyond providing access to medical care. They have provided clean water and simultaneously broken down entrenched social barriers by digging wells in the poorest areas of villages. They have engaged with farmers to develop methods for thriving in an arid climate. Perhaps the hallmark of CRHP is an obvious lack of a traditional central control, of top-down governance without community input. The success of CRHP emerged through efforts of the entire community toward their shared vision. Indeed, the Aroles had approached other communities prior to Jamkhed. They settled in on Jamkhed because a shared vision of population health and equity emerged over time.

## 9.3.3 Billings Clinic

During the 1990s, the Billings Clinic in Montana, USA, underwent a fundamental change in management style: from a linear, rigid, plan-and-implement approach to hospital administration, toward a nonlinear, positive deviance, self-organization, and emergence-based approach. The impetus for change initially came from pressure to decrease MRSA infections in the intensive care unit where traditional infection control methods were not working. The proverbial tipping point came when hospital administrators—some of whom were fluent in complexity concepts—opted to experiment with a systems approach.

After remarkable success in decreasing MRSA infections in the intensive care unit, complexity concepts began to permeate the larger hospital administrative strategy. Over time, the clinic began to look less like a command-and-control organization and exhibited more characteristics of a decentralized complex adaptive system. The Clinic's mission and vision became shared among various stakeholders, and care providers established nine simple rules to govern behavior. Indicators improved and so did the hospital environment, but these changes did not come easily. As is common in complex systems, there was substantial pushback and difficulty throughout the transformation process. From the beginning in the intensive care unit, some administrators, physicians, and other care providers were skeptical at best and overtly oppositional at worst. But as time progressed and outcomes improved, attitudes changed and the Clinic evolved into a robust healthcare organization nationally recognized for exceptional quality and safety [29].

## 9.4 Conclusion

Our current health systems are far too costly, produce poor population health, and perpetuate gross inequities. With the growing complexity and interdependence of our world, our traditional way of thinking and acting is no longer sufficient; we need another revolution in health and medicine similar to what resulted from Flexner's report—from a way of thinking dominated by biomedical reductionism toward an approach that embraces uncertainty and fosters new partnerships.

Complex systems thinking—a conglomerate of ideas and approaches from disciplines such as systems thinking, complex adaptive systems, and adaptive design—provides a promising complement to biomedical reductionism. CST has the potential to change the way we view the world, change the questions we ask, change the way we approach health, and even change our values and institutions.

Although there are substantial barriers to changing the way we think and act, from institutional resistance to powerful vested interests, we see an increasing number of successful initiatives based on CST. Three of those examples—Arizona State University, Jamkhed, and the Billings Clinic—illustrate the practicality of using CST approaches to improve population health.

**Acknowledgements** We gratefully acknowledge the work of Eliza Swanson in preparing the figures for this manuscript.

## The Journey

*Chad Swanson* I first recognized that things could be much, much better in the way that we as a global society approach health improvement while involved in humanitarian health aid in Africa. Foreign organizations, local clinics, donors: we were all, it seemed, focused on our particular, limited activity, without adequate consideration of what we all wanted most: coordination to alleviate needless suffering while increasing local capacity long-term. Once I stumbled across systems thinking and complexity concepts as a global health advocate, emergency physician, and part-time academic, I found that their application is needed in every aspect of health education, practice, research, and policy. A shared vision around what we as a society really want is desperately lacking in health policy discourse. Optimal feedback leading to ongoing learning and improvement is not part of the culture in healthcare. Mental models are deeply engrained and not adequately challenged in health education, leading to path dependent institutions and curricula. Current challenges such as healthcare reform, obesity, and the opioid epidemic cross sectors and professions. Health research is too focused on fragmented biomedical reductionism. I am convinced that a historical transformation in health is needed, a revolution with complex systems thinking at its core.

During my systems and complexity intellectual journey, I have crossed paths with the ideas of many systems advocates and experts, including Henry Mosley, Peter Senge, Donella Meadows, Allan Best, Joachim Sturmberg, Martin Reynolds,

Bob Williams, Michael Crow, Jean Boulton, Peter Allen, Cliff Bowman, Scott Page, David Peters, Don de Savigny, Taghreed Adam, Scott Leishcow, Paul Plesk, Trisha Greenhalgh, and Helen Bevan, to name a few. The journey has been and continues to be rewarding and invigorating. I resonate with Scott Page's discussion of social change in complex systems: change agents need to explore the landscape widely for high leverage opportunities, activities that might lead to a tipping point. Then they need to exploit those opportunities. As such, I am currently involved in an eclectic collection of activities (academic papers, advocacy and organization, teaching, clinical improvement) and hope to settle into a long-term activity or partnership soon that will have historical impact.

*Matt Widmer*  I first became acquainted with the need for a paradigm shift in health while working with impoverished inner-city families in the American Midwest. It was clear to me—and to them—that despite the efforts of their local health system, they were still living needlessly short, painful lives. At the time, I was perplexed and despondent under the load of a recurring question: "how do you make any lasting difference when the determinants of health are so complex and carry such momentum?"

It was not until a few years later when I was exposed to the ideas of complex systems thinking and found an answer—at least in part—to the question I had asked repeatedly during an undergraduate study of public health. This chapter provides historical context for the inadequacy of the current health paradigm and calls for a shift in health education toward a worldview better suited for the challenges of the twenty-first century.

Take-Home Message

- The biomedical reductionist paradigm which emerged after Flexner's report drives current health activities.
- Today's health challenges are complex and not amenable to interventions based exclusively on biomedical reductionist thinking.
- A complex social systems thinking (CST) perspective changes the way we see the world, the questions we ask, our approach to health, and the nature of our values and institutions.
- Arizona State University, Jamkhed Comprehensive Rural Health Project, and Billings Clinic are instructive examples of CST in practice.

# References

1. Flexner A. Medical education in the United States and Canada: a report to the carnegie foundation for the advancement of teaching. New York: Carnegie Foundation; 1910.
2. Hiatt MD, Stockton CG. The impact of the Flexner Report on the fate of medical schools in North America after 1909. J Am Phys Surg. 2003;8(2):37–40.

3. http://www.abms.org/member-boards/specialty-subspecialty-certificates/. Accessed 21 Aug 2017.
4. http://www.acr.org/Advocacy/Economics-Health-Policy/Billing-Coding/Prepare-Now-for-ICD10. Accessed 21 Aug 2017.
5. https://report.nih.gov/categorical_spending.aspx. Accessed 21 Aug 2017.
6. Merriam-Webster. Merriam-Webster's collegiate dictionary; 2004.
7. Williams B, Hummelbrunner R. Systems concepts in action: a practitioner's toolkit. Standford: Stanford University Press; 2010.
8. Plsek P. Appendix B: redesigning health care with insights from the science of complex adaptive systems. In: Committee on Quality of Health Care in America - Institute of Medicine, editor. Crossing the quality chasm: a new health system for the 21st century. Washington, D.C.: National Academy Press; 2001. p. 309–22.
9. Bogren MU, Berg M, Edgren L, van Teijlingen E, Wigert H. Shaping the midwifery profession in Nepal - Uncovering actors' connections using a Complex Adaptive Systems framework. Sex Reprod Healthc. 2016;10:48–55.
10. Caffrey L, Wolfe C, McKevitt C. Embedding research in health systems: lessons from complexity theory. Health Res Policy Syst. 2016;14(1):54.
11. Buchanan R. Wicked problems in design thinking. Kepes 2010;7(6):7–35.
12. Bernstein M, Linsky M. Leading change through adaptive design. Stanford social innovation review. Winter 2016. https://ssir.org/articles/entry/leading_change_through_adaptive_design.
13. www.revolutionizehealth.org. Accessed 21 Aug 2017.
14. Nichols B. Malnutrition in children in resource-limited countries: clinical assessment. UpToDate®. http://www.uptodate.com/contents/malnutrition-in-children-in-resource-limited-countries-clinical-assessment.
15. Trochim WM, Cabrera DA, Milstein B, Gallagher RS, Leischow SJ. Practical challenges of systems thinking and modeling in public health. Am J Public Health 2006;96(3):538–46.
16. Vollmer S, Bommer C, Krishna A, Harttgen K, Subramanian SV. The association of parental education with childhood undernutrition in low-and middle-income countries: comparing the role of paternal and maternal education. Int J Epidemiol. 2016;46(1):312–23.
17. Reynolds M, Sarriot E, Swanson R, Rusoja E. Evolution and application of systems ideas: toward principles for systems thinking in health practice. J Eval Clin Pract. 2018. doi: 10.1111/jep.12856.
18. Sturmberg JP, O'Halloran DM, Martin CM. Understanding health system reform - a complex adaptive systems perspective. J Eval Clin Pract. 2012;18(1):202–8.
19. Frenk J, Chen L, Bhutta ZA, Cohen J, Crisp N, Evans T, et al. Health professionals for a new century: transforming education to strengthen health systems in an interdependent world. The Lancet 2010;376(9756):1923–58.
20. http://beyondflexner.org/. Accessed 21 Aug 2017.
21. http://www.thenextsystem.org/next-health-system/. Accessed 21 Aug 2017.
22. Halfon N, Long P, Chang DI, Hester J, Inkelas M, Rodgers A. Applying a 3.0 transformation framework to guide large-scale health system reform. Health Aff. 2014;33(11):2003–11.
23. https://president.asu.edu/about/michaelcrow. Accessed 21 Aug 2017.
24. https://chs.asu.edu/. Accessed 21 Aug 2017.
25. https://chs.asu.edu/programs/schools/school-science-health-care-delive. Accessed 21 Aug 2017.
26. Crow MM, Dabars WB. Designing the new American university. Baltimore, MD: Johns Hopkins University Press; 2015.
27. Perry H, Robison N, Chavez D, Taja O, Carolina H, Shanklin D, Wyon J. Attaining health for all through community partnerships: principles of the census-based, impact-oriented (CBIO) approach to primary health care developed in Bolivia, South America. Soc Sci Med. 1999;48(8):1053–67.
28. http://jamkhed.org/about/. Accessed 21 Aug 2017.
29. Lindberg C, Hatch M, Mohl V, Arce C, Ciemins E. Embracing uncertainty: complexity-inspired innovations at billings clinic. In: Sturmberg JP, Martin CM, editors. Handbook of systems and complexity in health. New York: Springer; 2013. p. 697–713.

# Chapter 10
# New Ways of Knowing and Researching: Integrating Complexity into a Translational Health Sciences Program

**Paige L. McDonald and Gaetano R. Lotrecchiano**

## 10.1 Introduction

Health science research is tasked with addressing ever more complex health issues, necessitating an interdisciplinary approach which encompasses the overlapping "biomedical, social, policy, and environmental factors" contributing to potential solutions [1, 2]. Correspondingly, the next generation of health scientists must be educated in ways that allows them to respond to "multidimensional problems" [1] with an interdisciplinary, collaborative approach required to meet this challenge. We at the George Washington University School of Medicine and Health Sciences (GW SMHS) have attempted to meet this demand by developing a PhD program in Translational Health Sciences (THS). Translational science focuses on the "process of translating basic scientific discoveries to clinical applications, and ultimately to public health improvements" [3]. Our PhD program seeks to develop the skills required for future graduates to "change health care culture through innovation, develop and apply new products and technologies, and apply discovery to practices and policies that will serve the larger health care community" [4]. Similarly, we focus on exposing future researchers, clinicians, and educators to cross-disciplinary methods for research, practice, and education grounded in a collaborative ecology and a systems approach to exploring complex problems. Ideally, this approach will promote systemic uptake of research findings for greater social impact and train the next generation of researchers, practitioners, and educators to meet the demands of our increasingly complex health systems.

Future participation in THS will require unique skills: the ability to generate new knowledge through cross-disciplinary inquiry, appraise barriers and facilitators

P. L. McDonald · G. R. Lotrecchiano (✉)
Department of Clinical Research and Leadership, George Washington University School of Medicine and Health Sciences, 2100 W Pennsylvania Avenue, NW, Washington, DC 20037, USA
e-mail: paigem@gwu.edu; glotrecc@gwu.edu

© Springer International Publishing AG, part of Springer Nature 2018
J. P. Sturmberg (ed.), *Putting Systems and Complexity Sciences Into Practice*,
https://doi.org/10.1007/978-3-319-73636-5_10

to knowledge generation and translation across the translational spectrum, communicate effectively across diverse settings and stakeholder groups, facilitate the development of shared mental models when leading collaborative research projects and incorporate diverse stakeholder perspectives in research design and practice, and translate findings to maximize system uptake and social impact. Developing these skills necessitates a cross-disciplinary, collaborative, and transformational approach to education which embraces a complex systems perspective. Adoption of this approach required a paradigm shift on the part of our faculty and students. Correspondingly, we sought to achieve a shared vision of the nature of our task and how it would be accomplished. In this paper, we explore how we met these challenges, making connections among the needs of various stakeholders and creating a model for learning design and delivery which embraces inherent tensions to allow for adaptation and emergence within our system.

## 10.2   A Complex Task at Hand

A complex adaptive systems perspective guides our consideration of the unique characteristics of the program of study we were challenged to create. Developing a signature pedagogy [5] for Translational Health Sciences doctoral studies requires the following:

- Creating a model and conceptual framework to guide our efforts toward expanding and extending traditional research practices
- Encouraging doctoral students to cull their interests with more system-wide intentionality
- Fulfilling the promise of greater social impact from dissertation research that integrates a translational, cross-disciplinary emphasis

The matrix in Table 10.1 shows how we align the inherent complexity in program design with the desired outcomes of translational health research.

## 10.3   Addressing the Needs of Diverse Stakeholders

Designing a doctoral program in Translational Health Sciences grounded in a *complex adaptive systems approach* requires meeting the needs of a diverse group of stakeholders and anticipating their potential reactions to the approach to program development. Stakeholders invested in our new program of study include internal stakeholders (university leadership, faculty, student) and external stakeholders (researchers, policy-makers, federal partners, industry, patients). To develop a program that would gain support across the multiple stakeholder sectors, we had to anticipate potential reactions to our approach to design and delivery and develop appropriate responses. Table 10.2 provides an overview of various

**Table 10.1** Addressing complexity in model design

| Dynamics | Epistemological tensions | Impact: significant or social | Credibility and relevance | Collaborative dynamics |
|---|---|---|---|---|
| **Tensions** between different epistemologies | x | | | |
| **Interdependence** among teaching team members | | | | x |
| **Crossing boundaries:** stakeholder and disciplines | x | x | | |
| **Dynamic** program and curriculum development | | | | x |
| **Minimum specifications** and structure | | | x | |
| **Emergence** of new research models | x | x | | x |

stakeholders within the system, identifying potential reaction or need on the part of each stakeholder and our program's response to the anticipated need or reaction.

As Table 10.2 highlights, recognizing and addressing the potential diversity of needs among stakeholder needs can prove challenging but is also critical to achieve the "buy-in" required at multiple levels.

At the university level, adopting a complex systems approach which integrates multiple stakeholder perspectives has the potential to attract and generate multiple impact streams to ensure sustainability.

For faculty, a shared understanding of the value of an adaptive approach serves as the pedagogical scaffolding necessary to develop and deliver an integrated, cross-disciplinary, collaborative curriculum aimed at producing agile researchers who can navigate the changing dynamics of the current healthcare system.

Students unaccustomed to systems thinking may question the value of the approach for problem exploration and research. However, developing capability in systems thinking will help to ensure the incorporation of multiple stakeholder perspectives within future research to maximize the potential contribution of research findings for social impact and change within the health system.

As future researchers, graduates may then influence the approaches of future collaborators toward the study of complex problems in health. Researchers, particularly those inexperienced with cross-disciplinary techniques, who work with our students may come to recognize that the translational research process functions "exactly" like a complex adaptive system and, thus, is continually evolving based upon changing systemic needs.

**Table 10.2** Stakeholder analysis

| | Stakeholder | Potential reaction/need | Program response |
|---|---|---|---|
| Internal | University leadership | How is a complex systems program an asset? | The program cultivates multiple impact streams |
| | Program directors | How do I show the value of complexity? | Demonstrate the application of complexity theory |
| | Faculty | How do I integrate complexity concepts with my teaching? | The program adopts a cross-disciplinary team approach toward design and delivery |
| | Students | Why a systems approach? | It is required to ensure implementation and uptake of research |
| External | Researchers | What does complexity have to do with translational science? | Translational science by nature is a complex adaptive system |
| | Policy-makers | How does the complexity of the system influence policy decisions? | The program promotes multi-stakeholder involvement in policy recommendations |
| | Federal partners | We need cross-disciplinary researchers! | The program prepares collaborative researchers trained in a variety of perspectives |
| | Industry | Who will translate science into products? | The program will develop cross-disciplinary translational scientists with an implementation orientation |

For policy-makers, program adoption of a complex adaptive systems approach ensures that policy recommendations represent multi-stakeholder input and engagement.

Industries are concerned about the translation of innovations into usable products, a task that can benefit from translational professionals familiar with cross-disciplinary approaches who can upscale knowledge translation across a complex health system.

Finally, patient outcomes, a hallmark goal in all health science scholarship, will benefit from multilevel, cross-disciplinary research that considers wellness needs from initial research design to implementation and uptake of innovation at a systemic level.

## 10.4 The Emerging Learning Model

A conceptual framework is essential to allow the emergence of a shared mental model [6, 7] among various internal and external stakeholders regarding our approach to educating future translational health scientists able to manage complex challenges. Three main elements form the basis of the complex adaptive learning model for this Translational Health Science program. The complex adaptive characteristics outlined in Table 10.2 challenge the traditional doctoral training; however, they provide a scaffold for learners to perceive and approach solutions to problems in a systemic environment. The model entails three unique characteristics:

- **Oscillations between subjectivism (problem-solving) and objectivism (hypothesis testing)**—These dichotomies are indicated by the brackets serving as boundaries between the problem-solving approach and hypothesis testing approaches.
- **Scaffolding of collaborative, integrative, and transformational learning**— The complex adaptive learning characteristics are represented by the transcending spring helix within the model. Ideally, the scaffolding of pedagogical approaches will combine to create a transformational learning experience.
- **From a basic science to translational learning approach**—The progression from a basic science approach to a more translational approach is indicated by the upward arrow within the helix with these labels.

Figure 10.1 depicts this learning model and its three unique characteristics. It emphasizes the progression toward a perspective of transformative learning and research aimed at achieving socially impactful solutions to complex problems. The subsequent discussion addresses the inherent tensions contributing to model development.

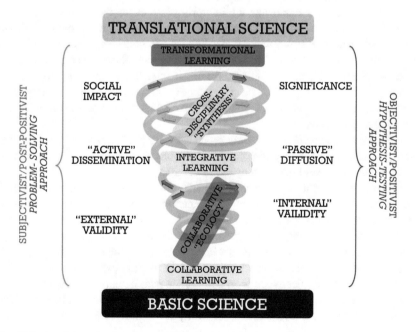

**Fig. 10.1** A collaborative learning model for Translational Health Sciences [4]

## 10.5    The "Hidden" Creative Tensions in the Model

While this model challenges the *status quo* and may make some feel anxious to move forward, it excites by creating creative tensions to accelerate the process.

### 10.5.1    Epistemological Tensions

The need to consider an expanded epistemological spectrum in Translational Health Sciences stems from the indelible characteristics of paradigmatic selection that has its roots in historical models of normal sciences [8]. Several normal sciences contribute to the array of translational health inquiry including but not limited to biology, chemistry, and physics. Within health sciences, the strands of science at work in understanding the human condition often intertwine in ways; as Jürgen Habermas has described, these represent several operative conditions that make up an expanded epistemological interest typology including the natural (technical), interpretive (practical), and critical (emancipatory) sciences, all of which are key to integrated health science inquiry.

The Habermasian *knowledge interest typology* provides clearer pairings of scientific interest with dominant epistemological lenses and methods while simultaneously recognizing their individual contributions [9]. Holistic healthcare, and the research that informs it, relies on conversations among the technical, narrative, practical, social, and emancipatory interests of science; ultimately such cross-paradigmatic conversations will produce new and novel technical, theoretical, and processual outcomes. From this perspective, we can consider personalized health, environmental factors to health, and the sociology of illness through a blending of paradigmatic interests drawing from normal science but not completely bound to any one science's limited scope. Epistemological paradigms serve to encourage receptivity to the potential of chaos and complexity in research activity and knowledge generation [10].

Paradigms of knowledge not only represent different scientific lenses, but they also symbolize ideological and political viewpoints that, as in all research, contain biases requiring careful attention by the researcher.

Quasi-experimental, experimental, and naturalistic approaches all contain political biases by nature as by their rules of engagement, they all focus their aperture on only small increments of the natural world. The act of choosing a paradigmatic lens for which to conduct inquiry serves as a mechanism for framing the knowledge that one hopes to acquire through research [11]. In health science research, certain paradigms prevail as more appropriate for certain expected outcomes. For instance, positivism/objectivism is an appropriate paradigmatic lens for conducting randomized controlled trials and even for conducting social surveys because these can be quantified to achieve potential reliability and to provide deterministic results.

In contrast, health science has incorporated constructivist paradigms like subjectivism, post-positivism, and critical theory that dislodge positivism, allowing for naturalistic knowledge to emerge from human experience. Analyzed and interpreted, these experiences inform how complex adaptive systems' understandings might reveal multiple insights into a problem, which in turn reinforces the need for a cross-disciplinary approach to inquiry.

Health science research can afford to look to different approaches as research designs evolve that solve more complex problems beyond those that can be normally solved through any one epistemological paradigm or within the boundaries of any one normal science [11]. The blending of research paradigms is representative of the complex process required to reach desired goals.

For these reasons, we believe skills that encourage scholars to oscillate between the extremes of the paradigmatic spectrum are an essential aspect to recognizing the relationship between different types of research and their models and methods. Recognizing the value of a cross-paradigmatic approach will assist future researchers in informing knowledge building in a complex adaptive world.

### 10.5.2   Impact: Significant or Social?

In a similar strain to the tension between deterministic and more subjectivist paradigms, measures of the value of research and its ability to impact intended audiences need to be considered if research is to be truly translational in character.

Significance, as a scientific term, is used in a specific way to indicate a measure of certainty as it applies to results often based in experimental or semi-experimental inquiries. Its meaning in naturalistic approaches differs greatly, as, by definition, naturalistic inquiry does not claim determinism as a goal. In the health sciences, "clinical significance," for instance, describes the extent to which a measure quantifies the impact of services [12] and treatment and/or quality of life [13]. In training future translational health scientists to negotiate the relationship between these approaches, competence must include skills in how to manage multiple meanings of significance in research.

As an alternative to the more reductionist measures that dominate some biomedical research, Translational Health Science depends equally on scientific significance as well as social impact. Health science research which emphasizes the translation of basic, human, clinical, social, and policy sciences to products must consider the effectiveness of research to move beyond quantitative significance to a measure that includes the potential and innovative qualities that allow for research to impact human health and wellness. Here additional emphasis is on the effect of an activity on one or more populations of a community and the well-being of individuals and groups.

The need for ensuring social impact in health science is not oppositional to supplying significance in research findings. Rather, social impact is a partner element in translational research as it serves as the tangible outcome that affects change through discoveries that are delivered to a needed public, population, or even professional community. Such products can be in the form of content analyses, software, healthcare technologies, public awareness campaigns, and teaching contributions [14] all of which depend equally on evidentiary science and the value of discovery to benefit society.

While research-intensive doctoral studies typically have not extended findings to this applied level, they have raised awareness of the need to incorporate methods and measures of the potential of discovery to impact health standards and quality. All phases of health research are required to consider what the social impact of research might be no matter what phase of the translational spectrum is in focus at a given time. The nature of multiphase translational research, in which basic human, clinical, and applied attributes of science inform one another simultaneously, illustrates the reciprocal nature of integrating various disciplinary and epistemological viewpoints.

Partnering of social impact and scientific significance will be a fundamental element to the doctoral dissertation process, so that the evidence-based biomedical sciences which often focus on deterministic factors can be paired with health sciences to accomplish pathways that impact humans and populations.

### 10.5.3   Credibility and Relevance

Focusing on measures of impact that research might have on the environment and the potential population health leads us to consider the validity of research for scientific inquiry and implementation.

Credibility is ultimately a combination of factors that contributes to the relationship between a source of knowledge and its trustworthiness considering its application [15]. Science relies on methods that assist in ensuring either that findings have been tested by some rigor of scientifically designed testing or that the new knowledge is relevant by nature of its ability to describe human and/or natural experiences [9].

Scientists often exploit credibility and relevance to convey the appropriate application of naturalistic or experimental findings. In other words, dependent on the epistemological stance, scientists assess the credibility of research on the reliability of the data collected either in vivo or in vitro. Ultimately, trustworthiness of this translation relies heavily upon the extent of the researcher's skills [16].

In Translational Health Science research, a combination of external and internal validity factors is more commonplace than in other more unidisciplinary sciences. No matter if they are more experimental, quasi-experimental, or naturalistic, in nature, basic discoveries depend greatly on internal validity grounded in the techniques and standards of host disciplines. These are often those sciences that dwell in the basic and exploratory regions of the translational spectrum (T0–T2). Conversely, external validity that strives to ensure that the scientific enterprise is in concert with external factors of implementation and application (T3–T4) is far less prone to identification and controlling factors and may provide alternative explanations for results [15]. Such sources of certainty, bias, and possible error need to be triangulated on a regular basis so that measurement of validity [17] for the real world, and feasibility of delivery to the targeted populations, is a constant goal for research findings no matter where on the translational spectrum such science dwells naturally [18].

The ability to translate evidence-based science to implementable results and products requires reporting factors that might influence external validity and ultimate uptake, such as dosage, time requirements, cost, training and certification, interdependencies, etc. This task of the research process can be challenging especially when hypothesis-testing research is normative to the discipline of the post-professional doctoral trainee. Trainees from a more controlled research environment with its focus on internal validity might find the creative task of ensuring both external and internal validity in research design and application challenging [19].

This Translational Health Sciences training program will guide doctoral students to synthesize and integrate these sometimes seemingly oppositional research frameworks. Collaborative and integrative learning principles and activities will expose students to the continuum represented by these mind models and their contributions to Translational Health Sciences. Thus, students will be exposed to increasingly higher levels of scholarly consideration.

## 10.5.4   Collaborative Dynamics

As a core concept, collaboration serves as the vehicle by which much of the translational process might successfully occur. Collaborative teaming is much of cross-disciplinary science and the skills required to perform under these unique conditions is a key aspect of learning. Much attention has been given to the mechanisms of collaboration as it is applied to health science outcomes [20–22].

Of particular note is the emphasis on the building blocks of teaming in science that draw our attention to an ecology that highlights:

- The practical aspects of interpersonal relationships between scientific stakeholders
- The intrapersonal factors of individual readiness and disposition to collaboration
- The organizational factors necessary that foster and support collaboration
- The growing technologic factors that continually impact science and research especially in teams
- The physical environments in which people work
- The sociopolitical climate that challenges and/or supports collaboration [21]

This seemingly complex set of concerns is only a starting point for doctoral students who hope to be able to engage in higher-order systems thinking, as they consider socially relevant and impactful research topics. This is achieved by building competencies in several important areas that allows doctoral students to gain the necessary confidence to emulate these in their scholarly work. These include growing in knowledge, skills, and abilities toward teaming, developing appropriate attitudes and growing in readiness to accept cooperative acumen, the ability to coordinate and to be part of a coordinating group, advanced skills in communication, cognitive abilities and maturity that lead to shared mental models, leadership insights, and an awareness of one's social and environmental conditions [23, 24].

Collaborative abilities are requisite skills, and their development will facilitate the performance of complex details associated with conducting cross-disciplinary research [25]. Systems thinking emphasizes the interrelationships among stakeholders within complex systems, such as healthcare systems [26, 27]. A systems approach to problem-solving and knowledge generation in healthcare is essential to anticipate how interactions among system stakeholders influence knowledge generation, implementation, and dissemination [27]. Adopting a systems approach when engaging in collaborative problem-solving and knowledge generation allows teams to recognize the value of multi-stakeholder representation in research. This in turn is a prerequisite to integrate diverse stakeholder voices into plans for future implementation and dissemination of innovations, which is ultimately required to ensure the systemic uptake of the newly generated knowledge [28].

Doctoral research that hopes to achieve high social impact and relevance must acknowledge the complexity in the healthcare system and seek to address the interrelationships among systems components by adopting collaborative, cross-disciplinary approaches that anticipate the potential impact new knowledge might have for stakeholders across the translational spectrum.

## 10.6   Conclusion

Going forward, our model will help to communicate the complex dynamics inherent within our program of study across various system stakeholders. It also helps support our reliance upon a team approach to course and curriculum design. Our next steps include evaluating the degree to which the model was applied in curriculum and course design and the resulting efficacy of this contribution. In our first semester, we have integrated a complex systems approach, through concepts such as stakeholder analysis, systems mapping, and influence diagrams, with critical components of collaborative dynamics, such as perspective differentiation and integration, and collaborative and team characteristics and principles. Artifacts from the semester indicate how students are operationalizing the tensions we have recognized and addressed within our model. Yet, it remains to be seen, and assessed, as to how this interdisciplinary integration will contribute to the achievement of semester competencies and overarching program goals.

This paper details our application of a complex adaptive systems lens to the task of designing a PhD program for future translational health scientists. Recognizing and addressing the needs of various system stakeholders prior to designing our conceptual model was essential to ensuring we achieved shared understanding of the tensions inherent in working toward our goal of developing translational researchers, particularly for faculty charged with curriculum design. As we are only two semesters into our first cohort of students, we cannot yet discern progress toward our end goal of research designed for systemic uptake and greater social impact. However, our students' application of complexity concepts within the first semester of the program indicates their recognition of the value of adopting a complexity lens to fully explore tensions inherent within healthcare system that may serve as barriers or facilitators to future research and knowledge generation, which is a critical step in considering how to design future research which navigates those tensions for systematic uptake of findings. While further assessment is needed regarding the relationship between our model and achievement of program goals, this application indicates we are on the right path toward educating future researchers who can apply complexity concepts for problem exploration and future research design.

## The Journey

I first encountered complexity theory in my doctoral studies. As a former naval officer with a minor in engineering, systems thinking came naturally. However, the concepts related to complex systems—self-organization, emergence, adaptation, unpredictable outcomes, minimum specifications—were initially a bit harder to grasp. But, when I started to work on my dissertation in blended learning, the increased complexity in the learning environment and the adaptation it would require on the part of the learner made the concepts of "minimum specification" and "unpredictable outcomes" more poignant when considering how to design systems that would allow for maximum adaptation but still support achievement of learning outcomes. From this point on, I could not look on a learning or leadership situation without questioning how a complexity lens might influence my approach to facilitation and problem-solving.

Later, when teaching leadership and change to healthcare professionals, I recognized the importance of teaching a complex systems perspective to problem exploration and resolution. Like me, so many of the healthcare leaders found static models of leadership and change limiting and found a complexity lens beneficial to anticipating the tensions within a system that might serve as barriers to change and innovation. For this reason, when I was designing the curriculum for our new PhD in Translational Health Sciences, I knew that a complex systems approach must be integrated at the beginning of the curriculum to encourage students to explore problems from a new lens from the very beginning of their program of study. Already, we have seen how this approach has influenced their discussions of stakeholder interdependence and barriers to change and innovation within health systems. I look forward to seeing what emerges from the minimum specifications we have provided! (Paige McDonald)

When I started my career investigating the science of team science (SciTS), I naturally gravitated toward cross-disciplinary knowledge generation and attempted to pair these fields of study. The origins of transdisciplinarity grounded in social learning and globalization fueled my interest in how we might train a new generation of translational scientists who are versed in crossing disciplinary boundaries as they attempt to solve wicked health problems while working in collaborative scientific teams. The intellectual and learning journey I am presently on has brought me to appreciate that collaboration and cross-disciplinary science exists as both complementary and conflicting constructs. Complexity science serves as a means that I might make sense of this relationship. Complexity science provides the framework by which to understand these reciprocal relationships and serves as a useful knowledge arena for new scientists to understand how they might successfully achieve these goals and generates new knowledge to inform practice in the ever-changing healthcare landscape we live in. (Gaetano Lotrecchiano)

Take-Home Message

- Adopting a complexity lens for exploring the task of developing a PHD program is essential to ensuring buy-in from many internal and external system stakeholders.
- Designing the PhD program required negotiating multiple, perhaps contradictory, stakeholder needs.
- Creating a model of the tensions negotiated within the program of study proved critical to promoting shared understanding among faculty of the task at hand.
- The learning model proposed adopts core tenets of complexity science that allow for minimal structure and emergence to serve students as they evolve in their perceptions of cross-disciplinary and collaborative science and scholarship.

# References

1. Lotrecchiano GR, McDonald PL, Corcoran M, Harwood K, Ekmekci O. Learning theory, operative model and challenges in developing a framework for collaborative, translational and implementable doctoral research. In: 9th annual international conference of education, research and innovation, Seville, November, 2016. ISI Conference Proceedings Citation Index.
2. Hesse-Biber S. Doing interdisciplinary mixed methods health care research: working the boundaries, tensions, and synergistic potential of team-based research. Qual Health Res. 2016;26(5):649–58.
3. Drolet BC, Lorenzi NM. Translational research: understanding the continuum from bench to bedside. Transl Res. 2011;157(1):1–5.

4. PhD in translational health sciences handbook. The George Washington University School of Medicine and Health Sciences. 2017. https://smhs.gwu.edu/translational-health-sciences/sites/translational-health-sciences/files/Handbook04-28-2017FINAL.pdf.
5. Schulman L. Signature pedagogies in the professions. Daedalus. 2005;134(3):52–9.
6. Cannon-Bowers J, Salas E, Converse S. Shared mental models in expert team decision making. In: Castellan N, editor. Current issues in individual and group decision making. Mahwah, NJ: Erlbaum; 1993. p. 221–46.
7. Ross LF, Loup A, Nelson RM, Botkin JR, Kost R, Smith GR, et al. The challenges of collaboration for academic and community partners in a research partnership: points to consider. J Empir Res Hum Res Ethics. 2010;5(1):19–31.
8. Kuhn TS. The structure of scientific revolutions. 2nd ed. Chicago: University of Chicago Press; 1970.
9. Habermas J. Theory and practice. Boston, MA: Beacon Press; 1973.
10. Sturmberg J, Martin C. Handbook of systems and complexity in health. New York: Springer; 2013.
11. Broom A, Willis, E. Competing paradigms and health research. In: Saks M, Allsop J, editors. Researching health: qualitative, quantitative and mixed methods. London: Sage; 2007.
12. Sloan J, Cella D, Frost M, Guyatt G, Sprangers M, Symonds, T. Assessing clinical significance in measuring oncology patient quality of life: introduction to the symposium, content overview, and definition of terms. Mayo Clin Proc. 2002;77(4):367–70.
13. Guyatt D, Osoba A, Wu K, Wyrwich KW, Norman G. Methods to explain the clinical significance of health status measures. Mayo Clin. Proc. 2002;77(4):371–83.
14. Smith R. Measuring the social impact of research. BMJ [Br Med J]. 2001;323323(7312):528.
15. Bocking S. Nature's experts: science, politics, and the environment. New Brunswick, NJ: Rutgers University Press; 2004.
16. Lincoln YS, Guba EG. Naturalistic inquiry. Newbury Park, CA: Sage; 1985.
17. Brewer M. Research design and issues of validity. In: Reis H, Judd C, editors. Handbook of research methods in social and personality psychology. Cambridge: Cambridge University Press; 2000.
18. Mitchell M, Jolley J. Research design explained. New York: Harcourt; 2001.
19. Whittemore R, Chase S, Mandle C. Validity in qualitative research. Qual Health Res. 2001;11(4):522–37.
20. Hall K, Feng A, Moser R, Stokols D, Taylor B. Moving the science of team science forward: Collaboration and creativity. Am J Community Psychol. 2008;35(2 Suppl):S243–49.
21. Stokols D, Misra S, Moser R, Hall K, Taylor B. The ecology of team science understanding contextual influences on transdisciplinary collaboration. Am J Prev Med. 2008;35(2 Suppl):S96–115.
22. Falk-Krzesinski H, Contractor N, Fiore S, Hall K, Kane C, Keyton J, et al. Mapping a research agenda for the science of team science. Res Eval. 2011;20(2):145–58.
23. Salazar M, Lant T, Fiore S, Salas E. Facilitating innovation in diverse science teams through integrative capacity. Small Group Res. 2012;43(5):527–58.
24. Salas E, Shuffler M, Thayer A, Bedwell W, Lazzarra E. Understanding and improving teamwork in organizations: a scientifically based practical guide. Hum Resour Manag. 2015;54(4):599–622.
25. Hess D. Medical modernization, scientific research fields and the epistemic politics of health social movements. Sociol Health Illn. 2004;26(6):695–709.
26. Norman C. Teaching systems thinking and complexity theory in health sciences. J Eval Clin Pract. 2013;19(6):1087–89.
27. Hawe P. Lessons from complex interventions to improve health. Annu Rev Public Health. 2015;36:307–23.
28. Tsasis P, Evans J, Owen S. Reframing the challenges to integrated care: a complex-adaptive systems perspective. Int J Integr Care. 2012;12:e190.

# Chapter 11
# Complexity of Knowledge in Primary Care: Understanding the Discipline's Requisite Knowledge—A Bibliometric Study

**Frauke Dunkel and Martin Konitzer**

## 11.1 Starting the Quest to Understand the Requisite Knowledge for Family Medicine

When I did my family medicine internship over 10 years ago, my tutor was reviewing the German version of Zollo's book *Fragen und Antworten zur Allgemein-medizin.* "*Medical Secrets*" (Questions and Answers about General Practice/Family Medicine. "Medical Secrets") [1] for some academic teaching journal [2]. So we talked about exam questions and medical knowledge, and skimming through Zollo's book, I found this table that aroused my interest (Table 11.1, first two columns from Zollo, 685p).

This table showed the ranking of *reasons for encounter* from the patient's point of view compared to that of their treating physicians. The book is nothing more than a catalogue of "need-to-know" questions and answers claiming—ironically—to entail the discipline's "Medical Secrets". Zollo's book title intimates that it conveys all of the essential knowledge required by a general practitioner/family physician (GP/FM). He implies that his book embraces the patient's perception of his illness and that it provides the clinician with the requisite skills to manage the patient's illnesses from his perspective.

However, the book's order and emphasis do not embrace the epidemiology of *reason for encounter* of either the patient or the clinician; rather it follows the

F. Dunkel
Praxis Drs Sieker, Rudolf-Breitscheid- Straße 1, D 06502 Thale, Germany
e-mail: frauke.dunkel@googlemail.com

M. Konitzer (✉)
Academic Teaching Practice, Medizinische Hochschule Hannover, Bahnhofstr. 5,
29690 Schwarmstedt, Germany
e-mail: m-konitzer@t-online.de

© Springer International Publishing AG, part of Springer Nature 2018
J. P. Sturmberg (ed.), *Putting Systems and Complexity Sciences Into Practice*,
https://doi.org/10.1007/978-3-319-73636-5_11

**Table 11.1** *Reasons for encounter*—The malalignment between patients', clinicians' and educators' perceptions

| Reasons for encounter—the patient's view | Reasons for encounter—the clinician's view | Content of Zollo's book |
|---|---|---|
| 1. General medical examination | 1. Essential hypertension | 1. Overview of internal medicine's conditions |
| 2. Hypertension | 2. Diabetes mellitus | 2. Endocrinology |
| 3. Progress visit, no other symptoms | 3. Chronic ischemic heart disease | 3. Cardiology |
| 4. Chest pain and related symptoms | 4. Acute upper respiratory infection | 4. Infectious diseases |
| 5. Cough | 5. General medical examination | 5. Gastroenterology |
| 6. Blood pressure test | 6. Osteoarthritis and allied diseases | 6. Oncology |
| 7. Diabetes mellitus | 7. General symptoms | 7. Nephrology |
| 8. Symptoms referable to the throat | 8. Chronic airways obstruction | 8. Haematology |
| 9. Abdominal pain, cramps, spasms | 9. Asthma | 9. Pneumonology |
| 10. Headache, pain in the head | 10. Bronchitis | 10. Rheumatology |
| 11. Upper respiratory infection (head cold, coryza) | 11. Neurotic disorders | 11. Allergology/immunology |
| 12. Back symptoms | 12. Angina pectoris | 12. Neurology |
| 13. Vertigo, dizziness | 13. Chronic sinusitis | 13. The consultation |
| 14. Shortness of breath | 14. Acute pharyngitis | 14. Primary care |
| 15. Tiredness, exhaustion | 15. Cardiac dysrhythmia | 15. Geriatrics |
| 16. Leg symptoms | 16. Miscellaneous (diagnosis missing or illegible) | |
| 17. Shoulder symptoms | 17. Other disorders of soft tissue | |
| 18. Neck symptoms | 18. Other respiratory symptoms | |
| 19. Ischaemic heart disease | 19. Peripheral enthesiopathies | |

"classical" discipline-focused textbook approach with its focus on organs and their pathologies (Table 11.1, third column from Zollo, 5pp).

As a family medicine resident, this table evoked a great deal of dissonance, does the discipline really have three sources of knowledge:

- One arising from the epidemiology of *reasons of encounter*
- One given by the weights attributed to them by the "experienced physician"
- One that satisfies examiners of students and vocational trainees

This observation of a possible *triple knowledge* about family medicine raised the following research question (and became the topic of my PhD project):

What kind of relationship exists between the epidemiology of illness experience, a GP's/FP's knowledge base to manage those illnesses and the knowledge expected of vocational trainees as represented in Family Medicine's vocational exam questions?

## 11.2 What Was Known?

Preliminary reading of the literature showed no data to directly compare the family medicine training programmes and examination formats either between European countries or internationally with, e.g. the USA or Australia.

### 11.2.1 Towards a Theoretical Framework

This study developed a theoretical framework based on empirically derived data, heuristics and data extracted from actual specialist examinations.

- **Empirical data**
  In the absence of empirical studies, a normative article by Braun and Halhuber [3] offered a "functional clinical thought and action framework based on clinical experiences", an approach that proved to be reliable even in the absence of "clinical disease".
- **Study samples**
  Examination questions from two German states[1]—Lower Saxony and Bavaria— were collected for comparison purposes and correlated to three paradigmatic frameworks of family medicine: Balint's relationship theory, Braun's professional theory and Cochrane's evidence-based medicine.
- **Exam topic clusters**
  Seven of the ten most common topics covered in the specialist exams in Lower Saxony and Bavaria (Table 11.2) show clustering around two threads— prevention (measles, vaccinations, undescended testis) and chronic disease (diabetes, hypertension, osteoporosis and elderly patients).
  The two samples are comparable across the seven most frequent topic domains— note the overlaps of topics of prevention with osteoporosis and geriatrics with diabetes.
  However, the 10 topics of the examination are twice as frequently in Bavaria compared to Lower Saxony.

---

[1]GP vocational examinations in Germany.
Because of the country's federal structure, the format of the vocational examination differs slightly between states but has a common structure: its format is oral, takes place at the local boards and lasts 40 min. The panel consists of three examiners (a chair from another speciality and two general practitioners). Questions are introduced in the form of patient-centred vignettes. As the number of main topics is limited, case vignettes are similar across exams. The questions about the case cover multiple clinical domains.

**Table 11.2** Exam inventory—ranking of topics, frequency of questions and consistency across exams

| Ranking of topics (Lower saxony 2005–2006) | No of questions[a] (%) | Consistency of topic across exams[b] | Ranking of topics (Bavaria 2003–2005) | No of questions[c] (%) | Consistency of topic across exams[d] |
|---|---|---|---|---|---|
| Diabetes mellitus—Types I and II | 50 (2.8%) | 18.6% | Acute coronary syndrome | 35 (10.0%) | 140% |
| Hypertension | 42 (2.4%) | 15.6% | Prevention (osteoporosis) | 34 (9.7%) | 38% |
| Measles | 37 (2.1%) | 13.7% | Geriatrics (Type II diabetes) | 26 (7.4%) | 29% |
| Signs of death | 35 (2.0%) | 13.0% | Vaccinations | 14 (4.0%) | 16% |
| Acute coronary syndrome | 34 (1.9%) | 12.6% | Measles | 10 (2.8%) | 11% |
| Vaccinations | 32 (1.8%) | 11.8% | Hypertension | 10 (2.8%) | 11% |
| Prevention (osteoporosis) | 31 (1.7%) | 11.5% | Diabetes mellitus–Types I and II | 6 (1.7%) | 7% |
| Geriatrics (Type II diabetes) | 29 (1.6%) | 10.7% | Lyme disease | 4 (1.1%) | 4% |
| Undescended testes | 28 (1.6%) | 10.4% | Undescended testes | – | – |
| Lyme disease | 27 (1.5%) | 10.0% | Signs of death | – | – |
| Total | 345 (19%) | | | 139 (40%) | |

[a]1778 questions
[b]269 examinations
[c]350 questions
[d]89 examinations

## 11.3 The New Approach: Professional Levels, Equivalents of Knowledge, and Bibliometric Method

A different approach to understanding the knowledge of GP/FM was inspired by a sociological perspective. Complexity of professional knowledge, as addressed by Abbott [4], means that each professional level of expertise repeats the knowledge of the profession fractally. Importantly distribution patterns of topics of the overall expertise are repeated by the distribution pattern between the "levels of expertise" in a self-similar fashion.

Based on the considerations by the German Association of Family Medicine (DEGAM) [5] and Braun [6], the knowledge base of GP/FM can be framed from three different perspectives (or domains):

1. Its underlying scientific basis
2. Its praxis
3. Its epidemiology

Based on these different perspectives, one would expect different levels of concordance between the topics explored in the exam and the GP/FM knowledge base assessed.

### 11.3.1 New Questions Emerged

These considerations raised four new questions:

1. Are there differences between exam topics and knowledge domains?
2. Which domain shows the highest level of concordance with the exam topics?
3. Are there "nested hierarchies" within some of the domains' knowledge that repeat themselves in a fractal pattern?
4. What can be said about the quality of the vocational exam based on the distribution of the topics covered in the exam?

These questions have been methodologically approached based on grounded theory (GT) as described by Strauß [7] and further refined by Reichertz [8]. GT arose in the qualitative domains of social research to explore and categorise the content of interviews and conversations—in this context, exam questions. GT organises materials based on their inherent properties (grounded) and then interprets these for their meaning (theory).

This approach uses deductive, inductive and abductive reasoning (as described by Reichertz [8]) to interpret the material and to reach logical and reproducible conclusions. This will be further explored in Sect. 11.6 in relation to this research.

It is not surprising that Strauß pointed to the usefulness of this method to reduce and understand complexities. This study aimed to discover "inherent patterns" in the "conversations of the examination material" and quantified by bibliometric approaches.

Bibliometrics[2] is a method to compare textual elements—in this study the comparison between examination topics and the knowledge domains of GP/FM [9]. The evaluation is carried out by comparing the fit between the exams' knowledge domains against its body of knowledge (pages in a textbook, frequency of topic in journals/year and general practice conferences [9]).

If there is a high concordance between the exam content and the discipline's underlying textual corpora in its scientific, praxis and epidemiological texts, it is worthwhile to compare these similarities quantitatively. High concordance between two comparative text corpora has been defined by Zipf [10] as "least effort" and by Polanyi [11] as the "law of poverty"; both terms arose in quantitative linguistics.

Quantitative linguistics [12] has shown that fictional and non-fictional texts have a fractal structure. Their constituent elements (letters, words, punctuation marks,

---

[2]Bibliometrics is the statistical analysis of written publications, typically used to explore the impact of those publications on the development of the field.

etc.) have a repetitive pattern, where the patterns at every scale repeat that of the whole text in a self-similar way.

Fractal linguistics states that concordance between a reference text (here the exam question catalogue) and a comparative text (here the discipline's main textbooks, guidelines, journal and conference contributions) is greater if a smaller rather than a larger amount of comparative text is needed to show concordance. Put differently, if a small amount of comparative text already shows the fractal pattern of self-similarity with the reference text, it conveys this message with the "least effort".

### 11.3.2  Comparing Corpora

The exam topics of the Lower Saxony and Bavarian general practice specialist examination were analysed for the knowledge covered across its professional domains: science, praxis and epidemiology. Comparative corpora, according to Fleck [13], include textbooks, periodicals and abstracts. The resources examined included:

- Science

  1. Textbooks
     For the period 2004–2007, "Google Books Ngram Viewer" [14] identified Kochen [5] and Mader and Weißgerber [15] as the most commonly used textbooks. According to N. Donner-Banzhoff, these textbooks can be taken as examples of the two main mental models of family medicine—a "strictly EBM" (anglophil or "atlantic") (Kochen [5]) and a "professional theory" ("continental")-oriented framework (Braun and Mader [16]) that remains influential in Germany and many European countries [17].
  2. Journal articles and abstracts
     For 2004–2007, we drew on the ZfA[3]-Archive [18] and the ZfA-Abstracts of the DEGAM Congresses 2004–2007 [19] as representing the leading periodical and congress of German family medicine.

- Praxis
  The corpora describing the praxis of GP/FM include DEGAM guidelines [20], European EBM guidelines for family medicine [21], the diagnostic protocols according to Braun's continental "Berufstheorie" [6] and a question bank generated by examiner participant observers [15].

---

[3]ZfA—Zeitschrift für Allgemeinmedizin is the Official German General Practice/Family Medicine Journal.

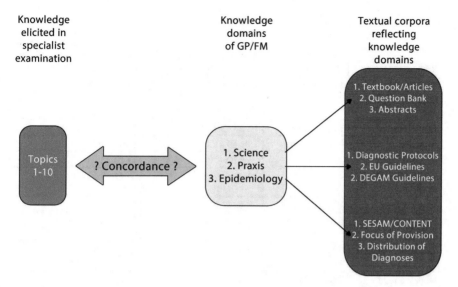

Fig. 11.1 HOW much are the exam questions concordant with the disciplines principle knowledge. For an examination (green box) to be valid, it has to represent its knowledge domains (yellow box) through its written textual *corpora* (red box)

- Epidemiology

  The epidemiology of German GP/FM was extracted from the *CONTinuous morbidity registration Epidemiologic NeTwork* (CONTENT) study [22] for the time period 2004–2007 and from the *Sächsische Epidemiologische Studien in der Allgemeinmedizin* (SESAM) [23] for the period 1999–2002.

  Figure 11.1 summarises the research question highlighting HOW much are the exam questions concordant with the discipline's principle knowledge base as mapped against its knowledge resources.

## 11.4 Outcomes

The concordance of examination questions to the GP/FM knowledge base is summarised in the following tables, and important deviations are highlighted.

### 11.4.1 Science

The science-based knowledge domains have been separately analysed for each source.

**Table 11.3** Coverage of exam domains in textbooks

| Ranking of topics | Kochen[a] [5] No of pages (%) | Mader and Weißgerber[b] [15] No of pages (%) | Mader/Weißgerber[c]—need-to-know-questions [15] No of questions (%) |
|---|---|---|---|
| Diabetes mellitus—Types I and II | 12 pp (1.92%) | 15 pp (3.08%) | 48 (3.27%) |
| Hypertension | 12 pp (1.92%) | 10 pp (2.05%) | 23 (1.57%) |
| Measles | 4 pp (0.64%) | 2 pp (0.41%) | 5 (0.34%) |
| Signs of death | – | 2 pp (0.41%) | 11 (0.75%) |
| Acute coronary syndrome | 4 pp (0.64%) | 12 pp (2.46%) | 21 (1.43%) |
| Vaccinations | 17 pp (2.72%) | 18 pp (3.69%) | 19 (1.15%) |
| Prevention (osteoporosis) | 6 pp (0.96%) | 4 pp (0.82%) | 24 (1.46%) |
| Geriatrics (Type II diabetes) | 30 pp (4.81%) | 1 p (0.20%) | 20 (1.21%) |
| Undescended testes | 2 pp (0.34%) | 1 p (0.20%) | 5 (0.34%) |
| Lyme disease | 4 pp (0.64%) | 2 pp (0.41%) | 11 (0.75%) |
| Total | 91 pp (14.58%) | 67 pp (13.75%) | 187 (12.75%) |

[a]624 pages
[b]487 pages
[c]1467 questions

1. Textbooks (Table 11.3)

   Both of the textbooks cover all of the topics. The top topics diabetes and hypertension are described in both textbooks [5, 15]. There are differences in the composition of other high ranks.

   Signs of death are absent but geriatrics are more extensively dealt with by Kochen [5], while myocardial infarction is more extensively dealt with by Mader and Weißgerber [15]. Mader's question bank does not cover his textbook content evenly as its questions were generated by the authors as examiner participant observers. Therefore its content—though incorporated inside a textbook—reflects praxis knowledge. The top 10 exam topics are covered by 13% of this question bank.

2. ZfA journal articles 2004–2007 (Table 11.4)

   Four of the ten top examination topics are covered in all 4 years of the observation period, and two are covered in 2 of the 4 years, and three domains are not covered at all. The journal provides extensive coverage of osteoporosis (overlapping with prevention) and to a lesser extent geriatrics (overlapping with Type II diabetes). Notably, prevention (rank 7) and geriatrics (rank 8) are significantly overrepresented in the journal. Despite this skewed distribution, 13–26% of the journal articles covered the top 10 examination topics through 2004–2007.

**Table 11.4** Coverage of exam domains in ZfA publications

| Ranking of topics | ZfA 2004[a] | ZfA 2005[b] | ZfA 2006[c] | ZfA 2007[d] |
|---|---|---|---|---|
| Diabetes mellitus—Types I and II | 3 | 2 | 1 | 3 |
| Hypertension | 2 | | 2 | |
| Measles | | | | |
| Signs of death | | | | |
| Acute coronary syndrome | 1 | | 1 | |
| Vaccinations | 1 | 1 | 1 | 3 |
| Prevention (osteoporosis) | 12 | 6 | 8 | 6 |
| Geriatrics (Type II diabetes) | 1 | 6 | 1 | 5 |
| Undescended testes | | | | |
| Lyme disease | | | | 1 |
| | 26% | 13% | 14% | 20% |

[a]76 articles
[b]111 articles
[c]99 articles
[d]90 articles

**Table 11.5** Coverage of exam domains at DEGAM meetings

| Ranking of topics | DEGAM abstracts 2004[a] | DEGAM abstracts 2005[b] | DEGAM abstracts 2006[c] | DEGAM abstracts 2007[d] |
|---|---|---|---|---|
| Diabetes mellitus—Types I and II | 2 | 1 | 2 | 5 |
| Hypertension | 2 | 4 | 3 | 1 |
| Measles | | | | |
| Signs of death | | | | |
| Acute coronary syndrome | 1 | 1 | 1 | 1 |
| Vaccinations | | | | 1 |
| Prevention (osteoporosis) | 5 | 9 | 8 | 13 |
| Geriatrics (Type II diabetes) | 4 | 7 | 8 | 10 |
| Undescended testes | | | | |
| Lyme disease | | | | |
| | 19% | 30% | 29% | 40% |

[a]80 abstracts
[b]74 abstracts
[c]76 abstracts
[d]78 abstracts

3. DEGAM conference abstracts 2004–2007 (Table 11.5)

   Five of the top 10 topics are covered at every conference, one topic is covered once, and four are not covered at all. Again, prevention (rank 7) and geriatrics (rank 8) are significantly overrepresented. 19–40% of the conference presentations covered the top 10 examinations from 2004–2007.

## 11.4.2    Praxis

The praxis of GP/FM covered by the top 10 exam topics has been compared to the DEGAM [20] and EBM guidelines [21] as well as Braun and Mader's [16] diagnostic protocols (Table 11.6).

Probably unsurprisingly, DEGAM [20] and EBM guidelines [21] covered the praxis of GP/FM by means of only 5% and 8% of the page numbers, respectively. Braun and Mader's [16] diagnostic protocols, while covering eight of the ten top examination topics, dealt with the praxis of GP/FM in 15% (Table 11.6).

**Table 11.6**  Coverage of exam domains in guidelines and diagnostic protocols

| Ranking of topics | DEGAM-LL guidelines[a] [20] | EBM guidelines family medicine[b] [21] | Diagnostic protocols[c] 2005 [16] |
|---|---|---|---|
| Diabetes mellitus—Types I and II | GL4-1 GL8-1 GL9-1 | 40 | 7 |
| Hypertension | GL4-1 GL8-1 GL9-1 | 19 | 7 |
| Measles | | 2 | 1 |
| Signs of death | | 2 | |
| Acute coronary syndrome | GL8-1 GL9-2 | 24 | 84 |
| Vaccinations | | 7 | 1 |
| Prevention (osteoporosis) | GL4-1 | 17 | 3 |
| Geriatrics (Type II diabetes) | GL4-1 GL6-2 GL9-1 | 7 | 3 |
| Undescended testes | | 2 | |
| Lyme disease | | 8 | 12 |
| | 14/273 = 5% | 128/1583 = 8% | 43/302 = 15% |

[a]273 pages of guidelines
[b]1583 pages of guidelines
[c]302 pages of diagnostic protocols

## 11.4.3 Epidemiology

The knowledge domains tested in the exam and their occurrence in GP/FM have been mapped to the frequency data of two epidemiological studies—CONTENT [22] and SESAM [23]. As in the epidemiology domain the only text type is "diagnosis", there is no other possibility to look for hierarchies than inside of this text type. Diagnoses were coded in ICPC-2.

One exam topic can be coded by more than one ICPC-2 code, e.g. measles as (A71) or as vaccination (A—general procedures) or diabetes I/II as (T89, T90) or as prevention (A—general/prevention). Coding differences thus result in differences in frequency between CONTENT [22] and SESAM [23], 68% reasons for encounter [22] and 32% of diagnosis for consultations [23]. The cumulation of A-, K- and T-diagnoses (prevention, circulation, metabolism) in the exam topics of diabetes, hypertension and related subjects (prevention, geriatrics) shows a high fit with general practice epidemiology; K- and T-diagnoses increase to 60% in CONTENT [22] and SESAM [23] for geriatric patients (Table 11.7).

## 11.5 Comparing Corpora

The match between exam topics and the discipline's textual corpora ("rank of fit") showed to be proportional to the number of topics assessed in the exam ("hit rate") and to be inversely proportional to the number of textual elements in the textual corpora that define the profession's knowledge base ("textual effort"). The latter displays the textual properties of Zipf's "least effort" [10] and Polanyi's "law of poverty" [11] (see Sect. 11.1—bibliometrical criteria of concordance).

Another way of comparing exam topics and the discipline's knowledge base looks at the number of times an exam topic appears in the discipline defining textual corpora (i.e. its "hit density").

If we consider the "hit rate" and "textual effort" as criteria for the fit between exam topics and the textual corpora of the knowledge domains, we see an overall descending hierarchy of concordance between praxis, science and epidemiology as follows (Table 11.8):

- praxis: as defined by EBM guidelines [21] and Mader/Weißgerber's question bank [15]
- science: as defined by Mader and Weißgerber's [15] and Kochen's textbooks [5]
- epidemiology: as found in the CONTENT survey [22]

We also see descending hierarchies inside the praxis-level corpora:

- EBM guidelines [21]
- Braun/Mader's diagnostic protocols [16]
- DEGAM guidelines [20]

**Table 11.7** Coverage of exam domains compared to their epidemiological frequency in CONTENT [22] and SESAM [23]

| Ranking of topics | Represented by ICPC-2 chapters | SESAM 2002 | CONTENT 2007 |
|---|---|---|---|
| Diabetes mellitus—Types I and II | T endocrine, metabolic and nutritional | 5.6% | 3.2% |
| | | T34, T63 | T90, T93 |
| Hypertension | K circulatory | 13.4% | 4.1% |
| | | K31, K50, K63 | K86 |
| Measles | A general and unspecified-A71 | – | – |
| Signs of death | A general and unspecified-A96 | – | – |
| Acute coronary syndrome | K circulatory-K75 | – | – |
| Vaccinations | A general-procedures | 3.5% | 2.6% |
| | | A44 | A98 |
| Prevention (osteoporosis) | A general-prevention | 25.0% | 12.1% |
| | L musculoskeletal | (A44), A63 | A98 |
| | K circulatory | K31, K50, K63 | K86 |
| | T endocrine, metabolic and nutrition | L01, L02, L03 | L86 |
| | | T34, T63 | T90, T93 |
| Geriatrics (Type II diabetes) | A general-preventions | 20.7% | 9.9% |
| | K circulatory | (A44), A63 | A98, K86 |
| | T endocrine, metabolic and nutrition | K31, K50, K63 | T90, T93 |
| | | T34, T63 | |
| Undescended testes | A general-preventions-A98 | – | – |
| | Y male genital system-Y83 | | |
| Lyme disease | A General-A78 | – | – |
| | S Skin-S12 | | |
| Total | | 68.2% | 31.9% |

the science-level corpora:

- Mader/Weißgerber's question bank [15]
- Mader and Weißgerber [15] and Kochen's textbooks [5]
- ZFA themes [18]
- DEGAM abstracts [19]

and the epidemiology-level corpora:

- predominance of prevention in the geriatric population in both CONTENT [22] und SESAM [23]

**Table 11.8** Coverage of exam domains in the discipline's knowledge corpora

| Rank of fit between exam topics and textual corpora | Textual corpora and professional levels represented by ... | Hit rate: Number of topics covered amongst the top 10 topics | Textual effort: Number of textual elements representing GP/FM (%) | Hit density: Number of times topic being mentioned in the corpora |
|---|---|---|---|---|
| 1 | EBM guidelines 2007 [21]; praxis | 10 | 8 | 15 |
| 2 | Mader/Weißgerber question bank 2005 [15]; praxis | 10 | 13 | 19 |
| 3 | Mader/Weißgerber textbook 2005 [15]; science | 10 | 14 | 6.7 |
| 4 | Kochen [5]; science | 10 | 15 | 10 |
| 5 | Braun and Mader [16]; praxis | 8 | 15 | 5 |
| 6 | ZfA 2004-7 [18]; science | 5 | 18 | 3.2 |
| 7 | DEGAM Guidelines 2004–2007 [20]; praxis | 5 | 5 | 2.8 |
| 8 | DEGAM Abstracts 2004–2007 [19]; science | 5 | 29 | 4.3 |
| 9 | CONTENT 2007 [22]; epidemiology | 5 | 32 | 2.6 |

## 11.6 Discussion

The questions of this project (Sect. 11.3.1) are initially answered at the level of comparisons (Sect. 11.5 and Table 11.8). There is a descending hierarchy of concordance between the exam question catalogue and the discipline's texts:

- Praxis
- Science
- Epidemiology

In addition we found a descending hierarchy of concordance within the texts representing each knowledge domain and the exam question catalogue:

- Praxis
    - EBM guidelines [21]
    - Diagnostic protocols [16]
    - DEGAM guidelines [20]

- Science

    - Mader/Weißgerber's question bank [15]
    - Textbooks [5, 15] and journal articles [18]
    - Conference abstracts [19]

- Epidemiology

    - Focus on prevention and geriatrics [22, 23]

Looking at the hierarchies of the corpora of each knowledge domain as a representation of that knowledge domain as suggested by Abbott's [4] "theory of fractal knowledge of disciplines", we find a fractal pattern between the discipline's knowledge domains and the exam question catalogue:

- Within the **praxis-level corpora**, EBM guidelines [21] represent the highest standard of praxis knowledge by European consensus, the diagnostic protocols by Braun and Mader [16] the high-level science domain and the "still young" DEGAM guidelines [20] the uncodified praxis knowledge most needed to answer epidemiological concerns
- Within the **science-level corpora**, the Mader/Weißberger question bank [15] represents praxis knowledge, the textbooks [5, 15] and journal articles [18] the scientific knowledge and the conference abstracts [19] still uncodified knowledge applicable to epidemiological questions
- The **epidemiology-level corpora** focus entirely on the diagnostic processes (as represented by the symptom chapter A- of ICPC) and diagnoses with a special focus on the K- and T-chapters [22, 23] and with a predominance on the geriatric-aged group

Figure 11.2 summarises the findings of the hierarchical patterns of concordance between the exam question catalogue and the texts that describe the three domains of knowledge and their repeated pattern within the corpora of each knowledge domain. This pattern shows the fractal pattern of nested self-similarity (as outlined in Sect. 11.3.1).

Metaphorically one can describe the knowledge base of general practice as a *Russian doll*—its innermost core being the discipline's epidemiology. Using the language of qualitative social sciences, the *Russian doll* metaphor translates: the exam question bank has a descending concordance pattern between praxis, sciences and epidemiology; the pattern is fractally repeated within the texts of each knowledge domain.

These findings were found deductively. Following Abbott's [4] rules, the data of this study confirmed the theory of the fractal pattern defining a discipline.

The answers to the emerging questions posed in Sect. 11.3.1 are as follows:

1. The exam question bank and the themes of the representative texts of each knowledge domain show a descending pattern of concordance between praxis, science and epidemiology

Knowledge elicited in specialist examination
         Knowledge domains of GP/FM
         Textual corpora reflecting knowledge domains

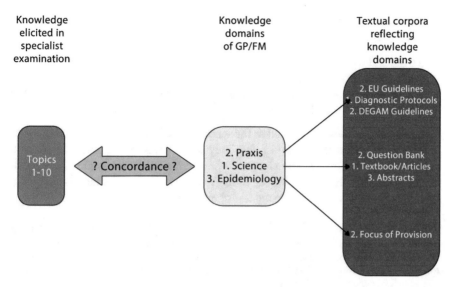

**Fig. 11.2** The fractal nature of general practice knowledge in the postgraduate examination. The examination (green box) indeed shows to represent the disciplines knowledge domain to have a fractal pattern (yellow box) and that each knowledge domain entails a fractal pattern of the disciplines overall knowledge as represented in its written textual *corpora* (red box)

2. EBM guidelines [21] show the highest level of concordance within the praxis-level corpora, and the Mader/Weißberger question bank [15] shows the highest level of concordance within the science-level corpora
3. The descending patterns of concordance within the praxis, science and epidemiology domains repeat themselves fractally (nested self-similarity)
4. The high level of concordance between the exam question bank and both the EBM guidelines [21] and practice epidemiology [3, 22, 23] attests a high level of "internal validity" of the exam question bank

## 11.7 Conclusions

The demonstrated complexity inherent in the general practice knowledge base raises at least two other aspects that deserve further exploration:

- GP/FM in Germany has a strong focus on prevention. This focus is reflected in the postgraduate examination; there is a high level of concordance between the exam question bank and EBM guidelines and general practice epidemiology.
- This pattern emerged without formal training of examiners or the evaluation of the examination itself. Such complex adaptive patterns are typical for general practice activities and have been previously described by Ellis [24]. To explore these issues further, it would be useful to initiate an international comparative study.

This research over a 10+ year period with its complex outcomes had a significant personal effect.

- It triggered the feeling of a "journey" (in old German, "queste") with an uncertain destination, nevertheless worth to pursue
- It triggered the feeling that one wound find a coherent background despite the obvious chaotic foreground [25]

Feelings of a "journey" as well as the sense of certainty of a coherent background despite a chaotic foreground—in psychodynamic terms—arise primarily from a perspective [26]. This emotional aspect of scientific work in complexity research has been emphasised by Kissling et al. in their work of transforming internal body images into externally visible pictures—or art [27].

**Acknowledgements** We thank Joachim Sturmberg for thoroughly reading the manuscript and helpful comments, our MHH reviewers Marie-Louise Dierks and Carsten Kruschinski for their helpful suggestions for reworking this book chapter and Nils Schneider for his support of the research project. Last but not least, we thank Rita Borkowski, exams office of the Medical Board of Lower Saxony, for her continuous institutional support.

# The Journey

I tried to understand the complex interactions of daily practice, which I neither understood nor mastered despite extensive psychotherapeutic studies and Balint experiences—that was what started my journey into complexity sciences. It was a qualitative, linguistically oriented research project that allowed me to create a coherent structure of my practice experience under the umbrella of "narrative-based medicine". Thure von Uexküll's biosemiotic model [28] provided the essential framework for a lot of studies concerning doctor-patient interactions, effects of complementary treatments and the placebo effect itself.

Following my habilitation, I found myself working in a large, mainly geriatric, rural practice with its high levels of diagnostic uncertainty. I aimed to understand and research these daily experiences based on the classical approaches of Braun's complexity categorisations. I linked up with the remaining Braun pupils Frank Mader, Waltraud Fink und Gustav Kamenski and the Karl Landsteiner Institut, Vienna. This ongoing collaboration has resulted in a series of joint publications. This work linked me to Joachim Sturmberg and his "complexity tribe" with which I feel connected, and I am curious to see how this journey will progress.

Take-Home Message

- The knowledge base of general practice/family medicine encompasses three knowledge domains—praxis, science and epidemiology
- The final postgraduate examination for general practice/family medicine in Germany reflects the knowledge domain of the discipline
- The knowledge domains show a fractal pattern between its components

# References

1. Zollo A (Hrsg.). Fragen und Antworten zur Allgemeinmedizin. "Medical secrets". Bern: Huber; 2004.
2. Rezension KM. Anthony Zollo, Fragen und Antworten zur Allgemeinmedizin. Zeitschrift für Evidenz, Fortbildung und Qualität im Gesundheitswesen 2004;98:487.
3. Braun RN, Halhuber MJ. Prüfungsfragen in der Allgemeinmedizin. Orientierung an der Lehre des funktionsgerechten Denkens und Handelns an der ersten ärztlichen Linie. Allgemeinarzt 1998;15:1440–47.
4. Abbott M. Chaos of disciplines. Chicago: The University of Chicago Press; 2002.
5. Kochen MM (Hrsg). Allgemeinmedizin und Familienmedizin. 3. Aufl. Stuttgart: Thieme, 2006.
6. Braun RN. Allgemeinmedizin - Standort und Stellenwert in der Heilkunde. Mainz: Verlag Kirchheim; 1982.
7. Strauß AL. Grundlagen qualitativer Sozialforschung. München: Wilhelm Fink; 1994.
8. Reichertz, J. Abduction: the logic of discovery of grounded theory. Forum Qual. Sozialforschung 2010;11(1), http://www.qualitative-research.net/index.php/fqs/article/view/1412.
9. Havemann F. Einführung in die Bibliometrie. Berlin: Gesellschaft für Wissenschaftsforschung; 2009.
10. Zipf GK. Human behaviour and the principle of least effort. Cambridge, MA: Addison-Wesley Press; 1949.
11. Polanyi M. Personal knowledge. Chicago: University of Chicago Press; 1958.
12. Du Bermoy W. Repetition and textual dimension: structural fractals in Edgar Allen Poe's Poesy; 2015. https://doi.org/10.13140/RG.2.1.3085.8724.
13. Fleck L. Entstehung und Entwicklung einer wissenschaftlichen Tatsache. 4. Auflage. Frankfurt/M: Suhrkamp; 2004.
14. https://books.google.com/ngrams. Accessed 19 Jan 17.
15. Mader FH, Weißgerber H. Allgemeinmedizin und Praxis. 5. Auflage. Berlin: Springer; 2005.
16. Braun RN, Mader FH. Programmierte Diagnostik in der Allgemeinmedizin. 5. Auflage. Heidelberg: Springer; 2005.
17. Donner-Banzhoff N. Matthäus-Effekte, Superstars und der Impact Factor. ZFA 2011;87(9):367–70.
18. http://www.online-zfa.de/. Accessed 10 Jan 17.
19. DEGAM - Kongresse: DEGAM-Kongress. ZfA 2004;80:377–402; DEGAM-Kongress Potsdam 29/9-1/10 2005. Blattsammlung; DEGAM-Kongress. ZfA 2006;82:1–26; DEGAM-Kongress. ZfA 2007;83:1–24.

20. www.degam.de/leitlinien.html. Accessed: 04 Jan 17.
21. Rebhandl E, Rabady S, Mader FH. EbM-Guidelines für Allgemeinmedizin. 2. Auflage. Köln: Deutscher - Ärzte Verlag; 2007
22. Kühlein T, Laux G, Gutscher A, Szecsenyi J. Kontinuierliche Morbiditätsregistrierung in der Hausarztpraxis. Vom Beratungsanlass zum Beratungsergebnis - CONTENT. München: Urban & Vogel; 2008.
23. Voigt R. Der Beratungsanlass in der allgemeinmedizinischen Konsultationssprechstunde (SESAM). Diss. Med. Fak. Univ. Leipzig; 2002.
24. Ellis B. An overview of complexity theory: understanding primary care as a complex adaptive system. In: Sturmberg JP, Martin CM, editors. Handbook of systems and complexity in health. New York: Springer; 2013. p. 485–94.
25. West BJ. Mathematical principles: tales of tails. In: Sturmberg JP, Martin CM, editors. Handbook of systems and complexity in health. New York: Springer; 2013. p. 63–80.
26. Bion, WR. Lernen durch Erfahrung. 2. Aufl. Frankfurt./M: Suhrkamp; 1997. p. 125.
27. Kissling B, Quarroz E, Fahrni A. Pictures in the Body - an interactiv dialog between art and science. In cooperation with the 2nd international conference "Putting Systems and Complexity Sciences into Practice - Sharing the Experience", Billings, USA, 9. -10.11.2016. https://docs.wixstatic.com/ugd/569094_a6e76b36b4974c90b08396daf4ae11d8.pdf (for a more detailed description see their chapter i this book).
28. Uexküll TV, Pauli HG. The mind-body problem in medicine. Advances J Inst Adv Health 1986;3(4):158–74.

# Chapter 12
# Journey to Refine Acute Care Hospital Process Improvement Projects for Ethically Complex Patients: Applying Complexity Tools to the Problem of Identifying Which Patients Need a Little More Attention than Most

Evan G. DeRenzo

## 12.1 Introduction

During my years at the National Institutes of Health (NIH, 1980–1998), much of my focus was on designing and approving clinical research protocols with the least prospect for confounders in drawing conclusions from the data collected. That meant stripping patient study populations of as many variables as could be identified and safely removed. When I completed my Fellowship in Bioethics at the NIH, I moved to what is now the John J. Lynch MD Center for Ethics at MedStar Washington Hospital Center (MWHC) (hereafter referred to as the "Center"). After about a year of orientation, I realized I knew virtually nothing about clinical medicine or clinical medicine ethics because clinical medicine is nothing like clinical research or clinical research ethics.

During the 8–9 years that I learned enough about clinical medicine to be more than minimally competent at clinical medicine ethics, I learned that the difference can be summed up in one word, "messiness." It is the messiness of clinical medicine that produces the medical and ethical complexities of clinical medicine. This messiness stems from the complexities of the relational dynamics of patients and their families, friends, and partners, of patients and physicians, of patients and other clinicians, and of the physicians and other clinicians.

One part of this messiness that has a common thread is its singular patient focus. That is, all the clinicians, support personnel, family, and friends are—or ought to be—focused singularly on achieving good outcomes for individual patients. But this is not nearly where the messiness ends. Layered on top of all this clinical, individually focused messiness are the complicating factors of administrative needs

E. G. DeRenzo (✉)
John J. Lynch MD Center for Ethics, MedStar Washington Hospital Center,
110 Irving St. NW, East Bldg., Room 3108, Washington, DC 20010, USA
e-mail: evan.g.derenzo@medstar.net

© Springer International Publishing AG, part of Springer Nature 2018
J. P. Sturmberg (ed.), *Putting Systems and Complexity Sciences Into Practice*,
https://doi.org/10.1007/978-3-319-73636-5_12

for improving outcomes for all the patients in the aggregate. That is, there is a messiness to creating different and multiple processes and systems for keeping patients safe and for meeting quality markers set by internal standards and outside oversight agencies such as meeting length of stay benchmarks, reducing 30-day readmissions, reducing legal costs, and improving patient satisfaction ratings [1].

Additionally, all this variability is seated within the context of the many systems within systems that have to come together like well-oiled gears [2, 3]. Just one example is the systems for managing a hospital's blood bank and its systems for tracking a patient through multiple admissions who had in the past identified as a Jehovah's Witness. The hospital's electronic medical record (EMR) would be expected to continue to show this religious belief which is an automatic barrier to blood transfusion. Needing to coordinate with these blood bank and hospital-wide systems for a patient who now lacks capacity, may need surgery and may or may not still be a believing Jehovah's Witness is the need to coordinate with the blood bank, the surgical team, and the surgical intensive care team (SICU), both of the latter two must discuss the matter with the surrogate in a way that successfully uncovers whether or not the patient is still a follower of the Jehovah's Witness faith and check to verify the surrogate's information in a way that neither endangers the patient nor destroys trust and good will with the surrogate.

Within the many and varied systems within a hospital and/or hospital system (sometimes referred to as an integrated, distributive healthcare system), each has its own core mission, some that may be at odds with others, but that are all created for one purpose—providing ever-improved care outcomes for patients. To achieve this end, many systems and variables within systems have to be harnessed to manage the medical and ethical complexities that impinge on achieving this goal [4, 5]. Then this mass of data needs to be analyzed by methods, some of which are yet to emerge, and examined against outcome measures, some of which are yet to be designed.

Soon after moving to the Center and developing my appreciation for this messiness, I began thinking about how best to manage it all toward the end of improving acute care hospital patient outcomes. My partner in this effort has been Jack Schwartz, JD, then a Maryland Assistant Attorney General and now affiliated with the Health Law Program at the University of Maryland, Carey School of Law. We realized that one path to figuring all this out was to use a hospital's own data with validated patient characteristic variables that predict problems in patient outcomes (Fig. 12.1).

Setting surrogate markers for poor outcome of

- Excessive length of stay (ELOS)
- Multiple admissions within a year, and
- Liability costs

we designed and implemented our first pilot study. We started by examining legal liability with an a priori set of variables.

**Fig. 12.1** Who is the
"ethically complex patient"

## 12.2    The Association Between Risk-Related Variables and the Cost of Legal Claims: A Proof-of-Concept Study at MedStar Washington Hospital Center (2012)

Investigators: Evan G. DeRenzo, PhD and Jack Schwartz, JD

### 12.2.1    Purpose

The study presents findings and conclusions of an examination of closed risk management cases from January 2004 to November 2009. The study identifies factors, which we termed "risk-related variables" (RRVs) and which we believe play a role in the filing of many of these claims. These RRVs fall into two categories: those that relate to certain patient characteristics, which appear to elevate the risk of a costly claim, and those related to clinicians and the systems within which they function.

### 12.2.2    The Study's Primary Question

In a series of closed risk management cases, do experience-derived, a priori RRVs predict a disproportionate amount of indemnity and expense costs for the hospital? The study supports a tentative "Yes" answer to this question.

### 12.2.3   The Study's Secondary Question

Will patterns emerge from this database that can suggest additional analytic steps, and potentially cost-effective interventions, to reduce risk management costs? Again, the study supports a tentative "Yes" answer to this question.

### 12.2.4   Methods

We reviewed 193 closed claims during the study period. Of those, we disqualified 118 for the reasons listed below. That left 75 claims that made up the universe of studied closed claims.

We examined every closed claim during the study period. An aspect of the review process, however, entailed the assessment of a claim against certain exclusion criteria. If a claim met one of these criteria, we did not analyze it further. That is, once we determined that a claim fell into one of three exclusion criteria, we did not examine the file to determine whether one or more RRVs were present. It is highly likely that some of the excluded claims also had RRVs. Hence, the costs associated with RRVs may well be higher than the 79% of total claims cost found.

The three exclusion categories were as follows:

- Exclusion category 1: small outlay cases—i.e., indemnity cost of zero and expense cost less than $2500.
- Exclusion category 2: technical error—i.e., claims which alleged an obvious breach of the applicable standard of care for a particular diagnostic or treatment service by an employed physician or nurse.
- Exclusion category 3: record does not include any hospital-related variables of interest. That is, although there may have been RRVs involved in these cases, the database did not contain information sufficient for us to identify any RRV, and on this basis, these cases were excluded.

Also, although not itself designated as an exclusion category, we did not examine informed consent issues, even when the risk manager's notes specifically allude to it and notwithstanding the fact that informed consent is often seen as the ethical issue par excellence. Our primary reason for this omission is the locus of legal responsibility: generally, liability for breach of the duty to obtain informed consent would fall on the attending physician, not the hospital [6]. Moreover, because informed consent is already addressed in Joint Commission requirements and hospital policy, we decided that we would contribute little if anything useful by discussing it.

The RRVs were derived by agreement between the authors as indicating medically and ethically complicated cases as documented in the closed case reports. This consensus process brought to bear the distinct analytic tools of the two investigators' disciplines, clinical ethics and law. Two decades of collaboration between the investigators has focused on using these distinct professional perspectives to arrive at shared understandings of the problems of caring for hospitalized patients [7].

The selection and shaping of the RRVs came out of this collaboration and are grounded in the almost 45 combined years of case consultation experience of the clinical ethicist investigator (DeRenzo) and of the attorney investigator (Schwartz) in healthcare law. The Center at which the clinical ethicist now practices and where this study was being conducted runs approximately 300 ethics case consultations a year and has done so for decades. This experience served as the conceptual underpinning for why an RRV makes for a case of ethically complex care.

The RRVs are:

1. Communication problems
   Definition: The case description or risk management notes identify a problem with communication among providers regarding a patient's condition or between patient/family and providers.
2. Decision-making complexity
   Definition: The decision-making complexity variable compresses a variety of circumstances that spell trouble for clinicians when making decisions with or for patients. These include difficulties with, or lapses in, assessment of decision-making capacity in a patient with dementia, stroke, or other conditions raising capacity issues; the full panoply of possible problems with surrogates, such as identification of the proper surrogate decision-maker or conflict—perhaps exacerbated or even produced by problematic communications between surrogates and clinicians—with or among surrogates; and behavioral disruptiveness on the part of a patient, family member, or friend when care-related decisions need to be made. In short, any wording in the case record that connoted difficulties in making decisions with or for patients led to the case's inclusion in this RRV.
3. Frequent admissions
   Definition: Based on information in the case report, the patient had at least two admissions related to the same medical problem within a 12-month period, regardless of where the hospitalizations were.
4. Life-sustaining technologies
   Definition: A case in which the file noted either the use of any device or medical intervention, such as dialysis, feeding tubes, tracheotomies, mechanical ventilators, or left ventricular assist devices, to sustain a function essential for life or the withholding or withdrawal of such a device.
5. Multiple comorbidities
   Definition: A case in which the patient is reported to have at least two organ systems involved.
6. Obesity
   Definition: A case in which either the terms "obese" or "obesity" are used in describing the patient or the data on height and weight permit the conclusion that the patient has a body mass index of 30 or higher, which is the accepted definition of obesity [8].
7. Neuropsychiatric conditions
   Definition: A case in which there is any mention of psychiatric illness, including explicit mention of a DSM-V diagnosis or of dementia.

8. Sentinel event

Definition: Any case in which the mention of a sentinel event was explicit. We presumed that the risk manager's use of the term was consistent with the Joint Commission's definition: "an unexpected occurrence involving death or serious physical or psychological injury, or the risk thereof" (Joint Commission [9, p. 2]).

9. Substance abuse

Definition: Any case in which there was explicit mention of alcoholism or abuse of drugs, prescribed or illegal.

10. Systems issues

Definition: Any case suggesting a failure of effective functioning of a system, which is a set of interdependent elements interacting to achieve a common aim. These elements may be both human and nonhuman (equipment, technologies, etc.) (IOM [10, p. 211]). A micro-system is an organizational unit built around the definition of repeatable core service competencies. Elements of a micro-system include:

(a) a core team of healthcare professionals
(b) a defined population of patients
(c) carefully designed work processes
(d) an environment capable of linking information on all aspects of work and patient or population outcomes to support ongoing evaluation of performance (IOM [10, p. 211]).

As a group, the RRVs represent characteristics or qualities about the patient (or sometimes those close to the patient) or the clinical context that are associated with problems in patient care.

## 12.2.5 Findings

We believe that these variables merit further attention because, even within the limited domain of closed claims, they were associated with a disproportionate share of legal costs; 39% of the cases were assigned to one or more of the RRV groups, but these assigned cases accounted for 79% of total costs.

## 12.2.6 Conclusions

The complexity of care in a large, urban teaching hospital increases the risk of anger-fueled negligence claims. Seriously ill patients (and, as importantly, their families) are acculturated to believe that skilled physicians, with the panoply of support services and technology in a service-rich, community teaching hospital, can make them well again. This sometimes unrealistic faith is reinforced when they observe clinicians demonstrating mastery of the technology and speaking an arcane language. Yet, this environment also heightens the possibility of misunderstanding and alienation. The emphasis on technology prowess can lead patients to feel that clinicians are more focused on lab values than the patient in the bed. The frequent changes in house staff, attending physicians, and nurses on a given service, which can be disorienting to patients and their families, contribute to a sense of unease and estrangement. In many ways, being hospitalized is like being lost in a foreign land. If the hope for recovery does not materialize, any shortfalls in communication or other perceived deficiencies in the personal aspects of care can generate anger. Preventing the situations that are most likely to generate anger might improve care and save money. Even claims that never result in indemnity payments impose meaningful costs [11, 12].

Once the report for Study 1 was written and submitted, Jack and I moved to run the next logical pilot. This time we needed to see if a hospital's electronic medical record (EMR) could be used to pull out one or more of our RRVs. If so we reasoned that we could, in fact, harness the complex system of a hospital's EMR to better understand a hospital's populations as identified by the RRVs. If we could run this study successfully, we then might be able to design quality assurance/quality improvement projects to support those particular populations and in so doing better care for medically and ethically complex patients.

To run this second pilot, we expanded our research group. Added was Juergen Klenk, PhD, now of Deloitte Consulting, who was the lead investigator on this study. At the time he was with Exponent, a consulting group in Alexandria, VA. Also added were Jack Kilcullen, MD, Inova Hospital System, Fairfax, VA, and Nneka Sederstrom, PhD, now of Children's Hospitals of Minnesota, Minneapolis, MN, then the Director of the Center. Our hospital partner was Main Line Health System (MLHS), Bryn Mawr, PA. Again, we produced positive findings; we could search a hospital's EMR and pull out the records of patients who had one or more of our RRVs in their records.

## 12.3 Ethically Complicated Cases (ECC) Feasibility Study: Ethics, Electronic Medical Records, and Quality Markers

### 12.3.1 Purpose

Investigators: Evan G. DeRenzo, PhD; Jack Kilcullen,[1] MD; Juergen Klenk,[2] PhD; Jack Schwartz, JD; Nneka Sederstrom,[3] PhD; Rosemary Wurster,[4] MPH, RN; and Frances Marchant,[4] MD.

---

[1] INOVA Hospital System.
[2] Then of Exponent Consulting Group.
[3] Previously of the Center.
[4] Partners at Main Line Health, Philadelphia, PA.

This study was intended to assess the feasibility of using MLHS's EMR data to predict ethically complicated cases. That is because although a literature around clinical ethics consultation has grown over the years, understanding what drives the development of ethically complicated cases, especially ones that result in clinical ethics consultation and quality-deficit markers such as excessive length of stay, 30-day readmissions, or legal claims, has never been attempted.

### 12.3.2 Methods

Our MLHS data collaborators provided specifically requested data sets to Dr. Klenk and his team. These data sets were selected to contain relevant information for the development of predictive models—i.e., to identify patients at risk for becoming ethically complicated patients who are already medically complicated (Fig. 12.2).

Some of the data fields sampled were:

- LOS (length of stay)
- BMI (body mass index)
- Advance directives

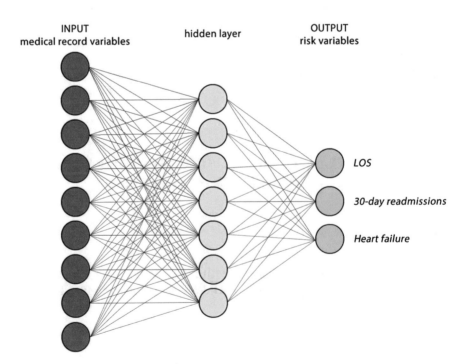

**Fig. 12.2** Patient characteristics that appear to identify "at-risk variables." The strategy to identify the potentially "at-risk patient" follows Neural Network Principles

- 30-day readmissions
- Ethics consult
- Neuropsychiatric diagnoses
- Admit date/discharge dates
- Psychiatric diagnoses
- Heart failure
- ICD-9 diagnosis
- Code status
- Palliative care consultation

### 12.3.3 Findings

Statistical analysis of the provided data showed preliminary evidence of correlation between outcome variables, such as length of stay and 30-day readmission, and clinical variables such as count of cardiac ICD-9 diagnosis codes and the patient's resuscitation orders as full code.

The analyses revealed sufficiency of data in both quality and quantity as well as initial patterns (correlations) that should allow for these big data analytic tools to provide, with additional positive research findings, the grounding for development of a predictive model of ethically complicated cases.

### 12.3.4 Conclusions

Although some questions regarding data contents and formatting remain, this second pilot, including some of the RRVs from the original pilot, provides promising findings that a predictive model for identifying risk for ethically complicated cases can be successfully created. This study found evidence of being able to define a single facility visit based on admission/discharge dates and times and obtaining large quantities of computer textual data sets from free text EMR fields. Although there are still kinks to be addressed in any larger and more definitive study, it appears that these analytic tools will allow us to predict what group or groups of patients in a particular hospital might become ethically complicated cases. From these data, a hospital should be better able to focus its QA/QI project budgets and, in so doing, better support the patients that most need increased attention.

**Acknowledgements** Study 1: This protocol was approved by the MWHC hospital's IRB on October 25, 2009. No personally identifying information was collected.
Study 2: This protocol was approved by the MLHS hospital's IRB on September 19, 2014. No personally identifying information was collected.

## The Journey

These are the study results I presented at the meeting in Billings, Montana. My journey, not nearly yet ended, has taken me along a path to Billings where I finally found my "complexity tribe." Although grateful to finally find the right group to present these studies to, even more joyous was that I felt intellectually at home. The group, small and collegial, was welcoming. The hospital in which the meeting took place, led by complexity tribe members of long-standing, was beautiful. The hospital's clinicians were also welcoming; they were happy to talk about the implementation of complexity research into their own processes, projects which were a revelation.

And so, for me, I continue to seek to advance this decades-old work of putting healthcare complexity analysis into practice at the bedside. Our research group is working on developing and implementing the next logical study, and I look forward to the continuation of this work with my long-standing colleagues. Additionally, I am excited about developing new collegial relationships with my "complexity tribe" and am grateful to have presented at this meeting and publishing the substance of the talk in these proceedings.

Take-Home Message

Thus far, it seems that this work has produced several insights that can be put to use while the next research steps go forward. The main two for now are:

- It is possible that by focusing on a few patient populations that likely are at risk for being medically, psychosocially, and ethically complex by adding systems improvements to their care, potential liability, excessive length of stays, and unnecessary 30-day readmissions may be minimized or avoided.
- These potential at-risk patient populations are likely to include such hospital care complexities as communications problems, decision-making difficulties, use of life-sustaining technologies, and multiple comorbidities.

Although we do not yet know what combination of QA/QI projects might be most profitable for these patient groups, we hope others interested in this work will conduct their own complexity research with these at-risk patient characteristics and present their findings, making the data available to those of us focused on how to improve such patients' hospital care.

# References

1. Manser T. Teamwork and patient safety in dynamic domains of healthcare: a review of the literature. Acta Anaesthesiol Scand. 2009;53:143–51.
2. IOM (Institute of Medicine). Crossing the quality chasm: a new health system for the 21st century. Washington: National Academy Press; 2001.
3. Wang MC, Hyun JK, Harrison M, Shortell SM, Fraser I. Redesigning health systems for quality: lessons from emerging practices. Jt Comm J Qual Patient Saf. 2006;32:599–611.
4. Stacey RD. Strategic management and organizational dynamics; the challenge of complexity. New York: Prentice-Hall; 2003.
5. DeRenzo EG. Individuals, systems, and professional behavior. In: Mills AE, Chen DT, Werhane PH, Wynia MK, editors. Professionalism in tomorrow's healthcare system: towards fulfilling the ACGME requirements for systems-based practice and professionalism. Hagerstown: University Publishing Group; 2005.
6. Gatter R. The mysterious survival of the policy against informed consent liability for hospitals. Notre Dame Law Rev. 2006;81:1203–73.
7. DeRenzo EG, Schwartz J, Selinger S. Harnessing complex hospital care: hospital practices must match the moral ends of treatment. Sci Prog. 2009. https://scienceprogress.org/2009/02/harnessing-complex-hospital-care/. Accessed 27 Mar 2017.
8. CDC (Centers for Disease Control and Prevention). Defining overweight and obesity. 2012. http://www.cdc.gov/obesity/defining.html. Accessed 17 July 2012.
9. Joint Commission. Sentinel event data, event type by year, 1995–2011. 2012. http://www.jointcommission.org/assets/1/18/Event_Type_Year_1995-2011.pdf. Accessed 19 July 2012.
10. IOM (Institute of Medicine). To err is human: building a safer health system. Washington: National Academy Press; 2000.
11. Carroll AE, Parikh PD, Buddenbaum JL. The impact of defense expenses in medical malpractice claims. J Law Med Ethics 2012;40:135–42.
12. Seabury S, Chandra A, Lakdawalla D, Jena AB. Defense costs of medical malpractice claims. Law Soc Rev. 2012;24:105–20.

# Chapter 13
# Relationship Between Health Outcomes and Health Factors: Analysis of 2016 Data in the Pacific Northwest Robert Wood Johnson Foundation *County Health Rankings and Roadmaps*

Russell S. Gonnering and William J. Riley

## 13.1 Introduction

A half century ago, an anomalously low incidence of cardiovascular disease in Roseto, PA, prompted a series of articles attempting to uncover the possible cause [1, 2]. Ultimately, it was understood that previously ignored elements of social support and a sense of community were the most likely cause of this improved Health Outcome [3]. When societal changes lessened the impact of these social support structures, the improvement in Health Outcome evaporated [4].

This story sets the stage for a number of questions. How do we improve Health Outcomes? The answer is not trivial. In the years 2010–2016, the Center for Medicare and Medicaid Innovation has spent $6.5 billion exploring new models of payment to improve quality [5]. Have *Health Outcomes* actually improved as a result of this expenditure of resources? Some have, and some have not. Has the improvement been worth the expenditure? How do we know? How do we measure it? These are timely, important and, in many ways, yet unanswered questions.

We have developed computational methods to explore these questions which have been described in detail elsewhere (R.S. Gonnering, W. Wiley, K. Love, The relationship between health outcomes and health factors: analysis of the 2016 Arizona data, Robert Wood Johnson Foundation *County Health Rankings and Roadmaps*, unpublished manuscript). For this report, we will concentrate on the

R. S. Gonnering (✉)
Arizona State University, 1780 San Fernando Drive, Elm Grove, WI 53122, USA
e-mail: Russell.Gonnering@asu.edu

W. J. Riley
Arizona State University, DTPHX Campus, Mailcode 9020, Tempe, AZ 85281, USA
e-mail: William.J.Riley@asu.edu

© Springer International Publishing AG, part of Springer Nature 2018                          177
J. P. Sturmberg (ed.), *Putting Systems and Complexity Sciences Into Practice*,
https://doi.org/10.1007/978-3-319-73636-5_13

relationships between Health Factors and Health Outcomes in the Pacific Northwest. We wanted to explore this question: **Are better Health Factors automatically associated with better Health Outcomes?**

## 13.2   County Health Rankings and Roadmaps

The *RWJF County Health Rankings and Roadmaps* compiles data on *Health Outcomes* and *Health Factors* from virtually all of the counties in the United States. The *Health Outcomes Data* consists of data on *Length of Life* and *Quality of Life*, both given equal weight. The *Health Factors Data* are broken down into four main categories (Fig. 13.1):

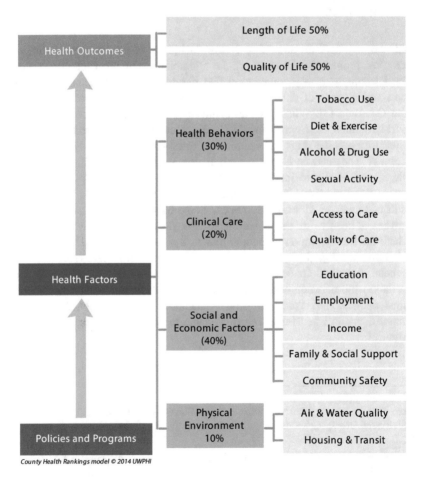

County Health Rankings model © 2014 UWPHI

**Fig. 13.1** County health rankings
http://www.countyhealthrankings.org/our-approach; Used with permission

- Social and economic factors (40%),
- Health behaviors (30%),
- Clinical care (20%)
- Physical environment (10%).

Each of the *Outcomes* and *Factors* is comprised of a number of subfactors listed on the website. While some subfactors are negative and others positive, the values are standardized so that a higher rank in each category indicates a better result. Within each state each county is ranked according to its *Health Outcome* and *Health Factors* taken as an aggregate as well as broken down into its main components. Ranking is given as to standing in the state as well as to the Z-score.[1] The rationale for assigning weights to the ranking data in the report is contained within the working paper of the University of Wisconsin Population Health Institute [6].

Our first observation is that there is a disconnect between the rankings of *Health Factors* and *Health Outcomes* for a number of counties in Washington, Oregon, Idaho, Wyoming, and Montana. The counties with a positive number had Health Outcomes better than would be expected by their *Health Factors*. Those with a negative number had *Health Outcomes* worse than expected. Those with a number close to zero had *Health Outcomes* expected by their *Health Factors* (Fig. 13.2).

However, the disconnection in the rankings gives only part of the picture. To explore the magnitude of the disconnection, we compared the Z-score of *Health Factors* and the Z-score of *Health Outcomes* (Fig. 13.3).

Interestingly enough, when grouped with the counties with the best *Health Outcomes* to the left, no pattern is identified (Fig. 13.4).

These graphs give a much more interesting picture of the relationships between *Health Outcomes* and *Health Factors*. The counties to the left of each graph show *Health Outcomes* better than expected from the *Health Factors*, while those to the right have worse *Health Outcomes*. The magnitude is given by the distance from the zero line. In general, counties that ranked higher in *Health Outcomes* also had *Health Outcomes* better than expected. However, there are notable exceptions, particularly in Montana.

In looking at the relationships between *Health Outcomes* and *Health Factors*, a binomial model was found to give the best fit (Fig. 13.5).

This binomial relationship between *Health Outcomes* and *Health Factors* appears to hold true for every state, with an $R^2$ varying between 0.45 for Idaho and 1.0 for Delaware and Hawaii (Fig. 13.6).

This binomial formula

$$Factors = a(Outcomes)^2 + b(Outcomes) + c \tag{13.1}$$

with differing constants $a$, $b$, and $c$ for each state forms a "signature" representing the relationship between *Health Outcomes* and aggregate *Health Factors*. This signature is fairly consistent and relatively unique over time for each state. The

---

[1]The Z-score indicates how many standard deviations an element is from the mean.

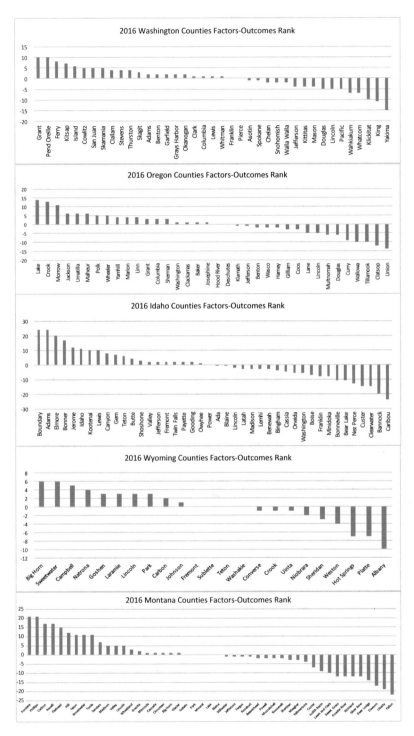

**Fig. 13.2** Counties factors-outcomes ranks

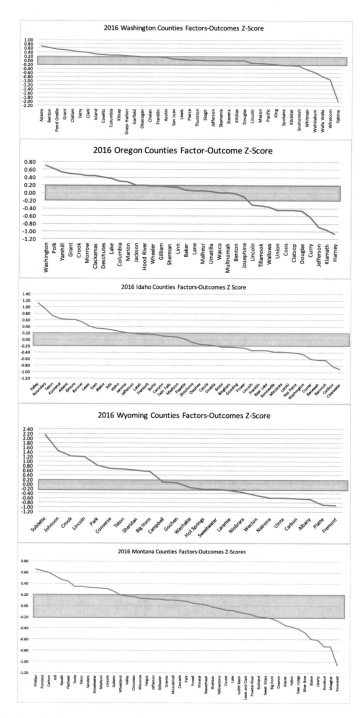

**Fig. 13.3** Counties factors-outcomes Z-scores

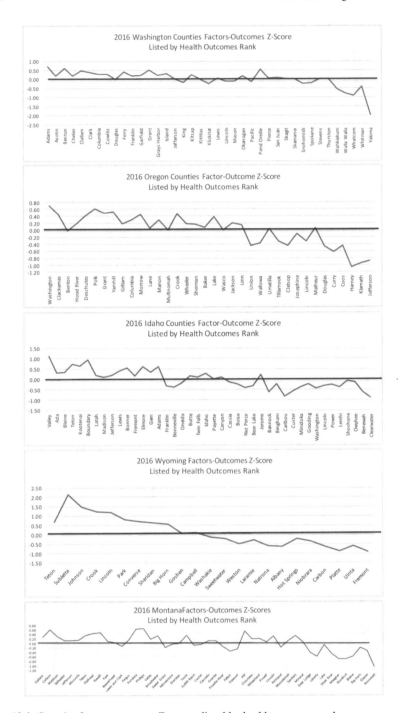

**Fig. 13.4** Counties factors-outcomes Z-scores, listed by health outcomes rank

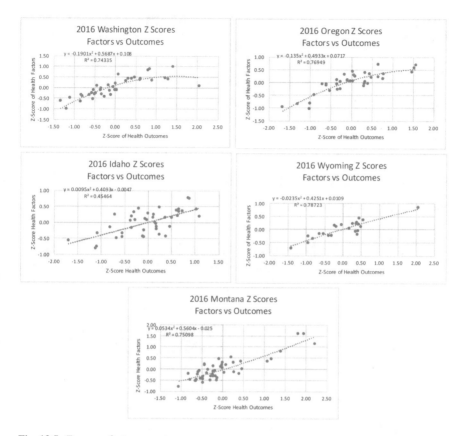

**Fig. 13.5**  Z-scores, factors vs outcomes

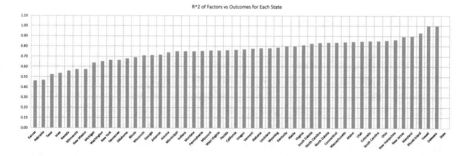

**Fig. 13.6**  Binominal relationship between health outcomes and health factors across all US states

state signature is further modified in each county, with a further adjustment of the impact of *Health Factors* on *Health Outcomes*. This is consistent with the initial figure showing the varying relative disconnect between *Health Factors* and *Health Outcomes*.

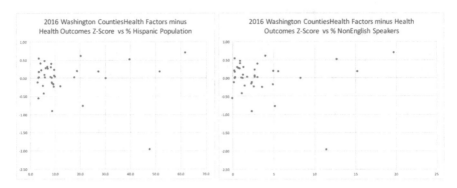

**Fig. 13.7** "Hispanic Paradox"

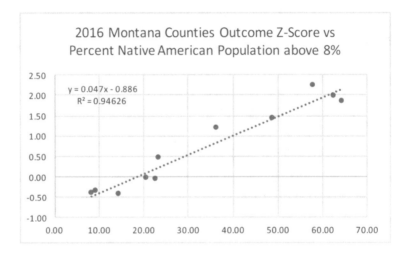

**Fig. 13.8** Native American population

In some states, particularly in the Southwest, an "Hispanic Paradox" is seen, with *Health Outcomes* better than would otherwise be expected [7]. In the Pacific Northwest, this was seen only in Washington when the percent Hispanic population was above 28% and percent of non-English speakers above 13% (Fig. 13.7).

In Montana, the situation with counties with predominantly Native American populations showed the reverse. In counties with greater than 8% Native American population, there was a linear negative correlation with *Health Outcomes* (Fig. 13.8).

Finally, examination of this graph of the Z-scores of *Health Factors* versus *Health Outcomes* for Montana is most instructive (Fig. 13.9).

Liberty county has significantly better *Health Factors* than Pondera, yet has significantly worse *Health Outcomes*. "Something else" is retarding the expression of these positive factors. Just as in Roseto, that something else defied the medical

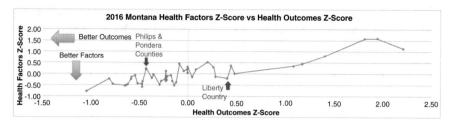

**Fig. 13.9** Liberty County Anomaly

logic of the time, so too other elements are at play in understanding the data contained in the RWJF County Health Rankings. The challenge will be in finding them.

## 13.3   Conclusions

The relationship of *Health Factors* and *Health Outcomes* is nonlinear and complex. The data compiled in the RWJF study on County Health Rankings is a landmark beginning for investigations into what constitutes "health." While it is true that in order to improve the health of a community, improving all aspects of health (health behaviors, clinical care, social and economic factors, and physical environment) will be helpful, it is equally clear that some efforts will be more productive than others. In a situation of limited resources, it is imperative that those resources be utilized wisely so the maximum improvement for the maximum population will be possible. This analysis points out this is not always intuitive.

For example, a mild "Hispanic Paradox" is seen in Washington when the Hispanic population is greater than 28% and the population or non-English speakers is greater than 13%. In Montana, strongly negative Health Outcomes are seen in counties with a Native American population greater than 8% ($R^2 = 0.93883$).

## 13.4   Recommendations

- In Montana, efforts should be directed toward improving *Health Factors*, such as increasing healthy behaviors like reducing obesity, increasing physical activity, and smoking cessation, especially in counties with a high percentage of Native Americans.
- In Oregon and Wyoming, such an effort in improving *Health Factors* will be most successful in those counties which already have high Health Outcomes. They exhibit *positive returns*.

- In Washington and Idaho, the use of *positive deviance* could identify possible other factors that improve *Health Outcomes* in those counties in which the *Health Outcomes* are better than expected.

## The Journey

This paper represents a way-stop on my own intellectual journey through Systems and Complexity Sciences for Healthcare. When I first learned of the concept of "complexity," I immediately attempted to apply that to health care. At least in my own experience, that was a mistake. I was applying my reductionist training to something that was the antithesis of reductionism. It was only after I investigated "complexity" in its totality that I was able to understand how it could be applied to my own experiences in health care. I am sure one is able to utilize the concepts of complexity science in isolation and concentrate on how they relate to the set of circumstances in health care. I am not able to do that. I need to be a "lumper" rather than a "splitter." I see health care as a seat at the larger table of complexity science, rather than a separate table by itself.

In *The Nature of Technology*, W. Brian Arthur makes the case that revolutionary jumps forward are often due to the combination of existing technologies and ideas in novel ways [8]. The "Pumps and Pipes" conferences in Houston bring together cardiovascular physicians, petroleum engineers, and aerospace scientists to discuss what actually are common problems from different perspectives. One of the organizers, Alan Lumsden, Chief of Cardiovascular Surgery at Houston Methodist Heart and Vascular Center, states "the answer to your problem is probably in the other guy's toolkit. The challenge is finding it" [9]. For my own journey, it is essential to interact with individuals outside of the health-care arena. I need to understand what is in their toolkit.

> Take-Home Message
> The relationship between *Health Factors* and *Health Outcomes* is ***complex*** and follow ***nonlinear dynamics***. Understanding this is necessary to improve health disparities.

## References

1. Stout C, Morrow J, Brandt E, Wolf S. Unusually low incidence of death from myocardial infarction in an Italian-American community in Pennsylvania. JAMA 1964;188:845–9.
2. Bruhn JG, Chandler B, Miller C, Wolf S. Social aspects of coronary heart disease in two adjacent ethnically different communities. Am J Public Health 1966;56:1493–506.
3. Gladwell M. Outliers. New York: Little Brown and Company; 2008. p. 3–11.

4. Egolf B, Lasker J, Wolf S, Potvin L. The Roseto effect: a 50-year comparison of mortality rates. Am J Public Health 1992;82:1089–92.
5. https://www.hhs.gov/about/budget/budget-in-brief/cms/innovation-programs/index.html. Accessed 26 Dec 2016.
6. Booske BC, Athens JK, Kindig DA, Park H, Remington PL. County health rankings working paper: different perspectives for assigning weights to determinants of health. University of Wisconsin Population Health Institute. 2010. http://www.countyhealthrankings.org/sites/default/files/differentPerspectivesForAssigningWeightsToDeterminantsOfHealth.pdf. Accessed 30 April 2016.
7. Gonnering RS, Riley W. The paradoxical "Hispanic Paradox": the dark side of acculturation. Unpublished manuscript.
8. Arthur BW. The nature of technology: what it is and how it evolves. New York: Free Press; 2009. p. 129–30.
9. http://www.tmc.edu/news/2015/02/guys-toolkit/. Accessed 26 Dec 2016.

# Chapter 14
# Positive Deviance in Health Care: Beware of Pseudo-Equifinality

David C. Aron, Brigid Wilson, Chin-Lin Tseng, Orysya Soroka, and Leonard M. Pogach

## 14.1 Introduction

The adoption of "best practices" constitutes an important strategy for organizational improvement [1–4]. Best practices can be sought from high-performing outliers [5–7]. This is the first step in using the positive deviance process, a strategy that is gaining popularity in healthcare improvement [8–16].

The "positive deviance approach" to social/behavior change began in the area of childhood nutrition when it was noted that within communities with high levels of childhood malnutrition, some families had well-nourished children [17, 18]. These families, referred to as positive deviants, evidenced uncommon but successful

D. C. Aron (✉)
Department of Veterans Affairs, Louis Stokes Cleveland VA Medical Center, 10701 East Blvd., Cleveland, OH 44106, USA

Case Western Reserve University School of Medicine, Cleveland, OH, USA
e-mail: david.aron@va.gov

B. Wilson
Department of Veterans Affairs, Louis Stokes Cleveland VA Medical Center, 10701 East Blvd., Cleveland, OH 44106, USA
e-mail: brigid.wilson@va.gov

C.-L. Tseng · L. M. Pogach
Department of Veterans Affairs, New Jersey Healthcare System, 385 Tremont Ave, East Orange, NJ 07018, USA

Department of Biostatistics, School of Public Health, Rutgers University, Piscataway, NJ, USA
e-mail: chin-lin.tseng@va.gov; leonard.pogach@va.gov

O. Soroka
Department of Veterans Affairs, New Jersey Healthcare System, 385 Tremont Ave, East Orange, NJ 07018, USA
e-mail: orysya.soroka@va.gov

© Springer International Publishing AG, part of Springer Nature 2018    189
J. P. Sturmberg (ed.), *Putting Systems and Complexity Sciences Into Practice*,
https://doi.org/10.1007/978-3-319-73636-5_14

behaviors or strategies that enabled them to find better solutions to a problem than their peers, despite facing similar challenges and having no apparent extra resources or knowledge. A similar approach, termed bright spotting, has been applied in primary care to the identification of patients with diabetes at high risk of complications who have managed to maintain their health [19].

The term positive deviance has been used in different ways in management improvement and research. The concept of positive deviance has also been used to describe behavior of individuals within organizations [20–24]. More recently, this concept has been applied to organizations themselves, especially in healthcare. For example in systematic review, Baxter et al. identified four key themes of positive deviance:

1. Positive deviants were defined as high performers
2. Positive deviants demonstrated different or uncommon behaviors
3. Positive deviance is a bottom-up approach
4. Positive deviant solutions are sustainable within current resource [8]

Although definitions of positive deviance vary widely, the phenomenon of positive deviance is often mentioned in the context of complexity, whether complexity science, complexity theory, or complexity thinking. For example, Lindberg and Clancy identified complexity science concepts and related then to the positive deviance process in reducing the occurrence of intravenous line infections in the intensive care unit [25]. These concepts included:

- The number and nature of relationships
- Difference and diversity in perspective and action
- The extent to which power is centralized or shared
- The degree to which variability and order exist

In being attuned to the number and nature of relationships, the positive deviance process seeks to involve all whose behavior affects the problem and relies on facilitators who are skilled at nurturing open conversation and encouraging participation in small group conversation [25]. Similarly, Spindler and Wagenheim described positive deviance dynamics as "typically a 'grassroots' self-organising unit, within teams, organisations, networks or society yet often outside the formal structure, that has a different, even contrarian, perspective of the social system. Such deviants can be considered holons that contain all the characteristics of the whole system to which they belong yet operate with an entrepreneurial independence. This autonomy and unique perspective allows them to observe the system's blindness and realise different solutions (p. 647)" [26]. Thus, the positive deviance approach implies the necessity of thinking that the process unfolds in the context of a complex adaptive system, in short, complexity thinking. Further exploration of the philosophical (ontological and epistemological) underpinnings of complexity thinking is beyond the scope of this paper. Readers are referred to the work of Richardson and others [27, 28].

A structured approach to employing the positive deviance process includes the definition of the problem, the identification of positive deviant individuals or teams, and the discovery of the uncommon practices or behaviors that allow the positive deviants to be successful [29]. Addressing mortality in intensive care units following myocardial infarction provides an exemplar of this approach.

Bradley et al. noted that there was marked hospital variation in ICU mortality for myocardial infarction [9, 11]. Their first step involved identification of organizations that demonstrated exceptionally high performance in this area of interest—positive deviants. In this case, there was a well-established metric for the outcome. In addition, a criterion of consistent high performance was used. This was operationalized by analyzing data from two consecutive years. They then selected hospitals that ranked in the top and bottom 5% of performance during both years. In the original work on positive deviance in public health, the comparators were required to be those with similar access to resources. In contrast, Bradley et al. selected hospitals that were diverse in areas such as the volume of patients with acute myocardial infarction, teaching status, and socioeconomic status of patients. They were seeing to identify "information rich" participants that have certain characteristics, detailed knowledge, or direct experience relevant to the phenomenon of interest. Later studies examined what the positive deviants were doing that was different from other intensive care units, and those actions were shared with others.

Many hospitals have since adopted those practices with resulting improvement in outcomes. However, despite their good results, several questions are raised about extrapolating that approach to other issues. First, in this case there was a very well-established and uniform metric, something often lacking. In addition to there being a wide range of performance metrics, how the definition is operationalized can vary greatly. Both the length of time deemed necessary to demonstrate consistency and the procedures to identify high performance vary. In contrast to Bradley et al., others have examined performance during a single 1-year period based on 99 percentile confidence limits [30]. In addition, in the latter study, the comparator was limited to other hospitals in the same, albeit very large, organizational unit. In the original work on positive deviance in childhood nutrition, performance was assessed by simple observation rather than statistical analysis [18, 29]. The difference between malnourished and well-nourished children was obvious. This may or may not be the case with organizational positive deviance. There are no agreed upon methods to determine the criteria for high performance or to define an appropriate comparator. The identification of an outlier depends on the measures and statistical methods chosen, and different methods often do not agree [7, 31–34].

Diabetes, a common chronic condition, lends itself to this type of assessment because there are well-established performance measures [35]. Many of these measures have been based on assessment of glycemic control using hemoglobin A1c (HbA1c) levels and have focused primarily on rates of inadequate or undertreatment. Recently, more attention has been paid to the increasing problem of hypoglycemia which may be an unintended consequence of overly intensive glycemic control [36–39]. Overtreatment can result from setting HbA1c targets that are inappropriately low based on patients' life expectancy, comorbid conditions, and other factors [40–44]. We previously developed a measure of overtreatment [30]. The objective of our study was to determine the effect of different factors on identification of high-performing outliers—positive deviants, especially consistency of performance over time, and use of different comparators. In addition, we included a reciprocal measure, one of undertreatment. Such undertreatment could be a consequence of efforts to reduce overtreatment or the combination of high rates of undertreatment and low rates of overtreatment could reflect lack of attention to diabetes care in general.

## 14.2   Methods

### 14.2.1   Research Design and Healthcare System Under Study

The design was serial cross-sectional, using yearly Veterans Health Administration (VHA) administrative data (2009–2013) [30]. VHA provides healthcare to eligible veterans of the Armed Services in >100 hospitals and their related clinics. During the period 2009–2013, VHA was organized into 21 regional networks (Veterans Integrated Service Networks or VISNs), each consisting of 3–10 facilities. The facilities vary by size, range of services offered locally, and other factors from which is calculated a complexity level. There are 18–32 facilities in each of the 5 complexity levels.

### 14.2.2   Outcome Measures

We used our previously developed measure for overtreatment and used an HbA1c threshold of 6.5%. Overtreatment rates were calculated at the facility level as the proportion of patients in the chosen population with HbA1c<6.5%. In brief, the population at high risk for hypoglycemia (hence overtreatment) included patients taking a diabetes drug known to have a relatively high frequency of hypoglycemia (insulin and/or sulfonylurea agents) plus having at least one of the following additional criteria: age 75 years or older, chronic kidney disease (defined as last serum creatinine measurement in a year greater than 2.0 mg/dL/176.8 mmol/L, or an ICD-9-CM diagnosis of cognitive impairment or dementia in ambulatory care) [30]. Undertreatment rates were calculated in the same patient population as the proportion of patients with an HbA1c greater than 9%. Rates were calculated for each year.

### 14.2.3   Outlier Status

Outlier status was assessed by a facility outlier value measure standardized within a year and for each of three comparator groups:

1. All VA hospitals
2. Hospitals within the same VISN
3. Hospitals within the same complexity level

The facility outlier value was calculated as:

$$\frac{\text{facility observed rate-mean rate in comparator population}}{\text{standard deviation of rates in comparator population}} \qquad (14.1)$$

## 14.3  Analyses

We calculated yearly rates of over- and undertretment as well as outlier status.

### 14.3.1  Results

Outlier values for our primary measure ranged from approximately −1.5 to +3.5 (Fig. 14.1). There was little effect of facility complexity and VISN on outlier identification. Use of different HbA1c thresholds results in different sets of outliers with only modest overlap (data not shown). Of the 14 facilities identified in the highest-performing decile for overtreatment in 2009, only 7 were consistent high

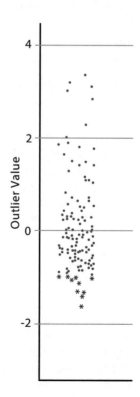

**Fig. 14.1** Overtreatment outlier values over time by 2009 deciles using 6.5% threshold and all VA facilities as comparator. Asterisk, top performing decile; filled circle, remaining 90%

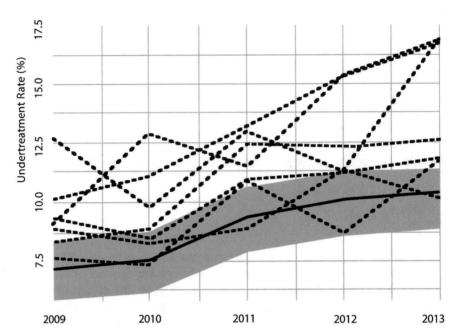

**Fig. 14.2** Undertreatment rates in the population at high risk for hypoglycemia. Undertreatment rates in the population at high risk for hypoglycemia over time among facilities with lowest rates of overtreatment (dashed lines) and the average rate +95% Confidence interval among all VA facilities (solid line within shaded area). Seven facilities were identified as high performers using overtreatment metrics; high rates of undertreatment were observed in many and looking at the undertreatment rates over time and comparing them to the undertreatment rates of all VA facilities, several high performers with regard to overtreatment have consistently high rates of undertreatment

performers in all the years from 2009 to 2013. While undertreatment in this population at high risk for hypoglycemia rose over time from a mean of 7.1% to 10.3%, consistent high-performing outliers for overtreatment had higher rates of undertreatment (HbA1c > 9%) in general. However, three of the high performers had overtreatment rates similar to VHA facilities as a whole; the remainder had higher rates at baseline that rose even more than facilities in general (Fig. 14.2).

## 14.4 Discussion

Statistical identification of positive deviants for diabetes overtreatment was dependent not only upon the specific measure used but also on time, i.e., high performance was consistent in only half of the facilities identified in the baseline year. Most importantly, our findings indicate the importance of including a balancing measure or countermeasure to identify unintended negative consequences. Thus, facilities which appeared to be similar based on one measure (equifinality) could be differentiated based on a balancing measure.

Equifinality and multifinality are each characteristic of open systems and represent opposite sides of the same coin. The principle of equifinality states that a given end state can be achieved by different paths or trajectories. In short, "all roads (may) lead to Rome," though the routes vary. In contrast, the principle of multifinality states that different end states can be reached starting from the same initial conditions. In short, every journey, regardless of where it ends, begins with the (same) first step. These principles make process improvement possible. Open systems exhibit change, but their end states are not ordained in a linear fashion from their initial states [45]. Different healthcare systems starting from different initial conditions reach a similar state of quality care. Moreover, different configurations of factors (and their interactions) may result in similar end states, a phenomenon that provides the basis for the methodology of qualitative comparative analysis [46].

The limitations of our study notwithstanding (e.g., single condition which is multidimensional and involves patients, providers, and organizations; single healthcare system; our focus on identification of high-performing sites rather than the best practices themselves) our findings have implications for the positive deviance approach because they illustrate the danger of taking a very narrow approach to what constitutes equifinality. Although there are numerous methods for outlier detection and differences in both criteria and comparator, our study suggests that considerable thought needs to be given to this issue at the outset, before attempts are made to identify performance outliers. Specifically, the end state of low rates of overtreatment may be observed under both desirable and undesirable conditions. Ideally, low rates of overtreatment occur as a result of specific attention to patients at risk for hypoglycemia. Less ideally, a low rate of overtreatment may occur as an artifact of widespread undertreatment and a facility-wide tendency toward higher HbA1c levels. We term this phenomenon pseudo-equifinality. In other words, two roads may lead to Rome, but one may lead to the Pantheon and the other to the Cloaca Maxima (greatest sewer).

**Acknowledgements** Funding. The work was supported by grants from the Veterans Health Administration (VHA) Health Services Research & Development Service and its Quality Enhancement Research Initiative (QUERI) to Dr. Aron (SCE 12-181), to Dr. Pogach (RRP-12-492), and to Dr. Tseng (IIR 11-077).
Disclaimer. The opinions expressed are solely those of the authors and do not represent the views of the Department of Veterans Affairs.

## The Journey

I came to complexity in the course of trying to do quality improvement, making incremental changes and moving up the linearly sloped "ramp of complexity." The reality of improvement followed every path. Some were dead ends and some traveled far without much effort. None (or perhaps very few) of those paths were linear. This taught me that my mental models did not reflect the world very well. I should have known this based on my experience as a physician. Patients with the "same" condition responded very differently to what should have been the correct therapy. To be a good physician involves dealing with every patient's complexities, using the term in its broadest sense. One particularly intriguing aspect has been the need to deal with unintended consequences, hence this study. Unintended consequences are seen in every sphere of activity—whether management of organizations or patients. This has led me on a journey of trying to better understand what underlies complex systems. Although thought experiments can be enlightening, the key to complexity is in the interactions and one only experiences interactions fully by interacting with others.

> **Take-Home Message**
> Identification of best practices from positive deviants constitutes an important strategy for organizational improvement. However, positive deviants may be difficult to identify and best practices dependent upon the context in which they are conducted. In a complex system of multiple interactions, unintended consequences are inevitable—some good, some bad. When evaluating a best practice, one's focus should not be so narrow that it ignores other factors which may mean that the "best" is not best at all.

# References

1. Bretschneider S, Marc-Aurele Jr F, Wu J. "Best practices" research: a methodological guide for the perplexed. J Public Adm Res Theory 2005;15:307–23.
2. Guzman G, Fitzgerald JA, Fulop L, et al. How best practices are copied, transferred, or translated between health care facilities: a conceptual framework. Health Care Manag Rev. 2015;40:193–202.
3. Maggs-Rapport F. 'Best research practice': in pursuit of methodological rigour. J Adv Nurs. 2001;35:373–83.
4. Mold J, Gregory M. Best practices research. Fam Med. 2003;35:131–4.
5. A systematic review of outliers detection techniques in medical data: preliminary study. 11 Jan 26; Rome, Italy: HEALTHINF 2011, 2011.
6. Hodge V, Austin J. A survey of outlier detection methodologies. Artif Intell Rev. 2004;22:85–126.
7. Shahian DM, Normand SL. What is a performance outlier? BMJ Qual Saf. 2015;24:95–9.
8. Baxter R, Kellar I, Taylor N, Lawton R. How is the positive deviance approach applied within healthcare organizations? A systematic review of methods used. BMC Health Serv Res. 2014;14 Suppl 2:7.
9. Bradley EH, Curry LA, Ramanadhan S, Rowe L, Nembhard IM, Krumholz HM. Research in action: using positive deviance to improve quality of health care. Implement Sci. 2009;4:25.
10. Gabbay RA, Friedberg MW, Miller-Day M, Cronholm PF, Adelman A, Schneider EC. A positive deviance approach to understanding key features to improving diabetes care in the medical home. Ann Fam Med. 2013;11 Suppl 1:S99–107.

11. Krumholz HM, Curry LA, Bradley EH. Survival after acute myocardial infarction (SAMI) study: the design and implementation of a positive deviance study. Am Heart J. 2011;162:981–7.
12. Lawton R, Taylor N, Clay-Williams R, Braithwaite J. Positive deviance: a different approach to achieving patient safety. BMJ Qual Saf. 2014;23:880–3.
13. Luft HS. Data and methods to facilitate delivery system reform: harnessing collective intelligence to learn from positive deviance. Health Serv Res. 2010;45:1570–80.
14. Setiawan M, Sadiq S. A methodology for improving business process performance through positive deviance. Int J Inf Syst Model Des. 2013;4:1–22.
15. Singhal A, Greiner K. Using the Positive Deviance approach to reduce hospital-acquired infections at the Veterans Administration Healthcare System in Pittsburgh. In: Suchman A, Sluyter D, Williamson P, editors. Leading change in healthcare: transforming organizations using complexity, positive psychology, and relationship-centered care. New York: Radcliffe Publishing; 2011. p. 177–209.
16. Marsh G. Are follow-up consultations at medical outpatient departments futile? BMJ 1982;284:1176–7.
17. Sternin J. Practice positive deviance for extraordinary social and organizational change. In: The change champion's field guide: strategies and tools for leading change in your organization. Hoboken, NJ: Wiley; 2013. p. 20–37.
18. Zeitlin M, Ghassemi H, Mansour M. Positive deviance in child nutrition - with emphasis on psychosocial and behavioural aspects and implications for development. New York: United Nations University Press; 1991.
19. Selby L. Public health project taps into superstar patients' expertise. http://thedo.osteopathic.org/2015/04/public-health-project-taps-into-superstar-patients-expertise/ (2017). Accessed 5 Jan 2017.
20. Mainemelis C. Stealing fire: creative deviance in the evolution of new ideas. Acad Manag Rev. 2010;35:558–78.
21. Spreitzer G, Sonenshein S. Positive deviance and extraordinary organizing. In: Cameron K, Dutton J, editors. Positive organizational scholarship: foundations of a new discipline. Oakland, CA: Berrett-Koehler Publishers; 2003. p. 207–24.
22. Spreitzer G, Sonenshein S. Toward the construct definition of positive deviance. Am Behav Sci. 2004;47:828–47.
23. Vadera A, Pratt M, Mishra P. Constructive deviance in organizations: integrating and moving forward. J Manag. 2013;39:1221–76.
24. Warren D. Constructive and destructive deviance in organizations. Acad Manag Rev. 2003;28:622–32.
25. Lindberg C, Clancy TR. Positive deviance: an elegant solution to a complex problem. J Nurs Adm. 2010;40:150–3.
26. Spindler M, Wagenheim G. Positive deviance: sparks that ignite systems change. Chall Organ Soc. 2015;4:647–9.
27. Richardson KA, Mathieson G, Cilliers P. The theory and practice of complexity science: epistemological considerations for military operational analysis. SysteMexico 2000;1:25–66.
28. Richardson KA. Complex systems thinking and its implications for policy analysis. In: Handbook of decision making. Boca Raton, FL: CRC Press; 2007. p. 189–122.
29. Pascale R, Sternin J, Sternin M. The power of positive deviance: how unlikely innovators solve the world's toughest problems. Boston, MA: Harvard Business Press; 2010.
30. Tseng CL, Soroka O, Maney M, Aron DC, Pogach LM. Assessing potential glycemic overtreatment in persons at hypoglycemic risk. JAMA Intern Med. 2013;174:259–68.
31. Bilimoria KY, Cohen ME, Merkow RP, et al. Comparison of outlier identification methods in hospital surgical quality improvement programs. J Gastrointest Surg. 2010;14:1600–7.
32. Mull HJ, Chen Q, O'Brien WJ, et al. Comparing 2 methods of assessing 30-day readmissions: what is the impact on hospital profiling in the veterans health administration? Med Care 2013;51:589–96.

33. Rothberg MB, Morsi E, Benjamin EM, Pekow PS, Lindenauer PK. Choosing the best hospital: the limitations of public quality reporting. Health Aff. (Millwood) 2008;27:1680–7.
34. Paddock SM, Adams JL, Hoces dlG. Better-than-average and worse-than-average hospitals may not significantly differ from average hospitals: an analysis of Medicare Hospital Compare ratings. BMJ Qual Saf. 2015;24:128–34.
35. Aron DC. Quality indicators and performance measures in diabetes care. Curr Diab Rep. 2014;14:472.
36. National action plan for adverse drug event prevention. Washington, DC: U.S. Department of Health and Human Services, Office of Disease Prevention and Health Promotion; 2014. https:// health.gov/hcq/pdfs/ade-action-plan-508c.pdf. Accessed 5 Jan 2017.
37. Trucil D. AGS unveils revised list of topics to talk about with older adults as part of choosing wisely®campaign. http://www.choosingwisely.org/ags-unveils-revised-list-of-topics-to-talk-about-with-older-adults-as-part-of-choosing-wisely-campaign/. Accessed 5 Jan 2017.
38. Duckworth W, Abraira C, Moritz T, Reda D, Emanuele N, et al. Glucose control and vascular complications in veterans with type 2 diabetes. N Engl J Med. 2009;360:129–39.
39. Miller ME, Bonds DE, Gerstein HC, et al. The effects of baseline characteristics, glycaemia treatment approach, and glycated haemoglobin concentration on the risk of severe hypoglycaemia: post hoc epidemiological analysis of the ACCORD study. BMJ 2010;340:b5444.
40. Inzucchi SE, Bergenstal RM, Buse JB, et al. Management of hyperglycaemia in type 2 diabetes: a patient-centered approach. Position statement of the American Diabetes Association (ADA) and the European Association for the Study of Diabetes (EASD). Diabetologia 2012;55:1577–96.
41. Ismail-Beigi F, Moghissi ES, Tiktin M, Hirsch IB, Inzucchi SE, Genuth S. Individualizing glycemic targets in type 2 diabetes mellitus: implications of recent clinical trials. Ann Intern Med 2011;154:554–9.
42. Montori V, Fernandez-Balsells M. Glycemic control in type 2 diabetes: time for an evidence-based about-face? Ann Intern Med. 2009;150:803–8.
43. Pogach L, Aron D. Balancing hypoglycemia and glycemic control: a public health approach for insulin safety. JAMA 2010;303:2076–7.
44. Pogach LM, Tiwari A, Maney M, Rajan M, Miller DR, Aron D. Should mitigating comorbidities be considered in assessing healthcare plan performance in achieving optimal glycemic control? Am J Manag Care 2007;13:133–40.
45. Kapsali M. Equifinality in project management exploring causal complexity in projects. Syst Res Behav Sci. 2013;30:2–14.
46. Ragin CC, Shulman D, Weinberg A, Gran B. Complexity, generality, and qualitative comparative analysis. Field Methods 2003;15:323–40.

# Chapter 15
# Understanding the Emergency Department Ecosystem Using Agent-Based Modeling: A Study of the Seven Oaks General Hospital Emergency Department

**Oluwayemisi Olugboji, Sergio G. Camorlinga, Ricardo Lobato de Faria, and Arjun Kaushal**

## 15.1 Introduction

The healthcare system is a complex adaptive system with many stakeholders and multidimensional interactions; it consists of agents, processes, and technologies. Given that agents, processes, and technologies can be configured in many different ways, simulation models are required to understand the system's behavior. Simulation is useful when direct experimentation is costly or infeasible. This will enable physicians to make logical and systematic decisions to address policy problems and make decisions that will deliver the most cost-effective care.

The complexity of the healthcare system is characterized by chaotic, nonlinear behavior and interdependencies among its agents. In this chapter, we analyze the complex behavior of agents in the Seven Oaks General Hospital emergency department (SOGH-ED). SOGH is an acute care community 304-bed hospital with the second busiest emergency department in Winnipeg, Canada.

O. Olugboji (✉) · S. G. Camorlinga
Department of Applied Computer Science, University of Winnipeg, 515 Portage Avenue, Winnipeg, MB, Canada R3B 2E9
e-mail: olugboji-o@webmail.uwinnipeg.ca; s.camorlinga@uwinnipeg.ca

R. L. de Faria
Seven Oaks General Hospital, University of Manitoba, 2300 McPhillips Street, Winnipeg, MB, Canada R2V 3M3
e-mail: rlobatodefaria@sogh.mb.ca

A. Kaushal
George & Fay Yee Centre for Healthcare Innovation, 753 McDermot Avenue, Winnipeg, MB, Canada R3E 0T6
e-mail: akaushal2@wrha.mb.ca

© Springer International Publishing AG, part of Springer Nature 2018
J. P. Sturmberg (ed.), *Putting Systems and Complexity Sciences Into Practice*,
https://doi.org/10.1007/978-3-319-73636-5_15

### 15.1.1 The Setting: Seven Oaks General Hospital Emergency Department

The Seven Oaks General Hospital Emergency Department (SOGH-ED) can be viewed as a black box that takes in patients as *inputs* and patients as *processes* that produce desirable *outputs*. The ED ecosystem comprises of agents and the available resources. The agents include the physician, physician assistants, nurses, nurse practitioners, and the patients. The patient agent serves as the input to the ED ecosystem, and interactions among all agents (i.e., patient agent, physician agent, nurse agent, etc.) determine the output of the ecosystem. Understanding the causal links in the ED ecosystem can bring about optimum utilization of the ED resources, saving costs and improving the quality of care. The challenge is how to properly identify and process those causal links that contribute to a given ED ecosystem operation.

### 15.1.2 Improving Patient Flow in the Emergency Department

Simulating the ED using a computer model developed on the agent-based NetLogo [1] software allows an understanding of the variations in ED process flows that arise from changes affecting the causal links between the ED system's agents. This can provide the ED management with a decision support tool to improve the quality of care and save costs by optimizing the use of resources.

## 15.2 Agent-Based Models

Agent-based models are used to simulate the complex and dynamic behavior of systems with very large number of entities in economics, politics, populations, and epidemics. They are computational models that usually involve numerous discrete agents. In this chapter, our agent-based models were analyzed using statistical methods, and we performed the simulations based on results of the statistical distributions.

Agent-based models are generally suitable for modeling complex systems. A complex system usually involves large number of events that have unpredictable system properties [2]. According to a study by the ISPOR Health Science Policy Council, there are three main methods for simulating complex systems in healthcare—systems dynamics, discrete event simulation, and agent-based modeling (ABM). Due to the autonomous behavior of the agent in the ED, ABM is the most suitable methodology [3].

## 15.2.1 SOGH-ED Model

Analysis of the SOGH-ED identified the core agents and their characteristics. We developed a stock and flow model followed by a causal loop diagram to describe the SOGH-ED processes. Simulations for modeling complex systems were carried out on processes in the ED ecosystem, and changes in the ecosystem were observed over time.

The stock and flow model is mostly used in analyzing the state of the system and its rate of change over time [4], while a causal loop diagram (CLD) is used to understand and account for the possibility of feedback in the system which in turn helps us in connecting the numerous variables and summarizing the result [4]. The next section describes both approaches as they relate to the SOGH-ED.

## 15.2.2 Current State Description (Stock and Flow Model)

Process and ecosystem analysis was performed to build an agent-based model.

### 15.2.2.1 Stocks vs Flows

It is worthy to note the differences between stocks and flows. A stock amounts to the quantity within a specific time period, while the flow constitutes the rate between two time periods. For example, the number of patients at a particular time in the ED represents the stock, while the number of patients within a certain time period represents the flow.

The stock and flow model is useful for understanding the arrival rates and inter-arrival rates of the agents in our simulation. This is very important in codifying the behavior of the system with greater accuracy.

The Seven Oaks General Hospital emergency department (SOGH-ED) stock and flow model is shown in Fig. 15.1. It describes the flow of patients through the SOGH-ED. There are two main stock values:

1. Patients in specific treatment phase
2. Hospital staff providing care

In the stock and flow diagram in Fig. 15.1, the stocks are depicted in rectangles. The stocks change over time depending on the inflows and outflows. The stocks also capture the state of the system and send signals to the rest of the system. Although stocks start with an initial value, they can only be changed by flows in and out of the system. In the SOGH-ED, the delays are usually caused by the values of the stocks at a particular instant.

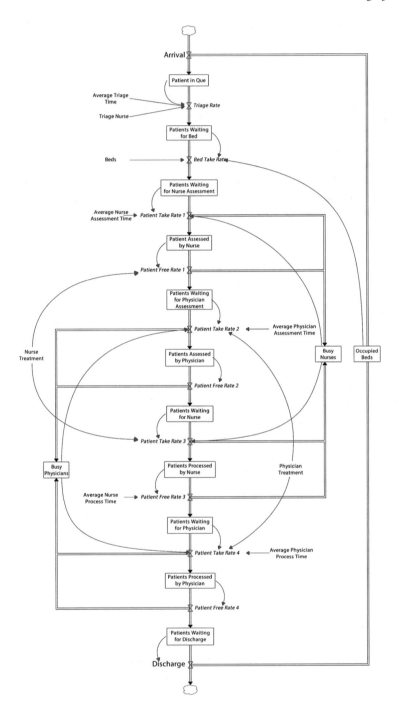

**Fig. 15.1** Seven Oaks General Hospital emergency department (SOGH-ED) stock and flow model. The diagram shows the flow of a patient from one phase to the other and highlights the dependency of flow in relation to the availability of staff at each treatment stage

The flows, depicted by the "data transmission" ⟨⟩ symbol, i.e., represent changes per time unit, for example, the rate of arrival per hour, rate of triage per hour, etc.

The major identified flow values are:

1. Arrival rate
2. Triage rate
3. Bed take rate
4. Patients take rate
5. Patients free rate
6. Bed free rate

The links in our SOGH-ED stock and flow represent influence, and the values outside the stock or flow represent auxiliary variables or parameters which are names given to constraints that directly influence the stocks and flows. Parameters are different from stocks because they do not accumulate over time.

## 15.2.3  The Patient's Journey Through the SOGH-ED

The patient journey through the ED consists of a triage phase followed a several post-triage steps. The dynamics of the patient journey are visualized in a causal loop diagram (Fig. 15.2).

The journey through ED has three phases and is influenced by its agents and behaviors as outlined above:

- Triage phase
- Assessment and treatment phase
- Discharge/post-discharge phase

From here on, phase names are placed between ** and agent states between <>.

### 15.2.3.1  Triage Step

As patients arrive at the hospital, they are put into <queue for triage>. As soon as the triage nurse becomes available, the patient from the queue is taken and moved to *triage* phase, and <nurse> is marked as busy. When the triage ends, the patient goes to <waiting for bed> state and the <nurse> is marked as free.

### 15.2.3.2  Post-triage Step

After triage, the patient <waiting for bed> goes through the following phases:

- *waiting for nurse assessment* (<bed is blocked>)

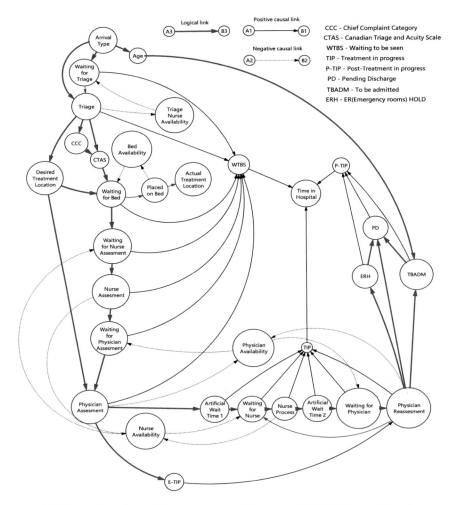

**Fig. 15.2** Seven Oaks General Hospital emergency department (SOGH-ED) causal loop diagram. *CCC* chief complaint category, *CTAS* Canadian Triage and Acuity Scale, *WTBS* waiting to be seen, *TIP* treatment in progress, *PTIP* posttreatment in progress, *PD* pending discharge, *TBADM* to be admitted, *ERH* ER (emergency rooms) HOLD

- *assessed by nurse* (<nurse is blocked>)
- *waiting for physician assessment* (<nurse is unblocked>)
- *assessed by physician* (<physician is blocked>)

Following the initial assessment, the treating <physician is unblocked>, and the *treatment* phase begins, which again entails a number of nurse and physician visits.

### 15.2.3.3   Discharge

When the treatment has been finalized, the patient enters the waiting for *discharge* phase and is discharged at some point in time, <unblocking his bed>.

Any of these phases can be interrupted depending on whether or not another consultation is needed.

## 15.2.4   Causal Loop Diagram of the SOGH-ED

The causal loop diagram aims to explore the systems dynamics of the SOGH-ED.

Each causal loop in Fig. 15.2 contains **two entities** (*nodes*) AND **one influence** (*connection*) as follows:

- Entities: The noun phrases (TIP, E-TIP, WTBS)
- Influences: The relationships between two entities
- Positive causal link: Causes an increase in the variable directly connected to it
- Negative causal link: Causes a reduction in the other variable directly connected to it

The causal loop diagram tells a coherent story about how different variables or factors affect the SOGH-ED flow. Such factors include:

- Chief complaint category (CCC)
- Canadian Triage and Acuity Score (CTAS)
- Waiting to be seen (WTBS) time
- Treatment in progress (TIP)
- Estimated treatment in progress (E-TIP)
- Pending discharge (PD)
- To be admitted (TBADM)
- ER (emergency rooms) HOLD (ERH)

In the SOGH CLD, a positive causal link (red arrow line) between two nodes indicates that the parameters will change in the same direction, while a negative causal link (blue arrow line) connecting two nodes indicates that the parameters will change in opposite directions. The black arrow line represents the logical connector link which shows a direct connection between two variables.

### 15.2.4.1   Reinforcing and Balancing Feedback Loops

A loop group with an even number of positive links in a CLD is called a reinforcing loop, while a loop with an odd number of positive links is called a balancing loop.

A reinforcing loop, as the name implies, will result in an outcome that influences the current state, hence producing more of the same effect, resulting in a growth or decline. A balancing loop, on the other hand, will help move a current state to a target goal.

Feedback loops help to make decisions that can regulate the behavior of a system in order to maintain some stability [5]. The positive loops in a CLD are called "reinforcing loops," while the negative loops are referred to as "balancing loop." Reinforcing and balancing loops help to determine the "weights" in a dynamic system; the discovery of patterns or formulas can help to determine how the combination of factors might lead to a "stable system."

$$T_1(\text{WTBS}) = \Delta t0 \left( \substack{\text{waiting for} \\ \text{triage nurse}} \right) + \Delta t1 \left( \substack{\text{waiting} \\ \text{for bed}} \right) + \Delta t2 \left( \substack{\text{waiting for} \\ \text{nurse assessment}} \right)$$

$$+ \Delta t3 \left( \substack{\text{nurse} \\ \text{assessment}} \right) + \Delta t4 \left( \substack{\text{waiting for} \\ \text{physician assessment}} \right)$$

$$+ \Delta t5 \left( \substack{\text{physician} \\ \text{assessment}} \right) \qquad (15.1)$$

The above formula was used in the simulation and helped to check the *waiting to be seen* (WTBS) time for its validity. The formula shows that WTBS is a function of several other factors; applying the same formulas in another emergency department will need some calibration to reflect that particular system.

The formula

$$F \left( \substack{\text{Assessment} \\ \text{time}} \right) = \gamma \left( \substack{\text{average} \\ \text{physicians}} \right) + h \left( \substack{\text{average} \\ \text{nurses}} \right) + b \qquad (15.2)$$

determines the assessment time for patient as a function of three main variables: the number of available nurses, the number of available physicians, and the number of available beds.[1]

## 15.3 Modeling and Simulation of the SOGH-ED

This section describes the algorithm used for the SOGH-ED simulation. It is based on the typical behavior of the agents and their interactions in the different sections within the ED environment.

---

[1] Where
- $T_x$ is a time required for "$x$" phase in the ED
- $\Delta t_x$ is a time required for "$x$" process in the ED
- $h$   is the number of available nurses
- $\gamma$   is the number of available physicians
- $b$   is the number of available beds

Both $T_x$ and $F(\textit{Assessment time})$ also depend on the patient's condition.

### 15.3.1   The Journey Through the ED

The patient's path is divided into three main phases:

- Waiting for treatment
- Treatment
- Posttreatment

The length of stay in the ED strongly depends on the severity of the patient's illness, which is measured by Canadian Triage and Acuity Scale (CTAS) [6]. The Emergency Department Information System (EDIS) datasets and simulation output can also be analyzed to ensure the assessment time intervals follow the CTAS guidelines.

### 15.3.2   The ED Environment

The ED ecosystem is divided into four zones (Fig. 15.3):

- Waiting room
- Triage zone
- Bed area
- Staff area

### 15.3.3   ED Resources

Patients go through various treatment procedures that involve any of the three resources:

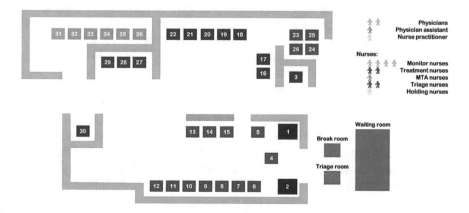

**Fig. 15.3**  Seven layout of the Oaks General Hospital emergency department (SOGH-ED)

- **Providers**.
  Physicians, physician assistants, and nurse practitioners
  They take part in treatment and posttreatment phases. Doctor types differ by
  effectiveness or experience, which is a defining factor in the treatment phase
  duration.
- **Nurses**.
  Treatment area nurses, minor treatment area (MTA) nurses, and holding area
  nurses
  Triage nurses play a KEY role in the waiting for treatment phase. Their function
  is to determine a patient's CTAS and to allocate him in the correct bed area.
- **Bed Areas**.
  Treatment, minor treatment area (MTA), and monitor or holding area beds
  The nurses associated with these areas take care of patients on those PODs. The
  first three types of beds are used in treatment phases, while the latter type is used
  in posttreatment. The most acute patients are put onto monitor beds, and the least
  on MTA beds.

## 15.3.4 Model Design

The experimental setup consists of three components, the simulation model, an
empirical dataset, and the steps of the care process.

- **The SOGH-ED NetLogo simulation model**. The SOGH-ED layout is divided
  into four zones as shown in Fig. 15.3: waiting room, triage zone, bed area, and
  staff area.
- **Empirical datasets**. The input file was generated from the SOGH Emergency
  Department Information System (EDIS).
- **The care process**.

  - *Waiting for treatment*
    The *waiting for treatment* phase begins with patients' arrival. The time of
    arrival was generated using distributions received by analysis of real patients'
    arrival times. The arrival rate strongly depends on certain periods of the day.
    After arrival, a patient is put into the waiting room. When the triage nurse
    becomes available, she takes the longest waiting patient to the triage zone.
    The triage nurse decides the patient's CTAS and where he should be allocated
    (DTL = desired treatment location). CTAS and DTL are generated based on
    derived probabilities. The probability of getting a specific DTL depends on the
    patient's CTAS. After triage, the patient goes to the waiting room until a bed
    becomes available. The bed the patient finally gets (ATL = actual treatment
    location) depends on his CTAS, DTL, and current bed availability. After the
    patient gets his bed, the *waiting for treatment* phase has finished.

– *Treatment*

The *treatment* phase consists of consecutive visits of doctors and nurses. The next steps on the patient's path are the initial nurse and doctor assessments. The nurse with the lowest number of patients adds a new patient to the end of her list. When she reaches the top of the list, the patient is assessed. After the nurse assessment, the patient can now be assessed by a doctor. The now doctor adds him to his list and carries out an assessment when it is the patient's turn.

Following the assessment, the doctor estimates the time required to treat this patient (E-TIP—estimated treatment in progress). E-TIP is generated based on average treatment times, and this depends on the patient's CTAS. E-TIP values are generated based on average treatment times, which depend on the patient's CTAS; CTAS in turn determines the number of necessary treatment steps.

One treatment course consists of first artificial wait time, nurse assessment, second artificial wait time, and doctor assessment. The duration of nurse assessment is 15 min. The wait time values and doctor assessment duration values are calculated based on E-TIP, the number of treatment steps, and the doctor's experience.

During the last doctor's assessment, the doctor will decide whether posttreatment is needed. If needed, the E-PTIP (estimated posttreatment in process) is generated, and the patient is moved to the waiting room, and the *posttreatment* phase begins. Otherwise, the patient is discharged. In both cases the *treatment* phase is considered to have finished.

– *Posttreatment*

A patient who is recommended for *posttreatment* stays in the waiting room until a bed in the holding area becomes available. Posttreatment time estimation is similar to that of the treatment time estimation, using E-PTIP instead of E-TIP. After the last posttreatment step, the patient is discharged.

– *Shift timing*

From 10:00 pm to 10:00 am, the MTA department is closed: The patients, MTA nurse, and nurse practitioner go home. Also, one of the physicians is at home between 2:00 am and 7:00 am.

There are short breaks for nurses every few hours. All nurses are divided into three shifts and they go on breaks by turns.

Nurses are also divided into PODs. If the nurse is free, but the other nurse in the same POD has patients, the first nurse will help with those patients. Table 15.1 shows how the patients are distributed in various treatment areas according to their CTAS.

## 15.3.5   Model Validation

The *waiting to be seen* (WTBS) time and the *treatment in progress* (TIP) time of our simulation output results are compared against the EDIS data using SAS statistical software [7].

**Table 15.1** SOGH-ED triage category distributions

| CTAS | 1 | 2 | 3 | 4 | 5 |
|---|---|---|---|---|---|
| % of patients | 1.6 | 16.5 | 54.5 | 20.9 | 6.5 |
| *DTL* % monitor | 92.13 | 72.77 | 37.93 | 24.98 | 14.40 |
| Treatment | 7.87 | 25.61 | 52.67 | 54.42 | 57.06 |
| MTA | | 1.62 | 9.40 | 20.60 | 28.54 |
| Average E-TIP (min) | 241.20 | 182.98 | 111.75 | 81.55 | 71.75 |

The simulation was run using all the parameters of the "real world" as captured by EDIS, i.e., the simulation took account of the process flow contingent to the urgency of care levels (CTAS) and the availability of service providers at the time of arrival. Table 15.2 shows the comparison of the simulation output to the actual historical ED utilization data for each CTAS category.

### 15.3.6 Stability of the SOGH-ED Model

Comparison of the data indicates the similarities between the simulation and the historical distribution of patients across the acuity categories (CTAS). Tables 15.3, 15.4, and 15.5 show the descriptive statistics for three simulation runs confirming the consistency in the time variable outcomes of the simulation model.

### 15.3.7 Comparison of WTBS and TIP Between Model and EDIS

Table 15.6 shows the comparison of the time variables (WTBS, TIP) between the simulation runs and the time variables in the EDIS datasets.

The null hypothesis assumes equal means between the time variables in the simulation output and the EDIS dataset. The *t*-test (Table 15.7) confirms that there is no statistically significant difference between the simulation output results and the EDIS dataset for WTBS and TIP.

## 15.4 Conclusions

This work provides SOGH-ED management with a tool that allows them to analyze the overall state of the ED system. Most importantly, the simulation model allows users to determine bottlenecks in the system and identifies not only the problem but also its cause.

It has been shown empirically that the model is able to recreate the outcomes corresponding with the "real-world system" of the SOGH-ED as evidenced by its

**Table 15.2** Comparison of simulation output and historical ED utilization data (EDIS) for each CTAS category

| CTAS | Frequency | | Percent | | Valid percent | | Cumulative percent | |
|---|---|---|---|---|---|---|---|---|
| | Sim. model | EDIS data | Sim. model | EDIS data | Sim. model | EDIS data | Sim. model | EDIS data |
| 1 | 22 | 14 | 1.1 | 0.7 | 1.1 | 0.7 | 1.1 | 0.7 |
| 2 | 279 | 232 | 14.0 | 11.6 | 14.0 | 11.6 | 15.0 | 12.3 |
| 3 | 972 | 986 | 48.6 | 49.3 | 48.6 | 49.3 | 63.6 | 61.6 |
| 4 | 606 | 568 | 30.3 | 28.4 | 30.3 | 28.4 | 94.0 | 90.0 |
| 5 | 121 | 200 | 6.0 | 10.0 | 6.0 | 10.0 | 100.0 | 100.0 |
| Total | 2000 | 2000 | 100.0 | 100.0 | 100.0 | 100.0 | | |

**Table 15.3** Descriptive statistics of time variables—first run

|                    | N    | Minimum | Maximum | Mean   | Std. deviation |
|--------------------|------|---------|---------|--------|----------------|
| WTBS               | 2000 | 22      | 904     | 169.74 | 157.531        |
| E-TIP              | 2000 | 51      | 349     | 130.67 | 51.438         |
| Post-E-TIP         | 284  | 16      | 1861    | 212.32 | 344.528        |
| Valid N (listwise) | 284  |         |         |        |                |

**Table 15.4** Descriptive statistics of time variables—second run

|                    | N    | Minimum | Maximum | Mean   | Std. deviation |
|--------------------|------|---------|---------|--------|----------------|
| WTBS               | 2000 | 21      | 801     | 97.62  | 100.880        |
| E-TIP              | 2000 | 55      | 327     | 132.91 | 51.849         |
| Post-E-TIP         | 310  | 16      | 1879    | 205.29 | 364.297        |
| Valid N (listwise) | 310  |         |         |        |                |

**Table 15.5** Descriptive statistics of time variables—third run

|                    | N    | Minimum | Maximum | Mean    | Std. deviation |
|--------------------|------|---------|---------|---------|----------------|
| WTBS               | 2000 | 21      | 812     | 108.404 | 101.294        |
| E-TIP              | 2000 | 55      | 326     | 131.19  | 51.892         |
| Post-E-TIP         | 301  | 16      | 1896    | 205.89  | 350.539        |
| Valid N (listwise) | 301  |         |         |         |                |

**Table 15.6** Sample statistics for WTBS and E-TIP

|        |            | Mean (min) | N    | Std. deviation | Std. error mean |
|--------|------------|------------|------|----------------|-----------------|
| Pair 1 | WTBS       | 123.96     | 6200 | 126.180        | 1.602           |
|        | WTBS_HIS   | 126.69     | 6200 | 96.798         | 1.229           |
| Pair 1 | Post-E-TIP | 131.39     | 6200 | 51.609         | 0.655           |
|        | TIP        | 128.04     | 6200 | 157.346        | 1.998           |

**Table 15.7** T-test results

|                             | Paired differences |               |                |                                                |        |       |      |                    |
|-----------------------------|--------------------|---------------|----------------|------------------------------------------------|--------|-------|------|--------------------|
|                             |                    |               |                | 95% confidence interval of the difference      |        |       |      |                    |
|                             | Mean               | Std deviation | Std error mean | Lower                                          | Upper  | $t$   | df   | Sig (2-tailed)     |
| Pair 1: WTBS-WTBS_HIS       | 0.269              | 153.535       | 1.950          | -3.552                                         | 4.091  | 0.138 | 6199 | 0.890              |
| Pair 2: E-TIP-TIP           | 3.346              | 164.116       | 2.084          | -0.740                                         | 7.432  | 1.605 | 6199 | 0.108              |

historical dataset (EDIS). This provides initial evidence that problems modeled by this simulation model could identify outcomes that most likely will reflect those encountered in the real world.

Although more testing and validation are required, our initial results are encouraging that the approach is feasible for this task. We have provided a tool that can be used to simulate the outcomes of changes to staffing levels and staff composition. It also allows the testing of new process streams without compromising patient safety like fast track treatment (FTT) [8].

In the future, we aim to integrate our model with the real-time EDIS datasets to enable mangers to make decisions based on real-time demands.

## The Journey

This project gave me my moment of opportunity to delve directly from theoretical applications of complex adaptive systems into its application in the real world—the emergency department. Walking into the emergency department for the first time as a non-patient, I recollect how the doctors and nurses were moving helter-skelter. There were stretcher patients in the lobby that were in the queue for bed space, and the ED seemed to have been over its capacity. I went ahead to discuss this project with the principal investigators, and after 2 h, I returned to meet an almost empty ED. The chaotic set of interactions I observed earlier had resulted in the emergence of an ordered system through self-organization among agents. At that point, I had started observing the systematic behavior of a complex system in the ED environment. Then, I realized I could potentially simulate the key components that drove the system between order and chaos.

---

Take-Home Message

- The careful analysis of individual parts in a complex system can result in the global emergence of a stable system
- Focusing on the important factors will give a good insight to the scale of complexity in the system
- Some approaches in multi-agent systems such as the stock and flow and feedback loops serve as a mechanism to better understand the complexity of the system
- The validation process can be performed iteratively to achieve the required level of confidence for the model results

# References

1. Wilensky U. NetLogo. Evanston, IL: Center for Connected Learning and Computer-Based Modeling, Northwestern University; 1999. http://ccl.northwestern.edu/netlogo/.
2. Hiroki S. Introduction to the modeling and analysis of complex systems. Geneseo: Milne Library State University of New York; 2015.
3. Marshall DA, Burgos-Liz L, Eng I, IJzerman MJ, Osgood ND, Padula WV, Higashi MK,Wong PK, Pasupathy KS, Crown W. Applying dynamic simulation modeling methods in health care delivery research-the SIMULATE checklist: report of the ISPOR simulation modeling emerging good practices task force. Value Health 2015;18(1):5–16.
4. Borshchev A, Filippov A. From system dynamics and discrete event to practical agent based modeling: reasons, techniques, tools. In: Proceedings of the 22nd International Conference of the System Dynamics Society; 2004, 22.
5. Diez Roux AV. Complex systems thinking and current impasses in health disparities research. Am J Public Health 2011;101(9):1627–34.
6. Bullard MJ, Unger B, Spence J, Grafstein E. Revisions to the Canadian emergency department triage and acuity scale (CTAS) adult guidelines. CJEM 2008;10(2):136–51.
7. SAS Institute. Base SAS 9. 4 procedures guide: statistical procedures. Cary, NC: SAS Institute; 2014.
8. Kaushal A, Zhao Y, Peng Q, Strome T, Weldon E, Zhang M, Chochinov A. Evaluation of fast track strategies using agent-based simulation modeling to reduce waiting time in a hospital emergency department. Socio Econ Plan Sci. 2015;50:18–31.

# Part III
# The Art-Science Project

The final part of this book describes a novel approach to sharing the experience of complexity—through art.

Why art? Art provides a means of expressing thoughts, feelings and responses that may otherwise be difficult to communicate.

As Shelley Esaak[1] emphasised, a piece of art tells a story in context, here the shared understanding of the nature of systems and complexity sciences in healthcare.

The final art installation—co-produced through intermittent conversations between the artists and the scientists/health professionals/health system managers—reflected the three key functions of art:

- The physical artefact
- The reflection of a collective understanding
- The stimulation of personal reflection

---

[1] https://www.thoughtco.com/what-are-the-functions-of-art-182414.

# Chapter 16
# Leo's Lions: An Art-Science Project

Bruno Kissling and Esther Quarroz

## 16.1 Introduction

A patient who gets overwhelmed by an unknown symptom creates inner pictures about his problem on the ground of individual and contextual singularities and influences. With these essences, he creates an individual illness narrative and tells it to his physician or therapist. The physician or therapist, him- or herself formed by own inner pictures, enters in a complex adaptive interacting dialogue with the patient and his or her narrative. Out of this dialogue, a trustful mutual therapeutic doctor-patient relationship emerges, and based on this, a therapeutic process evolves with unforeseeable further steps and outcomes.

Analogically, an artist reflects inner pictures composed of thoughts, innate and learned knowledge, social and cultural embedding, individual experiences and visions. Out of this personal reality, he or she creates art objects and by means of the finalized art objects enters in a dialogue with the observer.

With our everyday experience as art therapist and physician working interactively with patients in mind, we aim to go beyond this usual understanding of arts and create a social art sculpture (Joseph Beuys[1]). This means we enter in a dynamic dialogue with the observer—here with the scientists at the conference in Billings—

[1]Joseph Beuys (1921–1986) was a German Fluxus, happening, and performance artist as well as a sculptor, installation artist, graphic artist, art theorist, and pedagogue.

B. Kissling (✉)
Elfenau Praxis, Elfenauweg 52, 3006 Bern, Switzerland
e-mail: bruno.kissling@hin.ch

E. Quarroz
Perspectiven Entwickeln, Zähringerstrasse 61, 3012 Bern, Switzerland
e-mail: info@perspektiven-entwickeln.ch

© Springer International Publishing AG, part of Springer Nature 2018
J. P. Sturmberg (ed.), *Putting Systems and Complexity Sciences Into Practice*,
https://doi.org/10.1007/978-3-319-73636-5_16

at the beginning of our creative work. We integrate this complex adaptive artist-observer interaction within the creative process. With this procedure, we foster a mutual understanding of the unforeseeable emerging process.

## 16.2 Leo's Story

Leo, a 5-year-old boy from Bern, suffered from leukaemia. He flatly refused to have chemotherapy. His parents and doctors were desperate. How come that this 5-year-old boy was so adamant? As neither his parents nor doctors could find an answer, they sought help from an art therapist (EQ). Listening carefully to Leo's reasons to reject medical help, he told us about his very vivid inner picture and understanding of his illness—"I have white lions in my blood. They are my friends and protectors. I will never kill my friends."

"Leu-" in the word leukaemia means "lion" in Swiss German. It was the typical military oncological metaphor [1–4] of "killing" and "fighting against" that resulted in his strong rejection of therapy. What was needed was a new metaphor, one that would allow Leo to shift his inner image.

"The white lions are your friends. Your body is not the right place to live for them. We have to relocate them in a better environment." This new metaphor opened the way to *save the lions **and** the life of the child*. It allowed Leo to remain connected with his friends, something vital for his well-being.

## 16.3  Inner Pictures and Illness Narratives

Most of our thinking, memories, mental and physical perceptions, joyous and traumatic experiences, our feelings of well-being and pain, even our ideas, concerns and meanings about all of them are incorporated in the body as unique pictures and narratives [5]. These inner pictures strongly influence our explications and interpretations of our experiences and transform each disease into a unique personal illness journey. With them we construct our personal reality and our own universe. Inner pictures play a key role for the dynamic maintenance of personal health and influence the development of each individual's illnesses and recovery processes.

The inner pictures differ from one person to another being simultaneously influenced by culture, gender, profession, religion, education, etc. In the medical context, patients' inner pictures may not match with the medico-scientific anatomic and physiological knowledge. They may indeed be contradictory to the medical professionals' definitions/interpretations of health and disease. And they may also differ from physicians' scientific background as well as their own personal illness experiences and their associated inner pictures [5, 6].

The consultation is the meeting place of two universes, that of the patient's subjective experiences and the doctor's biomedical sciences [7–9]. The doctor with his responsibility for an effective therapeutic process must be aware of the possible divergent explications and interpretations of the patient's condition. For an effective therapeutic process/journey, the doctor and the patient have to create a *common reality* from these different universes. Thus, in addition to the disease-driven interrogations about symptoms, the doctor has to ask the patient explicitly about his personal illness narrative and inner pictures.

A mutual understanding—accordance is not needed—of the patient's and the doctor's different universes is an important part for the therapeutic relation and their common journey through the patient's illness.

## 16.4   The Art-Science Dialogue Project: Billings–Bern

This was the background to the inaugural *art-science dialogue* between the participants of the *2nd International Systems and Complexity Science for Healthcare Conference* in Billings and Esther Quarroz's art studio in Bern, Switzerland.

### 16.4.1   Structure and Method

We—Bruno Kissling, a family doctor; Esther Quarroz, an art therapist; and Andreas Fahrni, a photographer—are all visual artists who participated at the Systems and Complexity Science Conference in Billings, MT. We created an artistic installation in Bern, Switzerland. The installation, driven by aesthetic criteria, emerged from lively and mutually stimulating $4 \times 15$-min art-science dialogues over a 2-day period (virtual meetings via Zoom®). Following an initial *theme setting* conversation, the remaining meetings started with a presentation of the developments of the installation which was observed and photographed by Andreas Fahrni.

### 16.4.2   Aim and Purpose

With our art-science project, we want to explore:

- If a virtual interaction between an art project and a scientific conference is possible
- If art and science may find a common language

- If aesthetic criteria may influence scientific thinking
- If a visual aesthetic view and theoretic concepts may mutually enrich the understanding of complexity
- If art may help to create a new understanding of health/well-being and disease/illness at the patient-doctor level
- If art may contribute to societal reflections about purpose, goals, values and simple rules at a healthcare system level

### 16.4.3   The Consultation: As a Starting Point for …

In the consultation, patients and doctors share a common journey—the patient leads this journey presenting his symptoms and illness experiences, and the doctor interprets the narrative based on his medical knowledge. For it to be a common journey, they firstly have to recognize their different universes before engaging in the creation of a shared reality. A shared reality arises through the complex interactions in the conversation. Doctors must be cognisant of the complexity phenomena in conversation which are the basis for successful solution-oriented open therapeutic processes. There are successful simple rules to keep running the interactive communication between doctor and patient:

1. Relationship
2. Confidence
3. Mutual respect and curious interest

Interestingly all three reflect attitudes. As such they represent soft facts that can only be measured by qualitative means. They don't reflect technical instruments, hard facts which can get quantified.

### 16.4.4   … the Art Installation

So, the story of Leo's lions, the reflections about consultations, the virtual reality of our presence to the conference in Billings, MT, and our aesthetic criteria all shaped the process of our art installation.

## Starting Condition
Unstructured and disordered piles of PET packaging. This reflects the beginning of consultations collecting unstructured information that begin the vital movement.

## First Emergent Steps
Order created orientation and revealed new information and understanding.

But in this order, even though it had an aesthetic appeal—"froze the moment"—the situation became stagnant and technical. What had been left out could no longer be integrated.

As with blind spots, important things can be easily forgotten. In the consultation, one needs to look out for unappreciated information and unseen perspectives.

## Progression
Variations resulted in different and appropriate solutions; however, they remained static and technical.

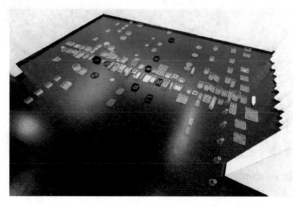

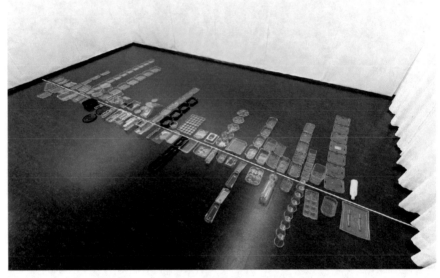

## Perturbations

A kick with a leg created partial disorder. This *perturbation* resulted to a new dynamic and a much greater vitality. This new state opened the opportunity to appreciate the situation with fresh eyes.

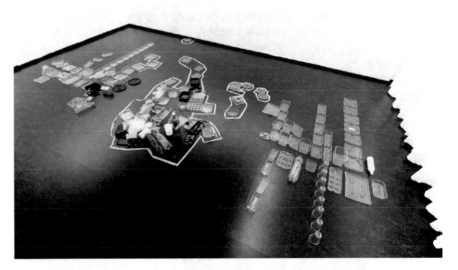

Perturbations have the power to start emergent processes that occur in the space between order and "creative" disorder. In the consultation, such perturbations may arise from a patient's utterance of "strange" sentences and non-logical thoughts; from suggestion of images, dreams, narrations, visions and pictures of hopes; from peculiar smells and from "by-the-way" mentions of feelings and thoughts or statements while standing in the already "half-open" door.

## Adaptive Work

The new partial disorder in an otherwise ordered structure allowed the emergence of higher-level information. Suddenly new insights could be integrated. The system became dynamic in the "balanced space" between order and a manageable amount of disorder.

In the consultation, perturbations provide new opportunities to enable the adaptive work to be carried out in the consultation. It facilitates an experience of tolerance in the space between order and disorder which helps to prioritize competing agendas.

*New Possibilities*  An unexpected new direction emerged. Doctor-patient encounters often "get stuck" focusing on seemingly unimportant things, when one suddenly sees totally unexpected solutions in one's peripheral vision.

## 16.5  Conclusions

The virtual contact between the scientists in Billings, MT, and the artists in Berne, Switzerland, by Zoom® worked well. The feedback and lively discussions showed that the four short presentations created a common reality halfway across the globe. The process of the artist's creation of this art installation was influenced by the interactive exchanges between the two groups.

The scientists and artists did not have any problems understanding their respective language. As the final discussions highlighted, the artists understood the *meaning of the scientists' words*, and the scientists understood *the artists' pictures* very well.

The purely aesthetic appearance of this art installation was able to stimulate reflections about the scientists' way of thinking and their way of practising as health professionals.

The visual aesthetic view achieved an understandable reflection of the theoretical concepts of complexity. Indeed, artistic visualizations have been shown to very helpful to make understandable quite abstract concepts like complexity.

This art project visualized and made understandable that well-being does not mean freedom from all disturbances. Rather to the contrary, it highlighted that each person's well-being and the healing processes of patients require a manageable amount of disorder and distress to achieve an environment that maintains necessary creative dynamic processes. This was a surprise. These insights expand the understanding of the meanings and tension entailed in the continuum of health/well-being, illness and disease for the doctor, patient and the health system at large.

The practical creating process of the art installation showed the importance of common purpose and goals. It pointed out that the values must not be identical but mutually respectable. It highlighted that the driving simple rules for achieving meaningful outcomes in the artistic as well as in the therapeutic discourse depend on attributes like relationships, confidence, mutual respect and interest—not only technical expertise.

The success of this art-science project encouraged us to continue our path. At the WONCA Europe Conference 2017 in Prague (28.6–1.7), a new art-science installation will take place in a large open space at the centre of the conference venue.

## The Journey

Looking for an appropriate space to create our first social art sculpture, which is based on a complex adaptive interaction, the cooperation with the participants of the Systems and Complexity Science Conference in Billings, MT, seemed to us to be an ideal platform. The artists, the photographer and the scientists we all are fully satisfied by the enriching and enthusiastic art-science dialogue which was mutually stimulated by the proceeding social art sculpture. And the reaction of the conference participants showed that they were also happy with this experience. We are convinced that the courage of both the artists and scientists to dare this novel endeavour was worthwhile.

With this success in mind, we all are courageous to continue our art-science dialogue with a second social art sculpture project at the WONCA Europe Conference 2017 in Prague.

**Acknowledgements** We very much appreciate and are grateful for the courage of the organizing committee, namely, Joachim Sturmberg and Curt Lindbergh, to provide space on the conference programme for this improvised art-science project and its unpredictable outcome. Neither side could be sure that this cooperation would work properly or could create appreciable results.

www.art-dialog.com
Bruno Kissling, family doctor, artist
Esther Quarroz, art therapist, theologian, artist
All pictures by Andreas Fahrni, photographer

Take-Home Message

- The consultation is art in its pure sense! (Ars medici)
- Every human being, patients and doctors, has rich inner creativity and inner pictures of understanding
- They have an individual narrative and unique journey of life
- Listening to these creative narratives is a very rich experience in every dialogue
- To share these individual "universes" gives important new information for healing processes and mutual understanding
- Aesthetic points of view and creativity are essential for reframing in therapeutic processes
- To give attention to aesthetic aspects in speaking and listening as well as in therapeutic processes can give a big amount of understanding, dignity and empowerment. This is an important way to find solutions

# References

1. Annas GJ. Reframing the debate on health care reform by replacing our metaphors. N Engl J Med. 1995;332(11):745–8.
2. Keiger D. Why metaphor matters. John Hopkins Mag. 1998;50(1). Available at http://www.jhu.edu/jhumag/0298web/metaphor.html.
3. Penson RT, Schapira L, Daniels KJ, Chabner BA, Lynch TJ. Cancer as metaphor. Oncologist. 2004;9(6):708–16.
4. Fuks A. The military metaphors of modern medicine. wwwinter-disciplinarynet; 2009. http://www.inter-disciplinary.net/wp-content/uploads/2009/06/hid_fuks.pdf.
5. Hüther G. Die Macht der Inneren Bilder. Göttingen: Vandenhoeck & Ruprecht; 2014.
6. Egger B, Merz J. Lösungsorientierte Maltherapie. Bern: Hogrefe, vorm, Verlag Hans Huber; 2013.
7. Tuckett D, Boulton M, Olson C, Williams A. Meetings between experts. An approach to sharing ideas in medical consultations. London: Tavistock Publications; 1985.
8. Olesen F. Striking the balance: from patient-centred to dialogue-centred medicine. Scand J Prim Health Care. 2004;22(4):193–4.
9. Kaminski M. Popping the question; 2015. https://pulsevoices.org/index.php/archive/stories/451-popping-the-question.

# The Programme

## Wednesday, November 9

| 8:00–8:15 | Impromptu Networking | To get participants engaged and connected. Two questions<br>• What attracted them to conference<br>• What questions did they bring to conference |
|---|---|---|
| 8:15–8:25 | Welcome, Orientation to Conference | |

© Springer International Publishing AG, part of Springer Nature 2018
J. P. Sturmberg (ed.), *Putting Systems and Complexity Sciences Into Practice*,
https://doi.org/10.1007/978-3-319-73636-5

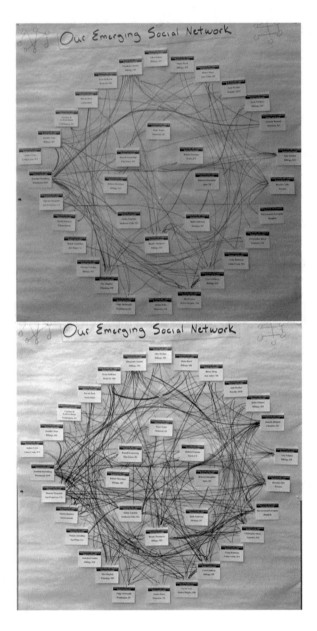

| 8:25–9:40 | Mini-TED Talks and Two Small Group Rounds | Five 5-min highlights of each presentation followed by two 25-min small group sessions. Participants invited to attend the two sessions of most interest |
|---|---|---|
| | David C. Aron | Pitfalls in Identifying High Performers in Diabetes Care. Positive Deviants May Be Neither Positive nor Deviant |
| | Eric Arzubi and Diane Hurd | A Tale of Collaborative Inquiry: Suspending Hierarchy, Liberating Innovation |
| | Christophe Herry, Nathan Scales and Andrew Seely | Transforming Monitoring and Improving Care With Variability-Derived Clinical Decision Support |
| | Virgina Mohl and John Scott | The Healing Journey. The Path from Suffering to Healing |
| | Joachim P. Sturmberg | The Multiple Networks of Multimorbidity |
| | Christine J. Ye and Henry H. Heng | Linking Elevated Genome Instability to Gulf War Illness: Searching for the General Mechanism |

## Keynote Address
Howard Leicester:
Simplifying Healthcare
for All with the English
Accessible Information
Standard

| 10:20–10:35 | Bruno Kissling and Esther Quarroz | A Body Is More Than a Machine, A Healthcare System More Than Machinery—Part 1 |
|---|---|---|

| 10:50–12:15 | Mini-TED Talks and Two Small Group Rounds | Five 5-min highlights of each presentation followed by two 25-min small group sessions. Participants invited to attend the two sessions of most interest |
|---|---|---|
| | Rebecca Kitzmiller, Jessica Keim-Malpass, Angela Skeeles-Worley, Theresa Simons, Curt Lindberg, Robert Tai, J. Randall Moorman and Ruth Anderson | Accelerating Technology Integration Through Emergent Design |
| | Paige L. McDonald, Gaetano R. Lotrecchiano, Kenneth Harwood, Mary Corcoran and Joseph M. Bocchino | New Ways of Knowing and Researching: Integrating Complexity into a Translational Health Sciences Program |
| | Bob Merchant | Impact of Relational Coordination on Care, Collaboration and Thinking |
| | Joachim P. Sturmberg | Putting Health Back into the Healthcare System |
| | Peter Tsasis | Enacting Interdisciplinary Thinking |

| 1:00–1:50 | Rounding with Billings Clinic | See part of the clinic, learn about complexity-inspired innovations and offer guidance on further development. Attendees pick one option<br><br>• Relational coordination in ICU—Pam Zinnecker and Jen Potts host<br>• Patient flow—Bob Merchant hosts<br>• Predictive monitoring in ED—Randy Thompson hosts<br>• Safe and reliable on inpatient medical—Dania Block hosts, Curt Lindberg attends |
|---|---|---|
| 1:50–3:05 | Mini-TED Talks and Two Small Group Rounds | Five 5-min highlights of each presentation followed by two 25-min small group sessions. Participants invited to attend the two sessions of most interest |
|  | Jeanette M. Bennett | Healthy Smoker: An Oxymoron? |
|  | Ben deBock | Dealing with Complex Clinical Decisions. Qualitative Empirical Research on an Intensive Care Unit |
|  | Henry H. Heng | Fuzzy Inheritance Challenges the Concept of Precision Medicine |

| | Elizabeth Ciemins, Robert Merchant, Randy Thompson and Curt Lindberg | Learning: Contemplating the Unexamined Core of Learning Health Systems |
|---|---|---|
| | Chad Swanson | Social and Institutional Change in Complex Health Systems: Lessons Learned |

| 3:20–3:35 | Bruno Kissling and Esther Quarroz | A Body Is More Than a Machine, A Healthcare System More Than Machinery—Part 2 |
|---|---|---|

| 3:35–4.25 | Putting Complexity Into Practice | |
|---|---|---|
| 6:00–8:00 | Evening Reception | Yellowstone Art Museum |

## Thursday, November 10

| 8:00–8:15 | Reflections on Day 1 |
| 8:15–8:25 | Orientation to Day 2 |

### Keynote Address

Ruth Anderson and Marcus Thygeson: Adaptive Leadership—A Complexity-Based Framework for Improving Healthcare at Multiple Levels: From Patients to Whole Health Systems

| 9:20–10:05 | Work in Progress Consultations | Wise crowds process to enable participants to solicit guidance from other attendees on their complexity-inspired projects or research |
| 10:05–10:20 | Bruno Kissling and Esther Quarroz | A Body Is More Than a Machine, A Healthcare System More Than Machinery—Part 3 |
| 10:35–12:15 | Mini-TED Talks and Two Small Group Rounds | Five 5-min highlights of each presentation followed by two 25-min small group sessions. Participants invited to attend the two sessions of most interest |
| | Elizabeth L. Ciemins | Why the Interdisciplinary Team Approach Works in Palliative Care: Insights from Complexity Science |
| | Evan G. DeRenzo | Using Systems Predictors of Ethically Complex Patients to Improve Care |
| | Martin Konitzer and Frauke Dunkel | Complexity of Knowledge in Primary Care. A Bibliometric Study |

| | | |
|---|---|---|
| | Amber Crist | ECHO (Extension for Community Health Outcomes): A Learning Partnership |
| | Oluwayemisi Olugboji, Sergio G. Camorlinga, Ricardo Lobato de Faria and Arjun Kaushal | Understanding the Emergency Department Ecosystem Using Agent-Based Modelling |
| | Geoff McDonnell, Dylan Knowles, Jo-An Atkinson and Ante Prodan | Visualisation in Simulation of Complex Systems in Healthcare |
| | Carmel M. Martin | Supporting Complex Dynamic Health Journeys. Using Conversation to Avert Hospital Readmissions from the Community |
| 12:55–1:45 | Panel Conversation Around Hot Topics | |
| 1:45–2:00 | Bruno Kissling and Esther Quarroz | A Body Is More Than a Machine, A Healthcare System More Than Machinery—Part 4 |

| | | |
|---|---|---|
| 2:20–3:30 | Open Space | Attendees organize into small group discussions around topics they nominate using Open Space process |
| 3:30–4:00 | Closing Reflections | Begin by viewing network map and follow with webbing process around relevant questions |
| 7:00–9:00 | Informal Discussion About Creating an International Complexity and Healthcare Society | Floberg House |

# Index

Genome
   genome heterogeneity, 91
transcriptome dynamics, 87

**A**
aetiology, 2
Agent Based Modeling, 200
allostatic model, 30, 33
antibacterial war, 37
antihistamines, 32, 33

**B**
bacterial adherence, 35–37
Bernard, Claude, 29
bibliometrics, 151
Billings Clinic, 43, 44, 129, 130
biomarker, 83
biomarkers, 55
biosemiotics, 162

**C**
Cancer
   cancer evolution, 84, 88
   cancer genome, 87
   evolutionary framework, 85, 90
   evolutionary mechanisms, 87
   gene-mutation centric, 84
   genome evolution, 87
   genome heterogeneity, 90
   genome instability, 87
   genome-mediated, 84

cancer evolution, 84, 88
cancer genome, 87
causal loop diagram, 201, 203, 205
cellular stress, 89, 91
chromosomal aberration, 84–86
chromosomal instability, 86
chromosomal translocation, 86
Chromosome
   chromosomal aberration, 84–86
   chromosomal instability, 86
   chromosomal translocation, 86
   non clonal aberration (NCCA), 85, 86, 88,
      91
   stochastic chromosome change, 84
co-morbidity, 66
Cochrane, Archie, 4
complex adaptive systems, 83–85, 87–89, 91,
      92, 122
complex disease, 84, 87
complex illness, 84, 87
Complexity
   adaptation, 36, 37, 39
   complex adaptive interaction, 217, 218, 227
   complex adaptive systems, 5, 6, 83–85,
      87–89, 91, 92, 122, 134, 136, 139,
      142
   complex disease, 84, 87, 90
   complex health systems, 133
   complex illness, 84, 87
   complexity of care, 169, 170
   complexity science, 190
   complexity sciences, 44, 91
   complexity theory, 122, 190
   complexity thinking, 87, 121, 122, 129, 190

© Springer International Publishing AG, part of Springer Nature 2018
J. P. Sturmberg (ed.), *Putting Systems and Complexity Sciences Into Practice*,
https://doi.org/10.1007/978-3-319-73636-5

Complexity (*cont.*)
   decision-making, 169
   design thinking, 121–123, 130
   ethics, 165
   loss of complexity, 5
   systems thinking, 121, 123, 125, 127, 130
   uncertainty, 73, 74, 91
   variability, 75, 76, 79
complexity thinking, 121, 122, 129
coping, 54, 55, 63
cortisol, 12, 13
cross-disciplinary, 133–136, 139, 141, 142, 144

**D**
depression, 12, 43, 47–49
design thinking, 121–123, 130
diabetes, 12, 191
diarrhea, 33, 34

**E**
electronic medical records (EMR), 166, 171,
   172
emergence, 87, 122, 134–136, 143
Emergency Department, 51, 52, 66, 199
   ED ecosystem, 200
epidemiology, 147
equifinality, 194
equity, 120, 123
Ethics
   communication, 171
   complicated patient, 172, 173
   risk management, 168
Evidence
   dynamic evidence, 45
   evidence based practice, 43–45
   evidence based treatment, 45
Evolution
   somatic evolution , 86
   cancer evolution, 87, 88
   cellular evolution, 87, 89
   evolutionary medicine, 91
   macro-cellular evolution, 90
   punctuated, 87
   somatic evolution, 90, 91
evolutionary, 85, 87
evolutionary mechanism, 83
extubation, 76–78

**F**
Flexner report, 119, 120, 130
Flexner, Abraham, 119

frailty, 51, 52, 55, 60, 63
fuzzy inheritance, 88, 89

**G**
Genome
   cancer genome, 87
   genome heterogeneity, 89
   genome inheritance, 84
   genome instability, 84–88, 90
   genome instability-mediated, 88, 90
   genome re-organization, 88
   genome theory, 83, 85, 87
genome instability, 83–88, 90
genome re-organization, 88
genome theory, 85
genome-level variation, 84
germ theory, 29
Gulf War Illness, 83, 87, 89

**H**
HbA1c, 191
health and well-being, 218, 219, 221, 227
Health Factors, 178
health outcome, 177
Health Outcomes, 178
   complex, 185
   episodic care, 125, 126
   equity, 120, 123
   length of life, 178
   nonlinear, 185
   population health, 120, 123, 126, 128–130
   quality of life, 178
   self-rated health, 55, 63, 66
health system, 4–6, 120
health vortex model, 5
healthcare system, 1, 4–7, 52, 199
heart rate variability, 73–75, 77
heterogeneity, 87–90
Hispanic Paradox, 184
histamine, 33
HPA axis, 12
Husserl, Edmund, 4

**I**
illness, 54, 56, 68, 147, 217–221, 227
infection, 31, 73, 76
Inflammation
   chronic inflammation, 38
Inheritance
   fuzzy inheritance, 88, 89
   genome inheritance, 84
   system inheritance, 83
interdisciplinary approach, 133

**J**

Jamkhed, 128, 130

**K**

Karyotyping
  spectral karyotyping (SKY), 84, 86
karyotyping, 84, 86
Knowledge
  GP/FM knowledge base, 148, 150–153,
      157, 159–161
  knowledge generation, 134, 138, 142–144
  knowledge translation, 134–137
knowledge generation, 134, 138, 142–144
knowledge translation, 134–137

**L**

Leadership
  adaptive leadership, 122
Learing
  online courses, 127
Learning
  co-learning, 43
  collaborative learning, 127
  innovation, 43
  single case, 43, 44
linear causation, 88
loneliness, 12–14, 16, 17, 19, 21, 23

**M**

macro-cellular evolution, 88
Maedows, Donella, 7
Mayo brothers, 4
McWhinney, Ian, 7
Medicine
  clinical medicine, 165
  clinical research, 165
medicine is a social science, 2
microevolution, 88
mindset, 1
Modeling
  flows, 201
  stocks, 201
Modelling
  decision support, 74, 79
  clinical decision making, 74
  predictive analytics, 74, 76
  predictive model, 173
  predictive modelling, 74, 76
MonashWatch, 58
Monitoring
  heart rate variability, 73–75, 77
  respiratory rate variability, 74, 75, 77

mucus, 31, 33, 35
multi-morbidity, 51, 60
multifinality, 195

**N**

NetLogo, 200

**O**

obesity, 169
Organisation
  interdiciplinary team, 43
  mission, 129
  organisational change, 43, 45
  organisational systems, 5
    purpose and goals, 5
    simple (operating) rules, 5
    values, 5
  organisational team, 43
  shared vision, 122, 124, 128, 129
  transformation, 129
Osler, William, 1, 4
otitis media, 29, 32, 35
Outcomes
  critical illness, 73
  efficiency of care, 74
  patient care, 73, 76
  problems in patients, 166
  quality of care, 166
  surrogate markers, 166
overtreatment, 194

**P**

PaJR, 56, 57, 60, 63, 64, 66–68
paradigm shift, 134
parasympathetic nervous system, 12
Pareto rule, 51
Pasteur, Louis, 29
pathology, 2
patient care, 45, 73, 76
Patient expectation
  emphasis on technology, 171
  non-compliant, 45
  unrealistic expectations, 170
Pauli, Hannes, 4
Pellegrino, Edmund, 4, 7
Performance
  performance measures, 191
  performance metrics, 191
person-centered, 2, 5, 8
pharmaceutical sampling, 32
phenotype, 87
physiologic defenses, 30, 34

positive deviance, 189, 190
primary care, 53, 56, 59, 65, 66, 190
psychological stress, 11, 12, 21
psychoneuroimmunology, 6

**Q**
quality of life, 178

**R**
reasons for encounter, 147, 157
reductionism, 39, 88, 91, 119, 123, 124
Research
    clinical research, 165
    ethics, 165
resilience, 54, 67, 68
respiratory infections, 31
respiratory rate variability, 74, 75, 77
rhinorrhea, 34

**S**
sense of community, 177
sepsis, 73, 74
smoking, 12–15, 17, 19, 21, 22
social determinants of health, 6
social impact, 133–135, 139, 140, 142, 143
social support, 52, 54, 60, 63, 64, 177
sodium-glucose transport system, 34
somatic evolution, 86–88, 90
Statistics
    Baysian statistics, 76
    multivariate techniques, 76
    ROC, 76
    time series, 74, 75
stochastic, 84, 90, 91
stochastic chromosome change, 84
Stress
    acute, 12, 21, 22, 24
    carer stress, 54
    chronic, 12, 21, 22, 24
    life events, 12, 16, 17, 21
    psychological, 11, 12, 21
    stressor, 54, 60

suicide, 49
sympathetic nervous system, 12
system adaptation, 90
system inheritance, 83
systems approach, 133–136, 142, 143
systems thinking, 121, 123, 125, 127, 130

**T**
taxonomy, 2
tipping point, 54, 55, 60, 62
tipping-point, 129
Transcriptome
    transcriptome dynamics, 87
Translational Health Science, 133, 134,
        137–141, 143
Treatment
    nonpharmacological, 47
    overtreatment, 191
    undertreatment, 192
triple chronotherapy, 43, 44, 46–48

**U**
uncertainty, 73, 74, 91
uncommon practices, 190

**V**
variability, 43, 76, 79, 166
Virchow, Rudolph, 2
vision, 122
von Uexküll, Thure, 4, 162

**W**
waveform, 73, 79
worldview, 1, 2

**X**
xylitol, 34–36
xylitol nasal spray, 35

Printed in the United States
By Bookmasters